'A riveting and moving read. Noorjahan's compelling life journey is a story of courage and resilience, and is a true inspiration to feminist activists around the world.'

— Jaspreet Kaur, poet, educator and author of *Brown Girl Like Me*

'Uncovering multiple dimensions of the varied landscapes of Bangladesh, England and the United States, *Daughter of the Agunmukha* tells the personal and political story of a life spanning the twentieth and twenty-first centuries.'

— Arizona State University, and author of *Women, War, and the Making of Bangladesh*

Arizona State University, and author of Women, War, and the Making of Bangladesh 'Knowing Noorjahan Bose through this fiercely honest autobiography is an honour. Her impossible journey is a heroic testament to the unbreakable spirit of the human soul. A gem of a book: inspirational, indomitable and tender.'

— Leesa Gazi, actor, filmmaker and author of *Hellfire*

'Bose's memoir unlocks a hidden nation before its identity was regionally and religiously determined. It's an incantation of love and violence, family secrets and resilience—by a deltaic daughter at the confluence of "rivers of fire".'

— Lipika Pelham, journalist, historian and author of *Passing: An Alternative History of Identity*

'An absolutely stunning and mesmerising account of life in a Bengal consumed by climate change and extractive greed. With lyrical prose and rich detail, Bose tells the captivating story of her life, revealing the fortitude and strength of the women she knew and the woman she herself has become.'

— Rafia Zakaria, attorney, political philosopher and author of *Against White Feminism*

# DAUGHTER OF THE AGUNMUKHA

NOORJAHAN BOSE

# Daughter of the Agunmukha

*Translated by*
REBECCA WHITTINGTON

*Edited by*
MONICA JAHAN BOSE

HURST & COMPANY, LONDON

First published in the United Kingdom in 2023 by
C. Hurst & Co. (Publishers) Ltd.,
New Wing, Somerset House, Strand, London, WC2R 1LA


Distributed in the United States, Canada and Latin America by Oxford University Press, 198 Madison Avenue, New York, NY 10016, United States of America.



A Cataloguing-in-Publication data record for this book is available from the British Library.

ISBN: 9781805260608

This book is printed using paper from registered sustainable and managed sources.

www.hurstpublishers.com
Printed in Great Britain by Bell & Bain Ltd, Glasgow

For my mother Johora Begum
and Manorama Mashima

The two great women whose love and guidance
inspired my journey

# CONTENTS

# PREFACE

As a child, I remember hearing everyone tell stories about the River Agunmukha—the Mouth of Fire. When I heard the name, a shiver of fear would run through me. In fact, the Agunmukha has six other rivers flowing into it: the Tetulia, Lohalia, Bura Gauranga, Rabnabad, Darchira, and Digri rivers. At one time, people called the Digri river a *khal* or channel. South of the Galachipa port, hugging the coast of the Bay of Bengal, many small islands or sandbars known as *char* have formed in the natural process of erosion and formation. Among them are Barobaishdia, Chhotobaishdia or Rangabali, Char Kajal, Char Momtaz, Char Biswas, Char Kukrimukri, Char Kalagachia, Andarchar, Sonarchar, and many others.[1] Around 200 years ago, pirates from Burma's Arakan region came and established the first settlements on some of the higher islands, such as Barobaishdia and Chhotobaishdia. They were attracted by the fertile land, the dense forest of the Sundarbans, and the abundance of fish. Bengalis came to the region later and gradually built settlements, living side by side with the Burmese.

The Agunmukha's frightening aspect was legendary. The people of Galachipa, Khepupara, Aamtoli, Char Kajal, and other villages and towns on the islands and on the banks of the Agunmukha had to cross the river for work or business. No one kept count of how many people lost their lives on the crossing.

Since the Agunmukha is an estuary or confluence of seven rivers, a billowing mass of water flows into it from every direction as far as the eye can see. The reflection of the sun's rays on the powerful waves reminded me of the flames of a blazing fire. When we crossed from one bank to the other, we could see nothing but water in every direction, masses and masses of water. I've heard from my mother, grandmother, and other villagers that women who were oppressed by their husbands would jump into the Agunmukha; that lovers who were ostracized by their families would leap together into the arms of the Agunmukha. My forefather, that is, my paternal grandfather's father, Chande Ali Sardar, settled in Katakhali village on Barobaishdia Island. Our family had another house near Galachipa, in Londa village, so we had to cross the Agunmukha often for weddings and other festive occasions. It took about twelve or thirteen hours in a big boat to go from our house in Katakhali to the house in Londa. We had to rely on the winds and the tides. When we went on a trip to the Londa house or when we needed to go to the city for medical treatment or education, a kind of terror would come over me despite my excitement. Crossing the Agunmukha was a game of chance. Some made it to the other side, some were lost in the Agunmukha. My father, Baba, never trusted any boatman completely with the serious responsibility of crossing the Agunmukha. He would hold the rudder himself with a firm grip. The raging waves often flung Baba's small frame onto the stern of the boat. Sometimes he would hit his head or injure his arms and legs. I would just close my eyes and hope that Baba wouldn't fall in the river. As soon as we crossed the Agunmukha, I would give Baba a big hug. His eyes would be bright with a sense of victory. I could finally relax and look around at the incredible scenery—flocks of cotton teals and seagulls flying overhead, the joyful dives of kingfishers. Over the years, the face of the Agunmukha has changed as the old islands have broken down and new ones arisen, part of a continuous cycle. Now it takes just four hours to go from our home in Katakhali to Galachipa. High schools have been opened in the region, and girls and boys attend in equal number. But it still takes twenty-eight to thirty hours by ferry-boat or launch to go from Dhaka to Katakhali.

Even today, the infrastructure is lacking for electricity, water, sanitation, roads, hospitals, or housing that is safe during the rains and storms. Exposed to storms, floods, and cyclones, which are increasing due to climate change, people are still at the mercy of nature. The region continues to have a high rate of maternal and infant mortality. Conditions in this area still have not received enough attention from the government and foreign NGOs.

The Agunmukha's impact on my life is endless. All the people of this region are my kin, close to my heart. Their stories are part of my story.

*Noorjahan Bose*
*Washington, DC*
*June 2020*

# ACKNOWLEDGMENTS

The driving force behind the writing of *Daughter of the Agunmukha* was my family: my late husband Swadesh Bose, my three children Jaseem, Monica, and Anita, and my granddaughters Tuli and Koli—especially Tuli, who refused to listen to any story other than the story of my life. In the end, even little Koli chimed in, "I want to hear Nanu's life story." My children said to me, now that you've told us all the story, why don't you write it? But we all know that telling a story and writing it are not the same thing. The difficult task of reading the original Bengali manuscript fell to my friend's daughter Simin Hossain Rimi and my oldest daughter Monica.

If Mr Toab Khan and Mr Swadesh Roy of the daily *Janakantha* (Voice of the people) hadn't published *Daughter of the Agunmukha* serially in their magazine, the book might not have gained such popularity. I must also mention Mafidul Haq of Sahitya Prakash. I am grateful to all of them. Ananda Publishers asked to publish the book in India. This was a huge gift for me. It makes me happy to think that readers in the other Bengal have the chance to read my book. I am grateful to Rebecca Whittington for making this book accessible to readers of English, and to my daughter Monica for working with Rebecca and me to edit the translation.

# AUTHOR'S NOTE ON BANGLA TERMS

Bengali kinship terms are complex, as relatives are divided into paternal and maternal relatives, biological relatives and relatives by marriage, and in some cases further differentiated by relational age; these same terms are used both for family members and for family friends, teachers, and others as a sign of respect and affection. As a child, I remember using the words Ma and Baba to refer to my parents and Kaka and Kaki to refer to my father's younger brothers and their wives. After we became part of Pakistan, I observed some linguistic changes as a result, I believe, of the influence of Urdu and the state's attempt to reduce the legitimacy of Bengali. Muslims started using the terms Amma and Abba for father and mother and Chacha and Chachi for paternal uncles and their wives. Today, there is a clear difference in use of kinship terms in Bangladesh depending on religion. Muslims also tend to use the Hindi/Urdu word for water, *pani*, whereas non-Muslims use the Bangla word *jal*. This translation retains Bangla and Urdu-derived terms used in the text for various relatives and friends as listed below.

| | |
|---|---|
| Ma/Baba | mother and father |
| Dada/Dadi | paternal grandfather and grandmother |

AUTHOR'S NOTE ON BANGLA TERMS

| | |
|---|---|
| Nana/Nani | maternal grandfather and grandmother |
| Phuphu/Phupha | paternal aunt (father's sister) and uncle (father's sister's husband) |
| Pishi/Pishemoshai | paternal aunt (father's sister) and uncle (father's sister's husband) (used more to refer to non-Muslims in Bangladesh) |
| Chacha/Chachi | paternal uncle (father's brother) and aunt (father's brother's wife) |
| Khala/Khalu | maternal aunt (mother's sister) and uncle (mother's sister's husband) |
| Mashima/Meshomoshai or Mashi/Mesho | maternal aunt (mother's sister) and uncle (mother's sister's husband) (used more to refer to non-Muslims in Bangladesh) |
| Mama/Mami | maternal uncle (mother's brother) and aunt (mother's brother's wife) |
| Apa | older sister (Urdu) |
| Suffix -di, short for Didi | older sister, Bangla equivalent of Apa |
| Suffix -da, short for Dada | older brother |

Other Bangla terms retained in the text and historical references are given in the footnotes and/or glossary.

PART 1

# GROWING UP ON AN ISLAND

*About my mother*

The story of my life must begin with my mother, Johora Begum. Ma looked like an ordinary Bengali girl: small in stature, with dusky skin, big doe-like eyes that seemed full of water, and a head full of thick curly hair that fell to below her waist. She didn't talk much; her eyes had a silent language. Yet my mother was an extraordinary woman, with a clear vision of the future she wanted for her children and community, a strong will, and an open mind. Her knowledge of traditional skills, her insistence on education for girls, and her ability to take the lead in new forms of community engagement have had a deep and lasting impact on me as a person and as a social worker and activist.

Ma was born around 1923 in the village of Tungibaria on Barobaishdia Island, East Bengal, in what was then British India. Ma didn't remember her own mother, Amena Begum, who died when Ma was little. Ma's father, Shirajul Islam Khan (nickname "Chand Mia"),[1] was always busy handling affairs related to his estate or with his various leisure activities. Ma was raised by her Dada, or paternal grandfather, Moulubi Abdul Ali Khan, and the domestic help.

Chand Mia, who was my Nana or maternal grandfather, came from a high-born and respected family. My mother's ancestral home was in Faridpur. Their forefather Shri Muktaram Banerjee was an influential Hindu *jomidar* or landowner. He had a social relationship with the local Muslim *jomidars* of Faridpur. They visited each other on Eid, various pujos[2] and festivals, and weddings and invited each other over to eat. Of course, every house had arrangements for separate cooking and serving vessels. The Hindu and Muslim cooks both cooked according to their masters' rules. Once, Muktaram Banerjee went with the other men of his household to a wedding in the house of a Muslim *jomidar*. After the meal was over, someone from that Muslim *jomidar*'s family beat a drum and announced in front of everyone that all the Hindus had eaten beef, and therefore they had accepted Islam. This news spread like wildfire through all the nearby villages. The men and women of Muktaram Banerjee's family started wailing, but the damage was already done. The men of the Banerjee family went home with their heads bent in shame. Later, when they wanted to attack the other family with spears, shields, and guns, their neighbors and friends stopped them, because fighting wasn't going to bring back their lost religious status. From then on, Muktaram Banerjee's family was Muslim. People who have converted are often particularly devout. In this family too, the likes of Maulana Shariyat Ullah, Pir Dudu Mia, and Badshah Mia were born. Because their ancestors were *kulin* Brahmins,[3] they held onto their *kulin* status even after becoming Muslims.

My Nana Chand Mia's father, in other words my great great-grandfather, Moulubi Abdul Ali Khan, was a man of expensive tastes. Legend has it that my great-grandfather's father-in-law, Azimuddin Talukdar, was very rich and wanted a high-born son-in-law, so he paid a lot of money to bring my great-grandfather from Faridpur to marry his beloved only child, Fatimunnesa. My great-grandfather Abdul Ali came to stay with his in-laws as a *gharjamai*.[4] He was extremely fashionable and wore silk clothes. On the wedding day, the father-in-law presented my great-grandfather and great-grandmother with a special new house on the same family property. But the wedding night was a disaster. My great-grandfather did not appreciate his bride's beautiful clothing and expensive silver jewelry. The next morning, my great-grandmother Fatimunnesa tearfully told her father that the groom had rejected her and complained about her jewelry and clothing. Her father became enraged and summoned his son-in-law to ask him how much money he needed for clothing and jewelry for Fatimunnesa. My great-grandfather asked for 1 lakh taka, an enormous sum at that time (the late 1800s). The princely sum was immediately handed over, and my great-grandfather Abdul Ali was sent shopping to Dhaka in a luxurious boat. Abdul Ali came back with a boatload of Benarasi saris, jackets, shawls, embroidered shoes, and jewelry made of pure gold and gems, none of which had ever been seen in these southern lands before.

Because of my great-grandfather's influence, the home my mother grew up in had reading tables and chairs, fine china, tea sets, and flower vases. The women of the family wore gold jewelry. Before the arrival of my great-grandfather from Faridpur, no one in our delta region had any of these things—you could say they were unacquainted with so-called civilization. My Nana, Chand Mia, born in that household. When he was a teenager, his parents arranged his marriage to Amena, a girl from a well-to-do family in the neighboring village of Chalitabunia. My mother, Johora, was the fourth child of Chand Mia and second child of Amena.[5]

When Ma was a child, she went to the school just outside the main gate of her homestead. My father, Abdur Razzak, the son of the *jotedar*[6] of the neighboring village Katakhali, went to the same school. In those days, people got their children married very young, so my Dada and Dadi or paternal grandparents, Munshi Yakub Ali Hawladar and Rosul Jan Bibi, decided to get my father married when he turned twelve. Baba said that if he had to get married, he would marry Chand Mia's daughter Johora—my mother—or no one else. My mother was only seven.

Dada and Dadi were floored that their son (my future father) wanted to marry a girl from the ostentatious Mia Bari. But my father, a stubborn and whimsical twelve-year-old, was unwilling to change his mind. Finally, my Dada hesitantly sent a proposal to my Nana's house. The people of Mia Bari were shocked to receive this proposal and immediately said no. A few days later, the proposal was sent again; it was rejected again. Chand Mia eventually agreed to marry his daughter to this farming family, feeling that since they were so eager to have her, they would probably take good care of Johora, his seven-year-old motherless daughter. Finally, after the families exchanged a lot of money and conditions, my mother and father got married.

The elders of Chand Mia's household arranged to make proper gifts to Dada's family: they bought dinner and tea sets and had a table and chairs made for Dada's house. The marriage contract stipulated that the groom's family would pay the bride's family a *kabin* or dowry of 1 lakh—a huge amount of money in those days. Wearing 52 *bhori* (1.33 lbs or 600 grams) of gold jewelry, an expensive Benarasi silk sari, a shawl, a jacket, and zari-trimmed shoes, seven-year-old Johora was married to twelve-year-old Abdur Razzak. During one of the wedding events, my mother Johora took off all her heavy jewelry and her sari and climbed up a tree naked, not coming down for hours.

Ma did not move in with Baba's family until she reached puberty, around age twelve or thirteen. When she moved to her father-in-law's house, her male servant Kalai went along to Katakhali to take care of her. All of us siblings grew up in Kalai's care. Kalai liked to do women's work—there was no match for him in cooking, arranging the house, and taking care of the women. Soon after my wedding, Kalai left our household, went to Dhaka, and became a well-known chef. Then he married and had a family.

Before my parents' marriage, Ma's family was considered elite and did not mix with Baba's farming family. Dada had money, but he didn't have a privileged background. In Mia Bari, where my mother grew up, some buildings even had attached bathrooms with huge copper bathtubs. The women never bathed outside in ponds or tanks like the other women of the village. In the afternoon, the women of the household would take a bath, drape their saris elegantly, apply powder and cream, line their eyes with *kajal* or *surma*,[7] and walk around like fairies. They didn't have to do any work besides reading fiction, sewing, or cooking a few fancy dishes. To me, it seemed like a dreamland. A dedicated washerman lived next to the house and only washed clothes for the women of this household. There were two or three big ponds within the compound for washing clothes. The people of my Nana's household didn't mingle with the ordinary village people.

Despite being the proud daughter of such an ostentatious household, my mother was somehow very different from many of her female relatives. She carried on with her work silently but with dignity. Ma was not considered especially beautiful. I never saw her wear jewelry, except for a small nose-stud. She wore simple clothes—ordinary saris, blouses, and petticoats—yet she was very particular about her clothes. She wore light-colored cotton saris along with her own hand-made *shemij* or slip when I was very young. Later, as styles changed, she would sew herself blouses and petticoats to wear under her saris. If my father ever gave her a sari with a wide border, she would cut off the lower portion of the border so that only a thin border would remain. Her daily needs were minimal. She never spoke loudly. She ate last, after everyone else had eaten. She preferred not to be noticed, but quietly fought for her girls to have a better life.

Ma was always doing something creative in her spare time. She would take old, faded saris, layer them and join them together with fine hand stitching to make *kanthas*, or light blankets. She would remove the borders of old saris (and border portions cut off from saris Baba gave her) and join them together to make gorgeous curtains. She would do embroidery on her sari blouses and on tablecloths and pillowcases. Sometimes she made embroidery just for the art of it. These small embroidered artworks would be framed and hung in our home. Her embroidery patterns were usually drawn from nature, with trees, flowers, and vines. In her free time in the afternoons, I would often find her on the veranda doing needlework, and that is where she taught me to sew and embroider. Ma was also expert at crocheting and created beautiful tablecloths for our small side tables, embellished with elaborate crochet patterns.

One of my mother's crafts that fascinated me as a child was basket weaving. It was a complex process. First, she would get the men to gather "*keya pata*" (screwpine leaves), the long, naturally water-resistant leaves of a salt-tolerant tree that grows in marshy areas. We children would eat the *keya* fruits, which look just like small pineapples and taste mild like avocados, but very juicy. To prepare for my mother's weaving, the thorns would be removed from the *keya* leaves. Then the leaves would be soaked in water until soft. Next, the softened leaves would be cut into thin strips. These cut strips would then be laid out in the sun to dry for several days until they turned brown. Finally, Ma would sit in her kitchen or veranda and weave these leaves into large, gorgeous baskets with intricate designs for storing or carrying food, *pati* or floor mats to sleep or sit on, and stunning *jaynamaz* or prayer mats, complete with minaret designs. She could manipulate the leaves in different patterns to make the designs she envisioned. Seeing her make these objects of great utility, versatility, and beauty from local renewable materials was my first lesson in sustainability as well as in valuing the many kinds of knowledge that women have and share.

In our big and bustling household, there was always someone cooking in the kitchen and always someone eating—no one ever left without eating. As the wife of the eldest son in my father's family, Ma had a lot of responsibilities, including cooking. I vividly remember the taste of Ma's special treats. Ma was famous for the delicious *nasta* or snacks and desserts she made. She had learned how to make these fancy treats in her childhood home of Mia Bari, so many of her recipes were unique, and no one else in our village could make them like her. Her *morobba*, or fruit candies, were legendary. Ma made *morobba* with the sour *bel* (wood-apple) fruit, which is the size of a grapefruit and has a hard shell that must be cracked open to reveal the pungent orange soft center. I loved her delicate *morobba* of *chal kumra*, a huge white gourd or pumpkin that grew on the roofs of our homes. Her papaya *morobba* had a beautiful pinkish orange color, and her *morobba* of ripe cucumber was a pale gold. She also made a scrumptious sweet and sour *morobba* with green mango. She would grind coconut and make *narkel borfi*, a type of *shandesh* or fudge. Ma also made a delicious flan or caramel custard that we called "pudding." Her *dudh lau*—a kind of rice pudding made with finely grated squash instead of rice—was incredible. She made all these treats with various locally available seasonal fruits and vegetables and would store them for several months. We had no electricity or refrigeration, so *morobba* would extend the life of our local harvest. She would store all these treats buried in *muri* or homemade puffed rice inside large old mustard oil tins. When the mustard oil was finished, we would save the tin container and take it to the market, where they would cut it in the middle and add a lid so that it could be used as a storage vessel.

Wintertime had a special magic for me because of Ma's *pithas*. *Pithas* are a seasonal dessert or breakfast food made with ingredients such as milk, *gur*,[8] sugar, coconut, flour, and rice flour. Ma knew how to make at least two dozen varieties of special *pithas*. One of her unique recipes was *taler bhapa pitha*. *Tal* is a fruit that looks a bit like a black coconut and grows on extremely tall palms. When you open the *tal* fruit, there are pulpy yellowish aromatic sections inside. Ma would extract this *tal* fruit, pulp it, and mix it with rice flour, coconut, and *gur*. She would let this mixture ferment overnight. The next morning, she would boil water in a narrow pot until it was steaming. Then she would cover the top of the pot with a tightly wrapped piece of cotton cloth and put a mound of the fermented *tal* mixture on it. The steam would cook this mixture into a fluffy yellow cake. It would melt in your mouth, and the flavor was divine. My mother is the only person I knew who could make this delightful dish. With the same fermented batter, she also made long skinny *lathi pitha* ("stick" *pitha*) on banana leaves that she would cook directly on a *tawa* or flat pan on our outdoor wood-fired clay stoves. Cooking was mostly done outdoors in these stoves, basically a hole in the ground for the wood fire with a beautiful handmade three-legged clay form on top to hold the pots.

In the summer, we would have so many mangoes on our trees that we could not finish them. Ma would harvest and pulp the extra mangoes to make *aam shotto*, or dried mango fruit roll. This was an elaborate process. The mango would be peeled and pulped and mixed with a little *gur* and salt. Then it would be poured out on the leaf *patis* she made. The mango mixture would dry into a leathery dark brown thin layer. Ma would add more layers of mango pulp each day until it got around a quarter-inch thick. When it was all dry, she would carefully roll up the *aam shotto*, which would have the imprint of her *patis*. Her *aam shotto* was so pungent and flavorful and just barely sweet. Even after we moved away from Katakhali, she would send us her special *aam shotto*. My daughters were particularly fond of it.

My mother had seven children in total, all of us born at home in Munshi Bari with the help of my Dadi, who was a renowned midwife. I was my parents' first child. I was born on 14 March 1938, when my mother was fifteen or sixteen. Most Bengalis do not know their exact birthdates, but we know mine because Dada wrote it down in his Koran. My mother had four daughters in a row—myself, Fatema, Lutfa, and Runu—before she had my two brothers. At that time, a woman had to bear sons to have value, and a mother was usually known by the name of her first son. However, it took so many years for Ma to bear a son that she became known by my name, her first-born daughter. Finally, around 1951 she had a son, my brother Taslim, followed by another daughter, Lina, and another son, Mahim, who was tragically killed in a cyclone. To this day, my mother is known in Katakhali as "Noorjahaner Ma," and I am known as Noorjahan's Ma's Noorjahan.

### *My mother's home, Mia Bari*

As long as my father was alive, my mother never called our household her own. She always thought proudly of her father's house, Mia Bari, as her home. The hope with which my Nana had married my mother to my father was not fulfilled. Ma felt she belonged to an aristocratic lineage, but in the eyes of her in-laws, she had neither looks nor talent, only pride. Ma held her head high and never bent it for anyone.

When I was small, I thought Ma was always sad. Her two big doe-like eyes seemed to be brimming with tears. Ma had thick black bushy hair. I thought she was very beautiful, but she was considered average by others. In our house in Katakhali, I rarely saw my mother smile. There was a teacher who lived in our house for thirty-five years. He said to me one day, "I've been in your house for so many years, but I've never seen your mother's face. I've never even heard her voice."

But when we went with Ma to Nana's house (Mia Bari) in Tungibaria, suddenly the whole place would fill with her open-hearted laughter. It felt so good to hear her laugh, and I wondered why my mother didn't laugh like that all the time. Baba never let Ma go to her father's house alone; she could only go with him. They would go to Mia Bari for a meal and some conversation, and then he would bring her back to our home. Everyone praised Baba highly for this, thinking it was a sign of love, but I didn't like it at all.

I would often climb onto Ma's lap and ask, "Why are you crying all the time? Why aren't you going to your father's house?" Ma would smile and say, "No, silly, I'm not crying. How could I feel sad when I have you all?" But I knew there was more to this than she wanted to admit. I promised myself that when I grew up, I would try to bring her happiness.

When we were small, Mia Bari seemed like nothing short of a palace. It was a homestead consisting of six big wooden buildings and one brick building on a large piece of land in Tungibaria. There was a huge courtyard in the middle where children would play and women would promenade.[9] The two single-story buildings to the north and south had wood floors and a long open veranda in front, furnished with a long table and big benches with wooden armrests. From the open veranda, you stepped onto the covered veranda furnished with a big bed, a table and chair, a box of *paan*[10] and a hookah; there were always books and magazines on the table. Nana's interior veranda also had framed paintings of Gandhi, Abul Kalam Azad, and other leaders on the wall. Nana and my Boro Mama, or eldest maternal uncle, used scented tobacco. Boro Mama lived in the North Building and Nana lived in the South Building.

In the North Building where Boro Mama lived was a huge bedroom with two enormous beds spread out on either end of the western side. Boro Mama's two wives lived in that room, but each slept on her own bed with her children. In my mother's family, besides Nana, only Boro Mama had more than one wife. However, Nana lived with only one wife at a time; he lost four wives one after the other, three of them sisters. Boro Mama's first wife was his own cousin. That marriage happened against Boro Mama's will when he was at most twelve years old. Later, Boro Mama married another woman of his own choice. We called Boro Mama's first wife Rani Khala. She had two sons and three daughters. Rani Khala and her two sons died in the cyclone of 1965; her three daughters are still alive.

On one side of the courtyard, on the eastern side of Boro Mama's bedroom, there was another bedroom where another uncle and his beautiful wife lived. The building also had a dining room, where people ate on the floor on beautiful spreads. Attached to the east side of the building was another huge veranda where the women worked and talked. There was always cooking and clamoring going on in the enormous kitchen. So many different dishes were cooked in those huge cooking pots, urn-shaped *handis*, cylindrical *dekchis*, and woks or *kadai*. But I never paid much attention to that. When we went to that house, either Boro Mama or Nana would supervise our meals. My own Nani or maternal grandmother was no longer living. Maybe that's why Nana looked after us himself.

Nana was one of seven brothers and four sisters. Each of the brothers had a nickname: Chand Mia, Lal Mia, Manik Mia, Mohan Mia, Moti Nana, and so on.[11] We were very close to all their children too. Three of Nana's brothers (whom I also called Nana or grandpa)—Lal Mia Nana, Manik Nana, and Mohan Mia Nana—lived in the Nayabari or New House, which was outside of the Mia Bari homestead, just a few houses south. Moti Nana lived in the Boro Bari or Big House, a long building on the eastern side of the Mia Bari homestead, with his wife and children. I was always very close to two of Moti Nana's children, Ala Mama and Ruzi Khala. Just south of the Boro Bari, there was another two-story building. The wife of my Nana's father, whom he had married late in life, and her son Shukur Nana lived there. Shukur Nana's older sister Parul Nani got married and moved to Moudubi on the south end of Barobaishdia.

On one side of the South Building where Nana lived there was a big bedroom with a huge carved bed fitted with a luxurious mattress, big, fringed head pillows, and side pillows. An elaborately embroidered canopy hung above the bed. When we went over to Nana's house, we stared at these things in amazement. In the inner rooms, there were huge wooden chests full of quilts, bedding, pillows, and sheets. The eating arrangements were equally fancy. We ate on a very beautiful carpet spread on the floor and covered with a hand-embroidered cloth. We washed our hands in shiny brass fingerbowls and dried them on towels. There were beautiful foreign-made plates, glasses, various kinds of bowls, cups, and glass pitchers. We had these things in our own house too, but we didn't use them every day; they were reserved for guests. We ate all kinds of *halwa*, *morobba*, and *pitha*.

We also went to Nana's house during mango and jackfruit season. Those were fun-filled times! In the evening, I played all kinds of games with my mamas and khalas (my mother's brothers, sisters, and cousins and the children of Nana's other wives)[12] in their huge courtyard—blindman's bluff, catching fireflies, and so much more. I still treasure the bright memories of those golden childhood days.

In the corner between the west and south buildings of Nana's homestead, there was another big building called Konar Bari or the Corner House. An old woman lived there with her son, whom we called Alamgir Mama. He was very handsome and married Begum, the beautiful daughter of Afsar Master.

The two-story building to the north and west side of Nana's building was the only *dalan* or brick building in Mia Bari. I think the domestic help lived downstairs. Just up the stairs was another world. There was one large bedroom with an ornately carved canopy bed. A veranda wrapped around on all four sides. The room and veranda were beautifully arranged with fabric and paper trees, flowers, vines, and many other kinds of handicrafts. I spent many days and nights in that room when I was small. My mother's Dadi's stepbrother, Salimullah Talukdar, lived in that house with his wife, four daughters, and one son. His wife was from Swarupkathi in Barisal. She was very beautiful. I could never figure out how Salimullah Talukdar came by such a beautiful and talented wife, because Talukdar Shaheb seemed half-crazy to me. When he was good, he was very good. But when he wasn't, he gambled and abused alcohol, marijuana, and *bhang* too. He was always going off somewhere to feed his gambling addiction. He had another family in Rangabali. When he would go to Rangabali to be with his family there, that would become his whole world. Sometimes he would spend three or four years there. His two wives in these two places made their homes with their respective children. I called Talukdar Shaheb "Taloi" and his Katakhali wife "Maoi." They were both very affectionate with me. Maoi's younger brother Benu Mama lived with them. He married Achiya from our village and stayed in the area; he later studied and became a village doctor, serving many who had little means.

Maoi was an impressive woman and spent her whole life in that upstairs room. She read a lot. She was known for her delicate needlework. Her daughters were also accomplished in needlecrafts and drawing. Even the simplest vegetable dish Maoi cooked always tasted divine. She was a great talker, and I loved her stories. She had brought two domestic helpers from her father's house, named Ahmad and Zobeda. They worked for her all her life. Sadly, Maoi died in the 1965 cyclone. The two domestic helpers were also swept away with her. One day after the independence of Bangladesh in 1971, Taloi arrived at my place in Dhaka wearing torn and dirty clothes. I took care of him, arranging for his bath and giving him some nice clothes and a good meal. He ate and slept. When he woke up, he asked me for some money and left. That was the last time I saw him.

There was another great beauty in our region—my Bilkis Khala, the daughter of my mother's Chacha, my Manik Nana. Manik Nana was also very handsome, and well educated by the standards of the time—a "matric pass" or high school graduate. Everyone called him Shaheb. He had an impressive memory and knew the inside story of every one of our relatives. He kept in touch with everyone until his last days. He and his family, including Bilkis Khala and her sister Mamata, lived in the Nayabari.

The story of those two lovely sisters is a sad one. Bilkis Khala married my Khalu, Raju Biswas. His wife, Begum Khala, died early, leaving behind two children, Badol Bhai and Shefali. He married Bilkis Khala mainly so she could take care of the children. At the time, Bilkis Khala was only thirteen or fourteen. Sometime later, we learned that Khalu was beating Bilkis Khala. Everyone in the family was worried about this abuse and brought Bilkis Khala to our house on the pretext of a visit. Then when her husband came to get her, the family confronted him and forced him to give her a divorce.

A few years later, Bilkis Khala's older sister Baby Khala died of cholera, leaving behind two children. Bilkis Khala was again married off to Baby Khala's husband, that is, our Badshah Mama. But misfortune kept coming for Bilkis Khala. After Bilkis Khala had two children with Badshah Mama, he died of typhoid. Now she was widowed with four children (including Baby Khala's two children). Who would take responsibility for them? Bilkis Khala was again married off to Badshah Mama's asthmatic younger brother, Zulfu Mama, even though he already had a wife and children. I witnessed that marriage; I couldn't believe it was happening again. After that, every time I met Bilkis Khala she would hug me and cry. Zulfu Mama, his first wife Sufia, and several of their children were swept away in the 1965 cyclone. Bilkis Khala survived. But it's considered dangerous for a beauty like her to stay unmarried for long—men started eyeing her with bad intentions. So Bilkis Khala's relatives hastily tried to "save" her: she was married off to a man from the next village as his fourth wife. Long after this marriage, Bilkis Khala came to see me wearing a burqa and carrying a tiffin carrier full of food. She still had a smile on her face, but her eyes were sad. She died a few days later. I often think of Bilkis Khala and wish that I could have done something to help her.

Bilkis Khala's younger sister Mamata also had a terrible life. Mamata was gorgeous like her sister. She too was married off at the age of thirteen or fourteen. Her husband Ali Akbar was forty-five years old and already had eight children. His firstborn child was three or four years older than Mamata Khala. I felt that it would have been better to throw Mamata into the Agunmukha than marry her to this man thirty years her senior. I still feel depressed thinking of how her parents could be so cruel. I saw Mamata Khala only once after her marriage, and it broke my heart to see her sad face.

The stories of these female relatives are deeply entangled with my mother's life and my own. Ma would share their stories with me as examples of the terrible plight of women. They were a part of our family, and we loved them. But Ma didn't want me and my sisters to end up like them.

### *My village Katakhali and my childhood home, Munshi Bari*

I grew up in Katakhali in my family homestead known as Munshi Bari,[13] which consisted of six or seven wooden buildings, one brick building, two ponds, and a big courtyard with acres of agricultural land all around. Our building was on the western part of the homestead. My parents, siblings, and I lived on the second floor of the huge tin house, which had a balcony with a railing in front. The upstairs room had two levels. My parents' bed was on the higher level, next to our trunk with clothing and other items. Dada and Dadi slept on the lower level. There was a huge granary in the room itself. A year's supply of paddy and rice were kept above, and below was a place to keep different kinds of squashes and fruits for later—ripe sweet pumpkins, *chalkumro* (ash gourd, named for the way the vine grows on the roof or *chal* of the house), and dry coconuts. You could call it a pantry. When we were a little older, another two-story house was built on the southern part of the homestead for Dada and Dadi. When I was very small, before the 1947 Partition, I remember we cooked with coal. There was a mountain of coal stored in the small garden on the south side. I still have a vivid memory of reading books in the space behind the coal-heap. Nobody went looking for me there. The air was heavy with the sweet smell of pineapples. There were a lot of mosquitoes too. I'd go home in the evening with mosquito bites all over my neck and legs. My mother often gave me a slap for this, but my grandfather put himself between us and tried to resolve it.

On the east side of the small garden were wonderful mango trees. Many of them had been there for a long time. I remember two big mango trees, but I don't know who planted them, probably my Dada's mother or father. The first one had smallish mangoes, round and pale green like young banana leaves at first, then pure yellow when ripe. On the outer side was a tree with big, long, dark-green mangoes with a lot of fiber. I didn't like those very much. That was called the "*kala aamgach*" or black mango tree.

There were two big mango trees in the north garden too. One tree had long mangoes, curved at the tip like a "*joal*" or yoke of a plow. The other had similar mangoes, but smaller, so they were called "big joal" and "little joal." They had very thin seeds and were very tasty. The mangoes from these four trees were harvested and divided evenly between the two sides of the family. We took one half, and they divided their half in two again. Besides these four trees, there were many good mango trees planted by Dada or Dadi. The mangoes were of all different colors and sizes and had an incomparable scent and taste. Two Fazli mango trees Dada had planted gave very good mangoes.

There were two big ponds, one on the west side and one on the east. The one on the west was designated for the women, and the one on the east was for the men. On the north side of the west pond was a big mango tree with huge mangoes, almost the size of a big pomelo. These mangoes were not stringy at all and were bright yellow when ripe. Everyone was wary of sitting under that tree when the mangoes were ripe—if one fell on your head, that would be it!

In the summer, we spread out mats in the southern garden and listened to Dada and Dadi's stories. Sometimes a couple of ripe mangoes would plop down in the wind. It was even more fun to gather the windfalls than to eat them. There's a special pleasure in scraping a hole in the middle of the mango with a big spoon made from an oyster shell and cutting out slices of unripe mango to eat. There was a forge in the house, and every summer they made little knives, called "*batul*" or something, for each of us. There were rose-apples (*jaam*), mangosteens (*gaab*), coral-tree fruits (*deuwa*), sugar-apples (*sharifa*), custard-apples (*ata*), and so many other summer fruits.

How could I ever forget those days? In the big garden, there were rows of coconut and areca trees. On the east side was an orange or blood-orange tree; the fruit was very sour, better to look at than to eat. Right in the middle of the big garden was a patch of cardamom plants Dada had planted with great enthusiasm. He had cut a little moat all around it so that the patch was surrounded by water. This was to keep the ants out. I remember seeing the beautiful cardamom flowers, but I don't remember the cardamom pods.

Next to the pineapple plants in the small garden were a few *bel* trees. I don't quite remember where, but Dada had also planted a lychee tree. He kept it covered with a net to protect the fruit from birds. No other house in the village had a lychee tree. Outside our Kachari Ghar (office buildings)[14] to the west was a huge starfruit (*kamranga*) tree with beautiful clusters of pink flowers. I can still smell the sweet scent of those flowers. The tree was planted right next to the office, so we naughty children never used the stairs—we always went up and down the starfruit tree unbeknownst to our elders. A little farther west was a very good *amra* or hog-plum tree. We called it the "foreign *amra*." There was also a fruit tree called *deshi amra* or native *amra*, which was used only for cooking sour dishes.

Very early in the morning, while it was still dark, we mischievous children would go out to gather mangoes and *amra*. One day, my Phuphu Rupjan (the daughter of Dada's younger sister, who lived in our house) got bitten by a snake while she was gathering *amra*. She screamed, and everyone gathered around her. Baba first tied a *gamcha*[15] tightly around her upper arm, then cut her arm with a piece of glass to let the poisoned blood out. She wasn't allowed to sleep all that night or the next day. In any case, I think it wasn't a venomous snake.

After that, we didn't go out to gather fruit for a while. Ma was also very wary. There was a big pond on the south side of the house (I don't know whom it belonged to) surrounded by a thicket of a thorny wild bush called *kantabohori* (literally, "covered in thorns"). This grass had countless tiny green fruits that turned bright red when ripe. We went to gather these fruits early in the morning and made them into necklaces, then ate them ourselves—they were sweet and sour, not that tasty, but it was fun to pick them. Now looking back, I think eating all these fruits is probably why I've never had a vitamin C deficiency.

Between the house and the outer buildings was the old brick building, long like a school. No one lived inside that building, only bats, sparrows, mice, and snakes. In the outer buildings lived an allopathic doctor, a homeopathic doctor, and a confectioner. My Shejochacha or third paternal uncle Rashid used this southern room for a small business. Shejochacha had a variety store where he sold all kinds of fancy things, scented oil, powder, face cream, red syrup for making *sharbat*, soap, peanuts, lozenges, Lily Biscuits—very small round biscuits, easy to break in half—colorful ribbons, and combs. And, of course, *beedis*[16] and cigarettes. Shejochacha studied at the school near my mamas' house. I think he lived with Afsar Master (a friend of Mejochacha, my paternal second uncle). The shop closed when he was at school and opened again when he came back. I loved Shejochacha and his little shop.

Whenever a newcomer arrived in Katakhali, everyone pointed to our homestead and said, "Go there." The doors of our house were open twenty-four hours a day to visitors, peddlers, beggars, and strangers. While the interior buildings were for family use, the two Kachari Ghar in the outer area of the compound on the north side of the property were for the men to carry out their business and social interactions, such as settling disputes or negotiating agreements. The eastern building was used by our relatives the Hawladar family for their employees, and Baba and Dada used the western one. Our two-story Kachari Ghar was furnished with big beds, tables, and chairs. Relatives and guests were always coming and going, and many stayed overnight. Dada loved to talk to people. I liked having visitors, too. Many unfamiliar Kabuliwalas (traveling merchants from Afghanistan or other northern regions) came to sell dried fruits, various kinds of Kashmiri *halwa*, and amazingly beautiful shawls. They gave loans with interest to the villagers. All of them took shelter in our Kachari Ghar. Ma looked after their meals from inside but did not venture out to the Kachari Ghar. Come to think of it, the head teacher at the primary school in front of our house lived in our office most of the year, except for the long summer holidays. We studied with him morning and evening. His name was Ismail Master. I started out talking about Katakhali and look where I ended up. Maybe that's what happens when you write from memory.

Many of our poor relatives and their children also lived in our household, sometimes for a few months, sometimes longer. Ma told us to treat them well, and she took care of all their needs, making sure that they had good food to eat and fresh clothes to wear.

Ma had eyes in every direction. Even as she juggled so many responsibilities and activities, Ma's keen attention ensured that we children bathed, ate, and studied regularly. She taught us to speak well and eat neatly. She also kept a sharp watch on what games we played and who our friends were. From the time we were small, Ma taught me and my siblings that we were different from the other villagers. She hoped that we would not suffer the same fate as the other village girls. She would tell us sisters, "You have to get a proper education and leave this house as fully developed human beings. I won't let you lead a life like mine." When she said this, I wondered where else I could possibly go and what I could do.

Moving beyond the boundaries of our compound, to the west in the middle of a marsh was a big house everyone called Biler Bari or the marsh house. It's still known by that name. On the south side of our house was Gajibari (the home of the Gaji family), and if you walked quite a way out east from the outer boundary of our house, you'd find the Sunday market. Then the Sonamoddis' house. Between the Sonamoddis' house and the market, along the river to the north, was a small fishermen's neighborhood, and next to it the Dalalbari (Dalal family home). The last house in this line, at a little distance, was the Kobirajbari or ayurvedic doctor's house. I don't know why it was called that, since I for one never saw a *kobiraj* in that house. I've never seen anyone as wily, devious, and litigious as Goyzoddi who lived in that house. Goyzoddi made even my life miserable for a while when I was small.

After that, there was another row of houses to the east. First Hajibari; maybe someone in that family had been on Hajj, I don't know when. The funny thing is, even though there were many well-off families in the area, going on Hajj was not common at all. Nowadays, going on Hajj seems like more of a way to show off than a real pilgrimage. As far as I know, only three people in the six or seven villages in our area had gone on Hajj: Taragaji in Phelabunia, Kalu Haji in Gabbunia (because his parents had made a vow that their only son would go on Hajj if he recovered from cholera), and the Haji of Hajibari in our village. Neither my Nana nor my Dada ever bothered their heads about going on Hajj. When my Dada decided to marry a young girl who worked in our house, as discussed in the next chapter, Baba and my Chachas tried to send him on Hajj, but Dada refused. There was no religious fervor on either side of our family. Both my Nana and my Dada were influential and wealthy, but there was no mosque or madrasa in either house. I never saw anyone but Dada and Ma doing *namaz* or keeping the Ramadan fast. *Parda* was not observed anywhere in the village, certainly not in our house.[17] And yet my Dada was a *koran hafez*, meaning he had memorized the Koran Sharif. When I went to live at my mother's cousin Surja Khala's house in Patuakhali to go to school, they set a condition that I had to wear a burqa. Dada was the first to object to this and said that wearing burqas was not mentioned anywhere in the Koran. In any case, we had the chance to grow up in a relatively open, free environment; we were untouched by religious conservatism.

When I was growing up in Katakhali, I was a daredevil. I was friends with the boys in our household and in the village. We caught fish, played soccer and *hadudu*,[18] and climbed all sorts of trees including coconut trees. A group of us went with Baba to the next village to see the bullfights. A funny thing once happened. Every winter, the local "*ostad*" ("master," or quack doctor who performed boys' circumcisions) came to do what's considered the needful for Muslim and Jewish men. I had no idea what this was about, but I knew it was something scary. My Choto Chacha[19] Abdur Rab and my cousin Khalek were both two or three years older than me. That year when the "*ostad*" came around, I ran away to the jungle with them. When we got tired after going all day without eating and went to the next-door house to find something to eat, they took us back to our house like criminals. I got a good drubbing from Ma, especially for my stupidity. The grownups never talked openly with us about these things. We discussed matters among ourselves and made decisions accordingly.

Anyway, after that was Sader Ali Khan's house. In the middle were the houses of the Boyatis, Adam Ali Haoladar, and Hafez Haoladar. After that was a house that belonged to us, where a landless family of the village lived for a while, and later our relatives lived there. Eventually, after many storms, and floods, sometime after the 1965 cyclone, my parents moved from Munshi Bari to a new home on that property, which was closer to the Darchira River. I was abroad then. That property also had two ponds and a lot of land, and my mother spent her final years there.

As I described earlier, Mia Bari, my *mamabari* or maternal grandparents' home, is in Tungibaria, on the eastern bank of the Digri River. The Katakhali *khal* or channel starts near Mia Bari in Tungibaria, flows past Munshi Bari to the east, and meets the Rabnabad River. On our side of the channel, a primary school and weekly market (both established by my Dada) have been running in front of our homestead for a long time. On the other side of the channel is the Burmese neighborhood; the Burmese in our area are now called Rakhine. The current village higher secondary school is also on that side of the channel on land belonging to our family. We didn't have a higher secondary school when I was a child; now the village children can study there in the school building, but the lack of roads makes the students' lives miserable in the monsoon. To the north of the channel are Gabbunia and Phelabunia, where I lived with my Phuphu during class five, and across the Digri River is Chalitabunia village, where my mother's *mamabari* is. This Katakhali channel was dug so that boats could come easily from across the Agunmukha right up to our house; it connects the Agunmukha to the Darchira River. But the channel itself is now a vast and frightening river; it has completely swallowed up Mia Bari. Nowadays sandbars are starting to show up. Mia Bari has broken up into fifteen or twenty households; the family is now scattered in Dhaka, Patuakhali, and Galachipa. Some have gone as far as the Middle East and Italy.

This gives you a picture of our Katakhali village. Today, each homestead has been split up into seven or eight houses, mainly due to population growth. When I was growing up, aside from a few families, most of the villagers were comfortable. They were all farmers. Now because of storms, floods, cyclones, and population growth, all but a few families are trying to make a living as fishermen. Many of them have gone to Dhaka to work in garment factories or as taxi drivers and day laborers. Little girls go to work for rich people in Dhaka and fall prey to emotional and physical abuse. I knew and still know every person in every household in the village.

*My mother's commitment to girls' education*

As I grew older, Ma pointed out to me the intolerable and unjust condition of women in our community and the world. For example, my cousin Rupjan was in school with me until class four. She was forcibly married to a man who was at least fifty years old and had grown-up children. Rupjan was absolutely against this marriage, but she had no choice. Ma said, "Look what happens to girls in this village! I want you to get educated and move out of this hell!" She made me aware of the behavior of the men of our household toward the women and girls who worked for us and our dependent female relatives. Many of our male relatives tried to exploit these women sexually. My mother tried to marry off our dependent female relatives quickly to get them out of harm's way. She had to suffer a lot of humiliation from the men of the family because of this, but she put up with it in silence.

Ma vowed to educate all of us girls and worked hard to prevent our early marriage. From a very young age, Ma sat us down beside her and taught us to read and write. Even though she was married young, Ma had been educated at the local school as well as at home and kept on studying until she was twelve or thirteen. In Munshi Bari, we could study at the nearby government-run Katakhali Primary School only up to class four. When I was nine years old and ready for class five, Ma sent me to my Phuphu's house in Phelabunia to continue my education. That was around March 1947. At the time, we were still part of British India, but there was talk that our region (East Bengal) would become part of a new country called Pakistan, which would be for Muslims. I didn't understand much about this, except I was sad to hear that our Hindu friends might be leaving. Partition happened in August 1947, while I was studying in Phelabunia; in that rural area, we had no inkling of what was going on politically. Unfortunately, I could hardly study at my Phuphu's house because I had to take care of two small children. My Phuphu, Asiya, was a child bride and mother of two by age fourteen.

Seventy years ago, my mother boldly sent me, a nine-year-old girl, to live and study at another relative's house because she wanted a different life for me. I knew that after sending me, my mother could not sleep at night. She used to worry about me all day long, wondering whether I had food, where I was sleeping, and whether I could study. Everyone was astounded that my Ma would send me so far away to continue my studies. But it turns out she was wise, and her determination made me who I am today. Because of Ma's constant battle, I became the first girl from my entire area to finish high school, and I went on to get higher degrees also.

I remember being home in Katakhali during the winter school break in January 1948 and asking Ma for food. She said, "I'm fasting. Please fix something for yourself." I said, "Why are you fasting? It's not Ramzan." She answered, "I'm fasting because Mahatma Gandhi was killed." I said, "Oh, but he's a Hindu," repeating something I had heard from my friends. Ma slapped me hard across my cheek. She had never hit me before and neither had Baba. She said, "How could a child born to me say such a thing?! I never taught you to distinguish between Hindus and Muslims. I never want to hear anything like that from you again. Did you know that Gandhi is called Mahatma, which means 'A Great Soul?'" I left crying, and Baba asked me what was wrong. When I told him what happened, he said Ma did the right thing. Ma was a devout Muslim and prayed five times a day, but we regularly interacted with Hindus and Buddhists, and she believed everyone was equal.

The next school year began in the spring of 1948, and Ma sent me to Moudubi, which was at the other end of Barobaishdia Island, a long journey by boat. One of Ma's phuphus, whom I called Parul Nanu, lived there. The Moudubi High School had just opened that year. Sending a ten-year-old girl so far away to someone else's house to study was considered completely crazy. Everyone was talking about my mother, but she remained firm in her decision. Ma sent me off with this advice: "I can't stand guard over you all your life. You will have to learn to protect yourself."

### *My grandfather's marriage to my playmate*

Around 1946, a skinny, sickly little girl of nine or ten named Hamela came to our house in Katakhali to fill her stomach by working as domestic help. My Dadi had brought Hamela from the house of a relative of ours. There had been a big flood in Bhola, and many people sold their daughters because they could not afford to feed them. There were boatloads of girls of various ages being brought to our area and sold. Across the ages in all civilizations, women and girls have been abused in this way, especially in times of war, conflict, famine, and floods.

Hamela's long, smooth head of hair was genuinely striking. But she had scabies all over her skinny body, a torn dress, and bare feet. My compassionate Dadi bathed her with her own hands in warm water and carbolic soap, then gave her my dress to wear. When I woke up in the morning and saw this sight, I was very jealous. I didn't want to share my Dadi. Slowly, with Dadi's love and care, Hamela regained her health. My anger also died down. I played with Hamela whenever I got the chance. Like all village children, we played with our homemade dolls, with mud and sand, and pretended to cook flowers and leaves. Hamela loved this playtime between her tasks.

In 1948, I was in Moudubi, studying in class six. Hamela was then around twelve or thirteen years old. I remember Dadi was planning to marry Hamela to our relative Hazrat Ali Chacha, who was around sixteen years old. Hamela and Hazrat Ali Chacha knew about their upcoming marriage, as it was being discussed openly. Ma was stocking up little by little on clothes, oil, soap, and other things for this wedding.

Then suddenly my world fell apart: when I came home to Katakhali for the Pujo holiday, I saw that my respected Dada had married Hamela. Until Dada's eyes fell on her, I didn't notice that Hamela had slowly grown into a beautiful adolescent. Only after this did I take a close look at her. With her small brown eyes and full red lips, Hamela looked a lot like the actress Sophia Loren. Her long, thick light brown hair fell to below the knee. She had a rebellious spirit that made her even more attractive. Despite the objections of everyone in the household and Hamela's endless tears, Dada would not be deterred. Ma went to Dada herself and asked him not to go through with this marriage. But Dada showed her his Koran and told her that, according to the Koran, he is not even obligated to marry Hamela to enjoy her body. He was marrying her only to uphold the family honor. After that, everyone held their tongues.

Dada's forcible "marriage" to Hamela shook me to the core. I could hardly look at my Dadi's face. Dadi, who was always smiling, wanted to sink into the earth from shame and sadness. That year, I spent much of the Pujo holiday sitting alone on the veranda of our home, the big building on the western side of our homestead. I stopped playing and even talking.

After Dada's marriage to Hamela, I slept with Dadi most of the time. She had come over to our building after Dada married Hamela. I couldn't even look at the South Building where Dada and Dadi used to sleep. Dada was now there with Hamela. I didn't speak to Dada, Dadi, or Hamela for a long time. Somehow, I felt angry at Hamela. I wondered why she didn't just run away somewhere. But she had nowhere to go. Every morning, I saw Hamela sitting outside the kitchen under a coconut tree, crying her eyes out. She hardly ate. The domestic help would force-feed her. In the evenings, they would comb her hair and dress her in nice clothes, and every night they would send her by force, sometimes hitting her, to Dada's room. It pained me to see her in this helpless and unbearable condition and not be able to do anything for her.

Meanwhile, my mother burned all the clothes she had bought for Hamela and Hazrat Ali Chacha's wedding and handed out the oil, soap, and other things to the domestic helpers. Seeing that, I felt even more love and respect for Ma. At the time, I shouted and fought with Baba and his younger brother Abdul Karim, or Karim Chacha, about how they could allow this marriage, but that didn't help either. Baba and Karim Chacha were afraid that if they objected to the marriage, Dada would disinherit them. Dada bribed them to let him indulge his disgusting desires; he placed almost his entire inheritance in his four sons' names. This meant that after Dada's death, Hamela, Dadi, their future descendants, and my two phuphus would be deprived of any share of his vast inheritance.

Whenever I saw Hamela, I realized that something like this could happen to me and my mother at any time. I began my inner rebellion during that visit home. At this time, marriage proposals began coming for me, too. Various relatives and other hateful men were trying to get at me, even though I was just ten.

*Molested at age ten*

My youngest nani, Nana's fifth wife, was the daughter of a panchayat[20] member in Moudubi. Nana's younger half-sister Parul Nani had married into that family in Moudubi. I lived in Parul Nani's house to attend school. Someone or other was always coming and going between Moudubi and Mia Bari, Nana's house in Tungibaria. One day before the end of my school break, we found out that Parul Nani's brother-in-law was going from Tungibaria to Moudubi. Ma quickly packed my suitcase, fed me, and sent me to Tungibaria with her domestic helper Kalai. That night after dinner, I was sleeping with one of my mamis. Suddenly she woke me up and said, we're all leaving for Moudubi right away, the river is in high tide. I got into the little dinghy with everyone else and sat on the deck. Parul Nani's brother-in-law sat right up against me. Mochan Mama went along too. After we got in, the boatmen released the boat. It was a moonlit night in the month of Ashwin, bright as day, with a light breeze. Suddenly it started to rain. In the month of Ashwin, rain showers often come and go without warning. Parul Nani's brother-in-law opened his umbrella and pulled me close to him. Then he grabbed me and pressed his face against mine and tried to stick his tongue into my mouth. Caught off guard, I didn't know what to do. I clenched my teeth shut, shaking with fear and disgust. I couldn't even scream. I don't know how long this went on, but it felt like an eternity. As soon as the boat reached the dock, the disgusting man let me go, closed the umbrella, got down in the mud, and stood there ready to pick me up and help me off the boat. I got off on the other side and ran into the house. I found Parul Nani inside and clung to her, but I couldn't tell her anything. Parul Nani probably thought I was sad to leave my mother. She lovingly washed my hands and feet and took me to sleep with her. I was prickling with fear all night. I was afraid that her horrible relative might come and attack me again.

That night when I went to brush my teeth, I threw up several times out of sheer disgust. From that day on, vomiting became a language of protest in my life. Whenever I am angry or disgusted with something, I throw up. This is my mind's silent protest. Meanwhile, the three months I spent in Moudubi after that cruel man's torture became unbearable. That nasty man had two wives and grown children at the time, but for sick people like that, being attracted to young children is like a game. I was only ten years old then and had not yet hit puberty. My body was skinny and light as a bird. That same sick man came to teach English in my classroom just to harass me. He wrote long love letters to me and proposed marriage. He would come to the house and send me gifts of biscuits and chocolate through Parul Nani. I was constantly shrinking in fear of him.

*Trying to escape disgusting men*

Then I somehow managed to do the final exam in Moudubi and came home to Katakhali. Even at home, I couldn't escape that man. He sent a marriage proposal through one of my chachas, Rashid Mia. He said if I married him, he would give me a lot of money and land. My mother was furious at this proposal. Ma said, "How dare he? With two wives at home, he still reaches out for my ten-year-old daughter!"

I was only ten years old, but there were more men after me. One of the teachers in Moudubi called Rashid Master also tried to marry me and sent multiple proposals. I think he had three wives and a daughter three or four years older than me. But that made no difference to him.

After all these proposals came, my mother and I became even more determined to try to change the trajectory of my life. Baba thought it was time to arrange my marriage. At that time, it was the custom in that region to arrange a child's marriage by age nine or ten. My mother was married at seven years old. But Ma had other plans for me, and her resolve saved my life. I had only one thought on my mind: I have to get out of this hell. The faster the better. Ma insisted that I should be educated and not get married yet.

My father's younger brother Karim Chacha was studying at BM College in Barisal at the time.[21] Ma begged Karim Chacha to put me in a hostel in Barisal and enroll me in school there. I also started crying and begging them to let me continue my studies. Karim Chacha was very affectionate toward me, and he was also very happy to see my extreme eagerness to study. He knew that I was devouring all the books and magazines in our household. When he came home for holidays, he would ask me lots of questions and tell me about famous women of our country and around the world.

The people of our village and several surrounding villages had great respect for my mother. Everyone listened to her. Ma had slowly established her authority in our household to the point that even my chachas listened to her every word. At Ma's repeated request, Karim Chacha promised to try to arrange for me to stay in Barisal and attend school. He upheld that promise.

### *The need for education*

In January 1949, I left my beloved Katakhali and went to Barisal. I readily gave up my carefree life in Katakhali and the people, plants, and animals I loved there to get away from the filthy men. Of course, even before coming to Barisal I had already spent two years in Phelabunia and Moudubi, away from the comfort of my home.

I was anxious about moving to the city. Would I be able to fit into urban, educated society? Baba and Karim Chacha both gave me a lot of encouragement on the way there. In Barisal, we rented a small tin-roofed room from Mochan Mia and stayed there. Karim Chacha bought some cloth and had some salwar kameez made for me. He also bought me new ribbons and hair clips to make me look more genteel before taking me for the entrance exam at Saiyadunnesa Girls' School. The school was named after the mother of Sher-e-Bangla A. K. Fazlul Huq Shaheb. There was a girls' hostel where around twenty to twenty-five girls resided. The school went from class seven up to matric (class ten and the high school diploma exam). It was at the end of Agarpur Road, a one-story building laid out from east to west and surrounded by a compound wall. Next to the entrance gate was the office and the teachers' lounge.

A girl named Halima enrolled in my class (class seven) a few days later, and we immediately became friends. We are still good friends after all these years and keep in touch with each other. Moji Apa, the fiancée of Karim Chacha's friend Mohiuddin Chacha,[22] her older sister Foji Apa, and their little sister Mini Apa also lived in the hostel. They had come there from Kolkata to take the matric exam. In class ten, there was Meruna, who was light-complexioned with a narrow forehead, and Sufia. In class nine, there was Anwara, who was very plump. Her little sister Sagardir went to the Baptist Mission School in Barisal. Fatima in class eight was very pretty, and clever. There was also Parul, who was tall and thin and looked young for class nine. A few other girls came for the matric exam, but I don't remember their names. The three sisters Moji Apa, Foji Apa, and Mini Apa took good care of us, but they left the hostel after a few months to live at Mohiuddin Chacha's elder brother's house.

The teachers I remember are the head teacher Shahanara Begum, Amena Apa, Gouri Sengupta, and Kochi Apa. A Moulubi Shaheb[23] with a salt-and-pepper beard taught Arabic and Urdu. There were two gates in the hostel. They were both locked twenty-four hours a day. They could only be unlocked with special permission from the school authorities. On Fridays, registered relatives could come and visit. But sometimes the older girls would pressure or bribe the gatekeeper to open the inner gate. I remember one such incident: one moonlit night, I woke up and saw the hostel room empty, except for Halima and me. I looked out of the window and saw that the other girls had secretly gathered in the school's big classroom for a midnight meal. The two of us just lay in bed pretending to sleep.

Amena Apa, who was our teacher and the hostel superintendent, was in love with Halima's brother Ali Ashraf. Ali Ashraf and Amena Apa used to sit in the teachers' room after school and talk over tea and snacks. Many people knew about their infatuation, and soon I figured it out too. Amena Apa took special care of me and Halima. Amena Apa had a lot of siblings. They lived at their Nani's house. Amena Apa's father was a *ghar-jamai*: he lived in his father-in-law's house. His father had a job in Patuakhali, I think. Amena Apa and Ali Ashraf got married in secret soon after that and went away to Dhaka. Ali Ashraf was a journalist who later worked at the *Dainik Bangla*. Amena Apa worked at a bank. They never had children. Many years later, Ali Ashraf got married again to a woman journalist. Amena Apa went back to Barisal broken-hearted.

After Amena Apa left the school, the recently widowed Sabita Sengupta took the post of hostel superintendent. She had four young children, and her husband had suddenly died at a young age. He had been a professor of commerce at BM College. Sabita-di was a relative of our teacher Gouri-di, who helped Sabita-di get the superintendent job after she was widowed. The first time I saw Sabita-di in a white sari, I felt so sad. The names of her children were Bubu, Tubu, Babu, and Bachchu. Bachchu was only a few months old then. I was very happy to have them around. Whenever I got a break from classes and studying, I would spend time with them. Sabita-di was very fond of me. Soon after Sabita-di arrived, I started eating my meals with her. Suddenly Sabita-di's youngest son Bachchu came down with a fever and died. We were all devastated to lose that sweet baby.

A few weeks after Bachchu died, we finished our exams. When the results came out, I saw that I had come second in rank in class seven. Sonia was ranked first. Her nickname was Baby, and she was very pretty. Her sister Beauty was also truly a beauty. Third in our class was Setara. After the exam, we were told that the school and the hostel were going to be shut down. I was crushed. I came to Saiyadunnesa School with such dreams, and with such difficulty, and now it was all over. It was almost the end of December. All the girls were heading home after the exam. Only Halima and I and a few other girls were still in the hostel, waiting for our relatives to come.

After the exam was over, we spent all our time having fun. One evening, our elderly cook made an excellent *khichuri* with coconut milk and scrambled eggs. Another afternoon she made a wonderful coconut rice pudding with *gur*. There were a lot of coconut trees around the building, and we got to eat the coconuts. I can still taste that coconut rice pudding with hot whole-wheat *rutis* (flatbreads). Our cook was a widow, and her only son had died of cholera. Her granddaughter Rokeya spent almost all her time with us in the hostel, helping her grandma. Rokeya was my age; I learned sewing from her. The cook's house was in Kaunia Road. One time, she invited all the girls from the hostel to her house. We rented a bus and went there. She cooked a lot of delicious things for us. There was such pride and elation on her face that day.

A few days after the exam, we were walking around in the field after dinner, talking and gossiping. Our cook was also relaxing in her room, chewing a *paan*. She had a habit of eating a lot of *paan-dokta* or betel and dried tobacco, which blackened her teeth. Rokeya's sudden screams brought us running to the cook's room. We saw the cook's eyes rolled back in her head. She was foaming at the mouth, and she couldn't breathe. We started stroking her and sprinkling water on her face. The gatekeeper ran to get the doctor, but our cook died before he got back. Hearing the news, the neighbors came and gathered outside the gate. The school authorities sent word to her house in Kaunia Road, and her relatives came running.

On one side of the hostel, the cook had kept her bedding and a locked suitcase under the stairs. When the suitcase was opened, we saw it contained more than twenty *dhutis*, saris, blouses, and petticoats—all our gifts to her. I think she was keeping them for her granddaughter Rokeya's wedding. The relatives took away her body, and Rokeya left crying.

A few days later, we all went home feeling very sad. Sabita-di went home with her remaining three children. I had one overwhelming worry in my mind: how would I continue my education?

### *The riots*

At the end of January 1950, Karim Chacha took me back to Barisal along with my youngest chacha Abdur Rab, our cousin Khalek Bhai, and Taloi's only son Shahjahan Bhai. Before we left, Karim Chacha told my mother that he would make some arrangements for me to study. When we reached Barisal, we rented a boat on the Bhatarkhal Channel and lived in it for a few days while we figured out another place to stay. Even in those days, when the big *jotedars* from the south came to Barisal, they would rent boats on the Bhatarkhal and live in them. They would go on shore to get medical treatment, do shopping, and enjoy the cinema and theater. These boats were really big, with three or four rooms, a bathroom, and a kitchen. The boatmen did the cooking.

Karim Chacha was trying to find a school for me. One day, Mohiuddin Chacha came and said it wasn't safe for us to remain on the boat. There could soon be trouble: communal riots between Hindus and Muslims. The District Magistrate of Barisal G. A. Faruqui was from West Pakistan. We heard that almost everyone in the Muslim Students' League was supporting the riots. But some members, including Karim Chacha, Bahauddin Shaheb of Fakirbari, and Imadullah, were against it. For my safety, Mohiuddin Chacha shifted me from the boat to his relative's house in Kalibari Road, called Aktar Manzil. The whole city was throbbing with fear of what might happen. One afternoon, Karim Chacha came to Aktar Manzil and took me to Bahauddin Chacha's house in Fakirbari, a Muslim area. Kalibari was a Hindu area, so there could be an attack there.

That night, everyone in Fakirbari finished eating early and went to their rooms. It seemed to me that the older boys in the household were very eager to do the virtuous work of murdering Hindus. Fakirbari was a huge house, with many rooms and a lot of people. I didn't know all of them. My mother's cousin (her Phupha's daughter), whom I called Anwara Khala, had married into this household. Later I became very close to Anwara Khala, Khalu, and their children.

One night in February 1950—I don't remember the exact date—I was in Bahauddin Chacha's house. He had a lot of siblings, including his sisters Mamata, Laili, Bulu, and Hashi Phuphu. Hashi Phuphu was in class eight at Saiyadunnesa School. She was strong and excelled at both sports and academic work. All of the sisters were very affectionate with me. I think I had gone to sleep with the youngest sister Bulu. In the middle of the night, sudden screams woke me up. When I looked outside, I saw everything engulfed in flames and heard cries of "Naraye takbir! Allahu akbar!"[24] I could hear the terrifying screams of men, women, and children. I stood with everyone, fearful and anxious. Fakirbari had its own big mosque, which is still standing today. The male members of the household were lining up all the women and children to take them into the mosque. Everyone took shelter there, carrying bundles of their most valuable possessions. I went with them. We spent the rest of the night there. Many were crying and saying "Allah, Allah." The men stood outside guarding us. In the morning, we came back to the house and ate breakfast. The fire was still blazing, and we could still hear crying, shouting, and constant cries of "Allahu akbar" and "Naraye takbir."

At breakfast, a few young men were sitting around a table talking about the night's experiences. I was very upset to hear about the carnage all around. I thought, what is all this? I don't remember how many days the riots lasted.

One morning, a few of us were sitting in the sun on the edge of the pond to the east of the house. A few women from the Hindu household next door came up to us fearfully and asked for shelter. Hearing their request, the women of Fakirbari said nothing and quickly went inside the house, thinking that if they gave these women shelter the house might be attacked. After the riots stopped, I heard that those Hindu women who sought shelter had all been killed in the riots. One of the women was tutoring the girls in Fakirbari, but they still didn't give her shelter.

I stayed in Fakirbari through the riots. Bahauddin Chacha told me many times not to get depressed. Karim Chacha came to see me one time and said that he and a few friends were trying as hard as they could to stop the riots. They had created volunteer brigades in various areas to stand guard over the Hindu neighborhoods. They had also moved the Hindu families who were scattered across Barisal into certain Hindu areas for their collective safety. Karim Chacha had moved some Hindu families we knew, including my beloved Sabita-di and Gouri-di, to Jhautala, an area dominated by wealthy and respected Hindu families. After the riots calmed down, Karim Chacha came and took me to Jhautala to visit people I knew. When we met, we cried and held each other. Sabita-di told her relatives, "Look, even at this dangerous time Noorjahan came to see us. Not all Muslims are bad." Later Karim Chacha personally escorted to the Indian border and helped save the families of Sabita-di as well another young woman whom I called Shobha Pishi. I never saw them again. Karim Chacha was in love with Shobha Pishi, but he knew an interfaith marriage would be complicated and hurt their families.

I remember one scene from those days of rioting. Every afternoon when the steamer came from Khulna, people would rush to huddle over the newspaper. Once they were done reading the paper, thugs would set out with sticks to murder Hindus. To protest something that happened to Muslims in Kolkata, they were determined to kill the innocent, peace-loving Hindus of Barisal. What kind of justice was this? I couldn't understand it. Is it religious to kill people in the name of Allah? What kind of religion is that?

After many days, the riots suddenly stopped. Then the government started arresting political leaders. The government had led the riots but now wanted to save face by arresting some of their own members. Hindu men and women were murdered systematically under the auspices of the government. Their homes were plundered and burned; women and girls were raped. After the 1950 riots, through the Nehru–Liaquat agreement, Hindus and Muslims were given the opportunity to leave their respective countries if they wished. But when it was time for the Hindus to leave Pakistan for India, the scene was even more frightening. They were supposed to be able to bring their clothes and jewelry, but I witnessed a different reality. They were stopped and "questioned" at the steamer dock in Barisal and deprived of everything. As for those who went on foot, who knows if they ever reached their destinations.

The year 1950 was a sad chapter in my life. After the riots died down, Karim Chacha moved me from Fakirbari to Karim Kutir, Ali Ashraf's middle sister's rented house. Her husband was a railroad employee, and they had to move around for his job. Her health was run down. She rented a place in Barisal so her children could go to the local school. On the way to her house, I saw the grotesque scene left by the riots. Houses and trees were half-burnt or totally burnt to the ground. Traces of blood remained on the streets. I felt as if I was walking through ruins. I couldn't understand why human beings were so cruel to each other.

My friend Halima was also living in Karim Kutir, and I was very happy to see her. Later Halima and I enrolled at the Sadar Balika Bidyalay, or Sadar Girls' School. After a couple of months, I don't remember exactly how many, I knew I couldn't live in Karim Kutir for long—there were already a lot of people in that tiny house. Then Shah Alam Mama came and took me home. My education was interrupted again. I felt helpless. I couldn't bear to look at my mother's sad face. I was scared thinking about my future. From the combination of the impact of the riots and the interruption of my schooling, I sank into a deep depression. I was only twelve years old, but I forgot about laughing and playing. Ma was worried about me and kept trying to find a way to continue my education.

During this post-riot period, I was also mourning the loss of some important people in my life. As I mentioned before, there were several people living in the outer part of our homestead in Katakhali, in a long brick building or *dalan bari*. One was an allopathic doctor named Bisweswar Babu. He had a younger brother, my dear Madhu-da. Another was a homeopathic doctor with a small frame and a bald head. Then there was a confectioner who made Bengali sweets. I don't remember his name. I knew that they were all Hindu because they celebrated Pujo. The allopathic doctor was a rather serious man. Every morning, he went out with an umbrella and his black medicine bag to travel from village to village. The homeopathic doctor mostly treated patients sitting at home. There's no telling how many times I ate the homeopathic medicines from his little medicine bottles. When he caught me, he would take me in his lap and tell me affectionately, "One day you might do something dangerous with my medicines. Then your parents will take me by the scruff of the neck and throw me out of the house. Then what will my children eat?" I would just respond, "Your medicines are made with sugar. I like them."

The confectioner made incredible sweets and desserts, and my favorite were *jilipi* and *amriti*. I used to call *amriti* "amiroti." When I woke up in the morning, I would run out of bed without brushing my teeth to where he was frying *amriti* and soaking them in syrup. Madhu-da would take me to brush my teeth at the pond and dry my face with the bright red *gamcha* tied around his waist. Then he would sit down on a stool with me in his lap and wait. The confectioner would give me these heavenly treats in a bowl specially reserved for me. In the middle of the day, he would curdle fresh milk and make *roshogolla*, *chomchom*, and *pantua*. In the afternoon, he'd make hot *boro goja* ("big sweets") and *angul goja* ("finger sweets"), which were finger shaped. Besides these, he made *jilipi*, which are like funnel cakes in syrup. The confectioner was a very good man.

Until I was one and a half or so, I was very sickly. I couldn't digest anything and had frequent diarrhea. One time, I was almost dying. Everyone thought I would not survive. Someone advised my parents that if they sold me to someone then I might just have a chance of survival. When the confectioner heard that, he came right away, bought me for 5 paisas, and took me on his lap. From then on, he never put me down unless I was sleeping. You could say I survived thanks to his care and affection. Several years later, one of my chachas bought me back from that confectioner for 5 rupees.

After the doctor Bisweswar Babu went out on his rounds in the morning, Madhu-da would do the food shopping for their meals—that is, for himself and his brother. Beyond the Kachari Ghar, a big courtyard and the family cemetery, in the northeast corner of our homestead, near the pond, was Madhu-da and Bisweswar Babu's kitchen. Madhu-da washed and cut the vegetables and cooked beautifully just like a woman. I would run over there whenever I got the chance and sit on the veranda chattering away at him. Madhu-da would finish his cooking and go take his bath in the pond. Sometimes he would take me along and bathe me. He never ate before his brother came home. I often sat in Madhu-da's lap and demanded a share of his food. Later, Bisweswar Babu brought his wife, his son Arun, and his daughter Madhabi to live with him on our homestead. A new building was built for them.

A weekly Sunday bazaar or open-air market was held right in front of our homestead. I don't know how long that market has been around, but it was there before I was born and it's still there now. Between the outer house and the marketplace, alongside the channel, my family built a beautiful Burmese-style house on stilts for the doctor's family. The house had a wooden floor. When they came to visit our house, they brought a wave of happiness with them. Arun and Madhabi were younger than me. I was happy to have more playmates. Where the marketplace ended and the rest of the houses of Katakhali village began, right in the middle along the Katakhali channel, there were five or six houses where fishermen lived. I could tell they were Hindu from their customs. One of the women was called Binar Ma, or Bina's mother. She wore a big dot of *sindur* on her forehead and a thick smear of *sindur* in the parting of her hair. She had no children of her own, and was named after Bina, the son of her husband's other wife. Binar Ma was busy all day with her washing and other chores. Every evening, she would roast *muri* or puffed rice all by herself. By contrast, in our family, roasting *muri* was like a festival; all the women and girls in the family would have a great time roasting *muri* all night. While one was roasting the rice, another would sprinkle it with salted water, so the rice didn't puff too early. On another stove, they would heat sand; someone kept checking the temperature of that boiling sand. One person would pour the roasted rice into a big vessel, put the sand in it, and swish the rice and sand around together. Another person stood ready nearby with a big earthenware sieve and the stalk of a banana leaf. These special sieves and a separate kind of vessel for catching the sand were sold as a pair by the potters. In the winters in our area, the big boatloads of earthenware were a sight to see. I always wondered how the potters managed to travel long distances with such a huge pile of pottery in those tiny boats.

The pleasure of eating fresh hot *muri* on winter nights was something else. Nowadays, our village girls don't roast *muri* like that. Not only could Binar Ma roast *muri* all by herself but she also made *moa*[25] and coconut *naru*.[26] Often, after school or when our teachers were dozing, we would go eat Binar Ma's *narus* and *moas*. I don't remember paying for them. Maybe this was a special perk for me because they lived on our land or because I was the daughter of the Boro Mia, the eldest son of a *jotedar* family. Bina lived in the room on the west side of their building with her two small children. In the room on the east side lived Bina's Pishi and Pishemoshai, her paternal aunt and uncle. They had a widowed daughter of fifteen or sixteen named Tepi. She wandered around sadly all day with her cropped hair and short, dirty white sari. I never saw her smile. And there was Sukumar, who was perhaps ten, and their little sister Gita. Sukumar and Gita were our playmates. I loved to hear fantastic stories of the gods from Sukumar. They would bathe a banana tree, dress it in a sari and jewelry, and worship it. During Pujo, we ate a lot of *muri* and *narus*. Other than these families, there were no other Hindus or Christians living anywhere in our village or surrounding area, though the Burmese or Rakhine had a strong presence in the area. All these people made up Katakhali village.

On days when Madhu-da cooked something special, he would always invite me and Baba. We would all sit and eat together. They also came and ate at our house on holidays or special occasions. They were Hindu but didn't bother much about caste, or at least they didn't show it.

Then suddenly, everything changed. Back at home after the 1950 riots, one morning I heard Shah Alam Mama's piercing cries and went to the outer house. In the dark of night, the two doctors, the confectioner, Madhu-da, Binar Ma, and the other Hindu families in the fishermen's neighborhood had left together on a boat. All their belongings were left behind: bedding, pots and pans, even the confectioner's special *kadai* for frying *jilipis*. The love and trust we shared for so long were shattered by the distant riots in Barisal and the threat of further religious persecution throughout the country. Even today, I wonder whether they were able to reach a safe place. We never heard from them again.

That day, no food was cooked in our house. No one ate. Everyone was miserable and silent with the grief of losing loved ones.

A vast part of the happiness and diversity of Katakhali village was lost forever. Later, many Burmese or Arakanese also left their homes out of fear of the Bengalis. Some went to Burma, some to the nearby village of Khepupara or across the Rabnabad Channel to Kuakata. They usually stayed in groups for safety.

### *Cutting off all my hair*

After the 1950 riots, I was extremely depressed. I had lived through such shocking violence. Important members of our community had been killed or uprooted. My school was closed, and I lost all my friends. I had been through such trauma and was now forced to move back home to the village. I felt very sad, angry, and empty at the same time.

I was around twelve years old and beginning to enter puberty. One of my uncles started touching my breasts around this same time. I was so upset and ashamed, but I didn't know what to do about it. I didn't want to tell my parents and upset them. Telling them would have caused who knows what consequences. It would have been a scandal. Perhaps they would immediately get me married to someone. I was always hiding and trying to get away from this pedophile uncle, but he would seek me out and grope me when no one was around. In fact, he kept molesting me whenever he could until I was seventeen and got married. During this time after the riots, I was suffering double trauma from the sectarian violence and sexual violence against my own body. I was constantly worried about being molested by my uncle or married off against my will to some other disgusting man. My world was oppressive, and I felt hopeless about the future.

I suddenly decided to cut off all my hair. I was famous for my thick curly hair that fell to my waist. People used to come from other villages to see how thick my braids were. Behind closed doors, I made my youngest chacha Abdur Rab shave my head. Abdur Rab was only two or three years older than me.

Everyone in the household was upset to see me bald, without my thick mane of curly hair. Baba gave Ma an earful. Ma thought her daughter had gone crazy. Maybe I had. But I felt I needed a new start. Somehow, shaving off my hair felt like an act of rage about what I had witnessed. I understand now that it was also rebellion against my gender, my developing female body, my pedophile uncle, and all the men who wanted to possess me. After my dramatic haircut, everyone seemed to realize that I needed to go back to school. Ma redoubled her efforts to get me educated.

Ma's cousin Surja Khala lived in a rented home in Patuakhali so that her children could go to school. In the end, Ma arranged for me to stay with Surja Khala to continue my studies at the Patuakhali Government Girls' High School. Surja Khala's husband's name was Ali Akbar Mia, and I called him Khalu. He had an MA degree and was deeply interested in children's education. He immediately agreed to let me stay in their home, but on one condition—I had to wear a burqa. I reluctantly agreed, even though my parents did not believe women needed to cover themselves.

I packed up my bags again and went to Patuakhali. I tied a black handkerchief over my shaved head. Everyone thought I was suffering from some illness. But pretty soon my head was covered with thick curly hair again.

*My first political action: a school walkout*

Surja Khala had five or six children, including a girl called Tara who attended my school. When we went to school, a woman who worked at the school would walk in front, Khala's trusted male domestic helper Karma would walk at the back, and Tara and I would walk in the middle, both wearing our burqas. In the afternoon when we came back, I would go straight upstairs. Downstairs, the stairwell would be locked from outside. Karma would bring us tea and *muri* upstairs. In the evening, he would bring our tutor upstairs, and we would study with him. That's how our life went.

Karim Chacha hired Khalek Sir to tutor me daily. In between teaching me mathematics, Khalek Sir gave me lessons in Marxist–Leninist thought. The door to a new world began slowly opening before me. Lying in bed at night, I read political chapbooks, sometimes until morning. In my social life, I was a prisoner, but my mind was flying free around the world. After a while, I became a member of Nirmalendu Library and started borrowing books. I became familiar with the writings of many great intellectuals of the world—Karl Marx, Engels, Tolstoy, Maxim Gorky, Romain Rolland, Mahatma Gandhi, Jawaharlal Nehru, Abul Kalam Azad, Mulk Raj Anand, Bernard Shaw, Ibsen, Bertrand Russell, Thomas Hardy, and so many others. Reading their books, I began walking in a dream world. I was reading these books in English; some were the full text and some were summaries. I had learned some English in school, but starting in class seven I taught myself English by reading every book

I could find. And of course, I read many books in Bengali. At some point, my Khalu suddenly became devoutly religious, a disciple of Sharshinar Pir Shaheb, a very famous Muslim spiritual leader at the time. The house filled up with heaps of Islamic books. To please him and to satisfy my book addiction, I started reading those too. Reading all these different kinds of books, I felt that the world was opening up to me.

Those years in Patuakhali were transformative. I came first in the annual examination in class eight. This ruffled a lot of feathers—a girl from some remote, unknown island suddenly came and outranked the other girls! The student who always came first in the school was Jharna Dasgupta, the daughter of a well-known lawyer. She was speechless with shock and anger. The one who came second that year was Nargis Ara Haq, whom we called Paru. Paru wasn't upset that I came in first. There was no match for her in dancing, singing, laughing, and talking.

Everyone in Surja Khala's household quickly became fond of me. My name was always on Khalu's lips. Whenever guests came to the house, I was the first to be called. I also took on a lot of household tasks. Making tea and breakfast, figuring out where everyone would sleep, what to offer to whom—I slowly became responsible for all these duties. The little ones didn't want to bathe, eat, or even sleep without me. If they got sick, I had no time to bathe, eat, or sleep, and it was hard to escape to school. Even with all this domestic work, I came first in the exam every year. I excelled at sports too. It was a small town, so word got around.

At first, seeing how everyone adored me, especially Khalu, his oldest daughter was quite naturally jealous. But later we grew close. My relationship with Surja Khala was more complicated. When Surja Khala was well, she was a wonderful person; but when she was in a bad mood, no one dared go near her. Actually, Surja Khala suffered from mental illness, but I didn't understand that then. Thanks to Khalu's limitless patience, all the children were able to grow up in an atmosphere of relative normalcy.

In 1952, at the time of the Language Movement, I was still in Patuakhali living in Surja Khala's household. News of the Language Movement came floating into Patuakhali. Newspapers weren't regularly available there. But I had heard that students in East Pakistan were demanding that Bangla also be a national language. The government, which was controlled by leaders from West Pakistan, had decided that only Urdu should be the national language. After the independence and partition of India in 1947, the region where my family lived, East Bengal, became East Pakistan, a province of the new nation of Pakistan. The majority of Pakistanis—close to 70 million—spoke Bangla. On 21 February 1952, the police shot and killed some peaceful student protesters at Dhaka University. Soon after that, my political guru Khalek Sir came by and gave me some posters demanding that Bangla be made a national language.

I didn't know what to do with the posters. I felt restless and agitated. The next day, I secretly bought some paper and pens and stayed up late making my own posters. I took them to school the following day. First, I went to Jharna and Nargis in our class and said, "We have to do something. They've killed many students in Dhaka. There are protests and strikes happening all over the country. We should do something too."

They said, "How can we do anything? Who's going to listen to us?"

I showed them the posters and said, "We should all walk out of our classes tomorrow when the bell rings. We can talk to the students in class ten and nine and tell them to send two students from their classes to inform the lower classes, and so on."

Jharna and Nargis agreed to help organize the walkout. Then we each went to a different classroom. I tried to make sure no one could guess who the leader was, although that plan ultimately didn't work. We asked the class ten students to tell the class eight students, the class nine students to tell the class seven students, and so on down to class three. I couldn't sleep all night wondering if our plan would work. I made more posters during the night.

In the morning, I went to school feeling very nervous and checked in with Jharna and Nargis and a few others. As soon as the bell rang, a few of us walked out of the school and stood in front of the gate holding posters. I was afraid no one else would come out. But I was elated when the tenth-grade girls came out and then, one by one, the girls from all the other classes walked out and joined us. We all came outside the school, while the teachers stared at us, transfixed. My nervousness disappeared, and I felt calm. We started walking to the right side of the big pond and past the SDO's residence and office.[27] Our school was in the Patuakhali city center, surrounded by businesses and government buildings. Everyone came out to see what we were doing. Next, we slowly crossed the street and walked in front of the Jubilee Boys' School. When we stopped in front of Jubilee, the teachers and boys came out to see us. Then we walked down the road by the west side of the pond and gathered again in front of our own school. Since we had brought our books and bags with us, we decided to go home. I told everyone that tomorrow we would be on strike and not come to school as a sign of respect and mourning for the students who were killed in Dhaka. I also told everyone not to reveal who organized the walkout and protest.

Tara and I left school and came home together. The news of the walkout and procession had spread like wildfire. We came home to find Khalu (Tara's father) waiting for us on the veranda looking worried. He was very nervous by nature and immediately asked me, "How could you be part of this outrageous scandal? Why did you do it?" I said, "The West Pakistanis won't let us speak Bangla. They shot so many Bengali students in Dhaka for protesting this. How can we keep quiet now?" I don't know what Khalu thought about it, but he didn't say anything more.

The next day, Tara and I stayed home, but I feared that perhaps we were the only ones who missed school. There was no telephone or internet back then, so there was no way for us to know what was happening with the other students. Khalu seemed worried that we weren't going to school but didn't force us. By this time, everyone in town was talking about us, wondering, "How did those girls do such a brave thing? Who was the leader?"

Two days after the walkout, I went back to school. The morning classes started as usual, but a little later they called me to the library. The headmaster Hem Babu and the SDO of Patuakhali, Khayer Shaheb, were waiting for me. Hem Babu called me over, grabbed my arm, and shook it hard. He said, "How dare you behave this way? You disgraced me by doing what no one else in the town dared to do. I'll beat you for this!"

I didn't respond. I couldn't figure out who had given them my name. SDO Khayer Shaheb stood up and said, "I can beat you up and arrest you right now."

I said in a strong voice, "I know you can arrest me, but you can't beat me."

They sent me back to my classroom. Later, I heard that when the teachers asked the youngest students who told them to join the walkout, they mentioned the girls in the class above them. Those girls also mentioned the girls in the class above them. And my own classmates, when threatened, gave them my name. For almost a week, all the teachers scolded me: Such a little girl dared to do such a thing! This girl is going to be a bandit when she grows up.

A well-known lawyer in town named Asad said to me, "Hey, little girl, you're a Communist. Don't you dare show your face in my house again." This made me sad, because I loved visiting his house. One of my favorite teachers, Dinu Apa, belonged to that family. When I took my exams, the lawyer's wife used to send a tiffin carrier full of food to school for me.

But when the Language Movement slowed down a little, the headmaster Hem Babu, who taught us English, called me over to him one day and told me affectionately, "I would be so happy if I had a daughter like you, Noorjahan!" I wasn't surprised by this statement. I knew that he was involved in the Congress movement when he was young. He spent a long time in jail during the anti-British movement. Satin Sen, that brave son of Patuakhali, was his older brother. I often went to Hem Babu's house to meet with the whole family. I came and went freely, sat on a *piri* (stool) in their kitchen and ate my fill. The two daughters of the house, Kalyani-di and Rama-di, tutored me.

And the SDO Khayer Shaheb, who had threatened to arrest and beat me, that same man later proposed marriage to me through Khalu and Karim Chacha.

# PART 2

# VIOLENCE AND LOVE

*Sexual violence by my uncle*

While I was away studying, my pedophile uncle was not easily able to touch me and grope me. But he still kept trying to get to me. When I was around fifteen years of age, he told my parents that he would pick me up from Patuakhali and bring me home by boat. My parents trusted him, and this was his way of getting to me. When he arrived to pick me up, I was nervous and tried to keep my distance from him. On the way back, he insisted on stopping the boat to rest at someone's house. I was asleep when he suddenly came into my bed and raped me. He didn't touch me or kiss me or speak to me—it was all over in a minute, and he left my bed immediately. I was so shocked that I didn't scream. I didn't even understand what happened, because no one ever talked about sex to me. My mother used to warn me about men, but she never explained any details or told me what to do if something happened. I was disgusted and angry about what my uncle did to me, but I was too ashamed and scared to tell anyone. What would I say in any case? And who would even believe me? I didn't even have words to describe what he did, but I knew I had been violated and that my uncle was an animal.

This same uncle raped me three more times until I got married and moved away. He couldn't do it when I was home with my parents, or when I was away at school. But he would slyly tell my parents that he would take me back to school or pick me up during vacations. Each time, it was an abrupt act in the middle of the night while I was sleeping during a break in our journey. Usually, there was no one else around. One time, however, he raped me when I was sleeping in a cot at a friend's home during school break. He somehow managed to invite himself over to spend the night with that family. Then he brazenly came in the room where I was sleeping. My uncle quietly attacked me in my sleep, even though there was an elderly woman asleep in the cot next to me. He knew that he could get away with his depraved actions and that I would be too afraid to tell anyone. I was shocked and froze when my uncle committed these violent acts. I didn't even understand what he was doing. I wonder now why I didn't scream out, but I would literally be paralyzed with fear and shame, and it was all over in moments.

Decades later, I found the courage to discuss my molestation with women friends and to utter the word "rape" to describe what happened to me. I also started talking about my experiences at women's conferences. When I disclosed my uncle's criminal acts, I found out that many other women had similar experiences. They would first seem shocked by what I said, but later these same women would call me and confide that that they too had been molested or raped by male relatives but were too ashamed to tell anyone. They would weep and speak about their horrible experience for the first time.

### *First love*

According to my Dada, I was born on 14 March of the English year 1938 and the 30th of Phalgun of the Bengali year 1345. As the first child of the "Boro Mia" or oldest son of a *jotedar* family, I was showered with love by the whole extended family. I was a restless and playful child, but I also loved reading and writing. Soon after I learned the Bengali alphabet, I started reading every book in sight. When I got a little older, I would even devour the grownups' books in secret.

Luckily for me, I was able to avoid getting married off at age ten and instead got the chance to study. In 1949, while I was in boarding school in Barisal, Karim Chacha was studying at BM College. But he was more excited about student politics than studying. He was a member of the Muslim Students' League, which had an office in Barisal. I used to go to that office all the time, even when I was only ten or eleven years old. I continued to visit there during the holidays even when I no longer lived in Barisal. Among the people I met there were Mohiuddin Chacha, Ali Ashraf, Imadullah, Abdul Gafur, Abul Hashem, Mosharraf Hossain Mochan, and many others whose names I don't remember.

Imadullah (also known as "Imad") was the handsomest of them all. No one could help noticing him. This tall, well-built young man was always sitting quietly in a corner of the office reading or writing something, or just thinking. From time to time, he'd make jokes: whenever he saw me and Halima, he'd say, "Hey, are you studying, or just wasting your parents' money?" Sometimes we'd answer, and sometimes just laugh. There was another reason everyone took notice of Imadullah. He wore baggy Afghan-style salwar pants and a white shirt. The combination of his height, thick mustache, and unusual outfit made him quite striking. His big wide eyes had a sharp and piercing gaze. Seeing my interest in reading, writing, and politics, Mohiuddin Chacha often said, "I've settled on a groom for you." Then he'd mention Imadullah. I was probably only eleven or twelve when this started. I would flare up angrily at his comments, and I didn't pay much attention to what he said. In the end, I married that same Imadullah. Later, I heard from Imadullah that Mohiuddin Chacha had mentioned me to him too.

Meanwhile, by early 1954, I was almost sixteen, and though I didn't know it, I was turning into a young woman. I was still living with Surja Khala in Patuakhali. Karim Chacha had been nominated by the United Front[1] in the East Pakistan Provincial Assembly[2] elections. Surja Khala's husband had also sought the nomination. One day, Surja Khala suddenly put me out on the street, yelling that "Because of Karim Chacha your Khalu didn't get the nomination!" I didn't know where to go; I decided to walk to my relative Shamsu Mia's house. I told Shamsu Mia that I had my matriculation exams in three months but Surja Khala had thrown me out. Shamsu Mia and his family were very kind to me and said that I could stay with them. But again, I was required to wear a burqa.

Karim Chacha became very busy with his election. That same year, he also got a Youth Star medal from the Jubo League.[3] Imadullah accompanied Karim Chacha on his election campaign. Imadullah rallied the public in support of Karim Chacha in the southern part of Patuakhali. Everyone was talking about Imadullah—he was charismatic, honest, and intelligent.

In that election, Karim Chacha, around age thirty-two, was the youngest parliamentary candidate in East Pakistan. I was busy studying for my matric high school exam in Patuakhali. One day, someone told me that Imadullah was leaving no stone unturned in our area to help Karim Chacha win the election. On hearing this, I suddenly became restless. I had trouble sleeping and couldn't concentrate on my studies. Just before the election, my Phupha Hamid Mia came to Patuakhali to take me back home. They needed me to help them in the last stage of the election. I was thrilled and quickly left with him by boat. They hadn't started running launches out there yet. Phupha and I were talking about the elections on the boat journey. Suddenly, he said, "He has all the qualities you could want in a son-in-law. He's as knowledgeable as he is handsome, and there's no match for his jokes."

I said, "Whose son-in-law?!"

Phupha laughed and said, "Everyone's saying the same thing."

I stared at Phupha in amazement wondering how he guessed what was on my mind. Phupha said, "I'll set up a meeting between you and Imadullah." I was ecstatic to hear this.

Over the next few days, we all worked hard to get people to vote. Then, the election was over, but the ballots were still being counted. I was sitting at home in Katakhali. Baba and Ma were pushing me to go back to Patuakhali because there were only ten days left before the very important high school matriculation exam. But I didn't want to listen to them. My mind was full of expectation for someone, and I hadn't seen him yet. Phupha and I were making various excuses to delay my return to Patuakhali. Finally, I had to leave; Phupha and I set out on a boat. My mother's Mama or maternal uncle's house was in Chalitabunia. Her brother, my Jalal Mama, had married the daughter of their Mama and was living there. On the way to Patuakhali, we stopped the boat in Chalitabunia to try to find out where Karim Chacha and Imadullah were. As it turned out, they too had stopped at that house to rest for the night on their way to Katakhali. We all spent the night in that house, but Imadullah and I didn't see each other, and I don't think he even knew I was there with my Phupha.[4] We were staying in different parts of the house, and it was not customary for women to meet men outside the family. The next day, their boat left for Katakhali again, and our boat followed them to Katakhali instead of going to Patuakhali.

When we arrived in Katakhali, our village homestead was full of people to welcome these two leaders, Imadullah and Karim Chacha. That evening, there was a huge feast. The whole night went by in laughter and stories. But again, I didn't meet Imadullah, as I was in the interior rooms with the other women and girls. The next day, I told Phupha that I was going to our own house. As I mentioned earlier, our extended family had several houses or buildings within the homestead called Munshi Bari. Karim Chacha had brought Imadullah to the southern building where Dada and Dadi and Karim Chacha lived. Baba had his own house right next door, and my siblings and I all lived in that house.

When I went home, I told Ma and Phuphu (my father's sister), "Your honorable guests will be coming to this house for tea and breakfast." They were thrilled and started making breakfast. I made up a bed in the front room or inner veranda to seat our guests and prepared myself to face Imad. At that time, we didn't use sofas in our house. I kept a *jalchouki* (a low wooden stool) next to the bed for myself. My whole body was trembling with excitement and nervousness.

Imad crossed the courtyard with long, strong strides and entered the room. Without thinking, I went to greet him respectfully by touching his feet. Imad stopped me midway, held me with both hands, looked into my eyes and said, "Don't bend your head for anyone, Noorjahan."

Then he said, "When did you get so big! And besides, nobody told me you were at home. I heard you were in Patuakhali for your matric exam."

Then Imad took off his shoes and sat reclining on the bed. I sat on the stool next to him. I knew that Ma, Baba, Phupha, and many others were listening to our conversation from behind the door.

I said to Imad, "I've gotten big in the usual way. You're a busy man, so you didn't notice. I'm definitely going to take the exam, but there are still four or five days before the exam starts." Then I said, "If I'm going to stay in my own house, do I need to beat the drums and announce it to everyone!"

He was listening to everything I said with astonishment and looking me over intently. We continued talking over tea and breakfast. When I gave a sly response to the question of whether I would pass the exam or not, Imad laughed and said, "I see you can beat even me in sly remarks!"

I said to him, "What, do you have exclusive rights to that?"

At this, he laughed out loud, filling the house. When he asked what I would do after the exam, I said immediately, "I'll do what all the other girls do around here. I'll get married and go to my in-laws' house."

Now Imad grew serious and looked into my face for a long time.

Just then, Karim Chacha suddenly came into the room and, seeing Imad, said in utter bewilderment, "When did you come here! Everyone's looking for you."

Imad said, "Why? Am I your prisoner! My work is done. You never told me that Noorjahan is here."

Karim Chacha said, "What is there to tell about that?"

Imad said in a hurt voice, "I hear you all have fixed her marriage?"

Karim Chacha burst out laughing and said, "Why don't you find us a good match for her!"

Imad didn't laugh at all. The two of them talked a while longer. Finally, Karim Chacha said, "Lala [Imadullah's other nickname], hurry up and take a bath and eat lunch. We'll leave for Patuakhali this afternoon."

Imad asked me if I would go with them. When I said yes, he seemed very happy.

That afternoon, we started our journey, with Karim Chacha and Imad in one boat and my younger sister Lutfa, my cousin Janu, and me in the other. They were going to Barisal to study. Imad seemed very disappointed to see the two-boat arrangement. I knew about this ahead of time, so I wasn't in the best mood either. Our two boats were going along side by side. After a while, I saw Imad half-reclining on the open deck of the boat, thinking about something; he'd taken his shirt off and had only an undershirt on. He had an amulet on a silver chain around his neck. He noticed me and said, "My mother gave me this amulet. I love my mother very much. This amulet will protect me from all kinds of danger." I just laughed, but I didn't realize that this amulet would be the cause of his untimely death.

The two boats were going along parallel to each other. For as long as possible, the two of us stood outside under the open sky, looking at each other.

When we got to Patuakhali, Karim Chacha and Imad went to a government rest house. We three sisters went to Shamsu Mia's place. I was supposed to take the exam from there. Once the election results came out, Janu and Lutfa would go with Karim Chacha to Barisal for school. There were only a few days left before my exam. I should have been studying hard. But no one understood how hard it was for me to focus on studying. In the meantime, the election results came out. Karim Chacha had won.

After the victory parade, I knew Karim Chacha and Imad would come to see me. So, I got Janu and Lutfa to make two beautiful flower garlands. In the evening, when Karim Chacha and Imad arrived, Janu and Lutfa garlanded them. I stood by watching. Imad smiled gently and said, looking into my eyes, "Why this garland for me? I haven't won yet!"

I laughed and said, "Who says you haven't won yet? Can you always tell by looking if someone's won or lost?"

Imad stared at me in astonishment.

They were in Patuakhali for two days. Both days, Imad came to the house and spent the evening sitting on the veranda, talking of this and that. Janu, Lutfa, and I were there at the house. Imad told stories about politics, about how they won the election, about his siblings, his mother, and his younger brother's son. Then Imad left for Barisal with Karim Chacha. Lutfa and Janu went with them.

Before leaving, Imad asked me a few times about my plans for after the exam and whether I was going to Barisal. I wished I could just drop everything and go with them, but that wasn't possible. When they left, my mind filled with dejection. I wasn't well prepared for the exam but somehow managed to finish. Then, the day it was over, I boarded a launch for Barisal.

As soon as I reached Barisal, around noon, I ran to visit one of my favorite people, Manorama Bose, whom we called Mashima, at Hiren-da's place.[5] Hiren-da's house was a commune in the true sense of the word. A hub for all political workers to stay and talk. A lot of leftist political leaders who'd been released from jail before the election were staying there. As soon as I went inside, I saw the house was full of people. A real crowd. Mashima saw me and came running, hugged me close, and said, "Your exam's over. Why are you here? The Jubo League is having their annual conference in your area. Everyone's leaving this evening for Galachipa. Aren't you going?" I'd been so busy with the exam that I hadn't paid any attention. Imadullah was the East Pakistan Jubo League's General Secretary. I had no doubt that he had a hand in holding the annual conference in Galachipa. I looked all around the room and saw that except for Imadullah, nearly everyone was there. Karim Chacha, Nikhil Sen, Mohiuddin Chacha, Khandakar Iliyas, Ali Ashraf, and many others were going to Galachipa. Preparations were under way. Everyone was busy. But because one person was missing, I felt my coming here was useless.

Mashima said she wasn't going to Galachipa and needed me to write a statement for her. I sat on the southern veranda writing the statement, with Mashima sitting next to me. Just then, Imad arrived. He stood between the room and the veranda. Even without turning my head, I could sense his presence. Then Imad asked Mashima, "How did the examinee's exam go?"

Mashima said, "Why don't you ask Noorjahan herself?"

At that, Imad said, "Will she deign to notice a person like me?"

I turned my head and said, "Is it right to allow myself to get distracted when I'm working?"

Imad stood there and kept talking to us. Mohiuddin Chacha told us not to waste time talking. Imad laughed and said, "Who can say who is doing the most important work?"

A little while later, Lutfa and Janu came from Nannu Mia's house.[6] They had enrolled in school. It must have been summer break, so they were going home. When he saw them, Imad got excited and said, "Come to my house. My mother was talking about you."

Now it was my turn to be dumbstruck. How did they become so close to Imad? He was inviting them to go meet his mother! I hadn't yet been invited. I felt like going with them, but they didn't ask me to come. Janu and Lutfa went off with Imad, and later they came strolling back.

In the meantime, everyone had gotten ready for the journey. All the workers and leaders went off in groups with their baggage, bedding, bundles of papers, posters, and placards, hopped on rickshaws, and took off for the steamer dock. Last of all was my rickshaw. In the rickshaw right in front of me were Karim Chacha and Imad. Imad's house was on Bagura Road. That house was surrounded by a fence. When we were passing by the house, he turned and said to me, "Noorjahan, my mother is waiting in front of the door for you."

I looked and saw a few women standing on the other side of the fence. When we got down at the steamer dock, I went straight to Imad and asked him, "Am I a mind-reader?! How should I know your mother was waiting for me?"

Imad said, "I thought you knew."

Everyone was getting on the steamer with their bundles. Before I could pick up my own small bag, Imad lifted it onto his shoulder. I objected strongly, but to no effect. We slowly boarded the steamer last of all. Janu, Lutfa, and I took a place in a room called Ladies Inter Class. Imad made up our beds for us. Then he stood outside the door and struck up a conversation. I was standing inside talking to him. A long time passed this way. Then he said suddenly, "You must be hungry. I'm sending food for you right away. I'll eat too. But don't go to sleep." With that, he left. Janu and Lutfa ate and lay down to sleep. I stayed up waiting for him. A little later, Imad came and sat next to me. There were no other passengers in the Ladies Inter Class that day.

There were a lot of books scattered around me on the steamer: Mahatma Gandhi's autobiography, Jawaharlal Nehru's *Glimpses of World History* (letters written to Indira from jail), *Discovery of India*, *Origins of the Nation and the Family*, *India and Soviet Central Asia*, *The Communist Manifesto*, and many more. I was a member of the Nirmalendu Library in Patuakhali and had checked out these books and read them. I was taking them home for the long break to read them more closely. Imad said, "Karim is going to the conference. Why is he taking so many books with him?"

I said, "These books are mine."

Imad said in a suspicious voice, "What do you do with all these books?"

I said, "I read them."

Imad stared at my face, dumbfounded. I laughed and said, "Try me and see if I'm telling the truth."

Then our conversation turned to many different topics. We talked into the night, the hours passing in a blur. There was an important political meeting happening that night in one part of the steamer.[7] Even though they called him again and again, Imad didn't go.

Just before morning, Imad was looking deep into my eyes and saying something. I looked and saw he had a pen in his hand. His eyes were begging me to take the pen. As soon as I touched the pen with my right hand, he took my hand in a firm grip and gently touched it to his lips. I was trembling. If I hadn't held on tightly to the bench with my left hand, I would have fallen. Then we both looked at the sky. A sliver of the waning moon was still awake in a corner of the sky. Next to it a huge star (maybe Venus) was burning. The eastern sky was growing blood red. It was almost morning. The steamer was slowly moving toward Galachipa. Imad hummed a few lines of "Sojan Badiar Ghat," a love poem by Jasimuddin,[8] then slowly let go of my hand and left. I had tears in my eyes. Why these tears, I didn't know. I wiped my eyes, wrapped myself in a sheet, and lay down. A new chapter of my life had begun.

Eventually, the steamer reached Galachipa. There were people running and shouting all over, and fierce competition over who would get down first. I was in a trance, thinking only of Imad. "My heart dances, today my heart dances like a peacock"—it felt as if the poet Rabindranath had written this song with me in mind. The moment before I got down at Galachipa, Imad came rushing up and said, "I think your Chacha is mad at you. Never mind—don't forget me, please, come and see me."

I went to see Imad once or twice in Galachipa. Lutfa and Janu came with me each time.

At the end of the conference, Lutfa and Janu were going home to Katakhali. Despite Karim Chacha's strong objections, I got on the steamer to Patuakhali with Karim Chacha and Imad. The Jubo League leaders held an all-night meeting on the steamer. I waited for Imad in the ladies' compartment. At some point, Imad came and handed me one of Karim Chacha's undershirts and left. When I opened the shirt, I saw there was a small paper package in it. Inside it was a small photo of him, taken in front of Dhaka University's Iqbal Hall. He had also written down Mohiuddin Chacha's address. He was asking me to write letters to him at this address and leaving this little gift for me to remember him by. I cried alone for a long time. I wasn't sure when I would see Imad again.

Imad got off the steamer with Karim Chacha at Patuakhali. Maybe he had some work there. I got down with them at Patuakhali too. I went to stay at Shamsu Mia's house. One day, Imad, Nikhil Sen, and Karim Chacha came to Shamsu Mia's house. I was thrilled by their unexpected visit. I had thought that this time around I would not see Imad again. Imad had a thick book in his hand. As he talked, he kept closing the book and opening it again. At some point, he handed the book to me. I took the book upstairs and found a ten-page love letter inside. The first love letter of my life, from a person I really loved. I read it right away and wrote a response, because he was going to Dhaka that same day. I don't remember what I wrote. When I finished writing, I put the letter in the same book and returned it to him. After everyone left, I spent the whole night tossing and turning, with Imad's letter clasped to my chest.

The next day, I left Patuakhali and went home to Katakhali. It was May 1954. Now I would have to stay at home for a while, until the matric exam results came out. What would happen after that, I didn't know. Even if I was able to enroll in college, there was still the issue of housing. A few days after I went home, Imad's letters started to come regularly. I had to tell Karim Chacha what was going on. Everyone else pretty much assumed that Imad was going to be the eldest son-in-law in our family.

All of Karim Chacha's friends and relatives were coming to congratulate him after the election. The house was teeming with people. I had to shoulder the huge responsibility of looking after them and entertaining them. Then, suddenly, I received a very upsetting letter from Imad. He wrote that the government of Pakistan had passed Section 92, broken up the elected parliament, and established military rule in the country. They were arresting patriotic leaders and workers and putting them in jail.

Imad had gone into hiding along with many other leaders and workers. It would no longer be possible for him to write to me, and there was no telling when and where we would meet again. Therefore, Imad was giving me my freedom and telling me that I shouldn't wait for him. Reading this letter, I broke down in tears. Within a few days, Karim Chacha was arrested. Nikhil-da was at our house at the time. With great effort, we managed to hide Nikhil-da. For many months, the whole country was sunk in deep despair and darkness. For almost fourteen months, there was no way to get news of anyone.

I felt suffocated in our village house. In the meantime, my exam results came out. With this excuse, I went to Barisal alone to get the results. Even in that era, my parents gave me enormous freedom to go about on my own. My main purpose was to go find a place to stay in Barisal and try to get enrolled at BM College. Karim Chacha was in jail. Imad was in hiding. I was sixteen, and there was no one I could turn to for advice. Not seeing any other option, I went to Mosharraf Hossain Nannu's house and asked him to let me stay. I talked to his mother. She was willing to let me stay. At one point, Janu and Lutfa had stayed in this house for a few months. Nannu Mia was very generous and a true gentleman. He worked for the Farmers and Workers' Party.

In Barisal, I did something brave, mostly out of curiosity. I suddenly had the desire to see Imad's house in Bagura Road. One day, I went to the house and knocked on the door. A beautiful woman opened the door and said, "You must be Noorjahan! Come in."

I was baffled. How did Imad's mother find out about me? Later, I learned that Imad's older brother had read my letter to Imad and told everyone in the family about me. Imad's parents welcomed me affectionately with tea and sweets. A little later, Imad's Nanu (maternal grandmother) also came to the house.

Her sharp gaze and pointed questions made me feel rattled. Still, I felt she liked me well enough.

When I was leaving, I asked them to call a rickshaw for me. A little while later, someone said, "The rickshaw is here." Then everyone came to the gate to see me off. I saw the rickshaw was covered with a sari, obviously at the request of the family. Women from Muslim families who practiced *parda* traveled in rickshaws this way. Just three or four months ago, I came out of the trap of the burqa, and I wasn't about to be imprisoned behind that curtain again. I asked the rickshaw driver to take down the sari. When he removed it, I hopped in and left. I was thinking, maybe they won't approve of me as a daughter-in-law because of this, but I don't need a marriage like that.

The decision I made that day turned out to be important. A few days later, Imad's younger brother Khosru went to Dhaka. He returned to Barisal with a letter from Imad, the first letter after an entire year. I was thrilled and couldn't sleep with excitement. I wrote a reply that I sent to Imad through Khosru. I wrote about my enrollment in college, that I was staying in Nannu Mia's house, and that I went to Imad's house and met everyone, and that I took down the rickshaw curtain. Imad sent a letter in response praising me for defying his parents and taking down the rickshaw curtain. Imad wrote that he himself never had the nerve to disobey his father's orders. By doing that, I became forever worthy in his eyes. I thought to myself that this is a strange relationship between a son and his parents. Of course, you should listen to your parents, but your own will is also important.

Everything about their family was different from mine. In my family, we valued individual freedom. One day after our marriage, Imad told me that when his father saw him playing cards before his BA exam, he beat him with an umbrella to the point of breaking it. I was astounded to hear this. No one in my family could even imagine beating grown children.

After a while, Karim Chacha got out of jail. Then he and I did a lot of canvassing and soliciting of the DC[9] and finally got permission to establish a girls' hostel in Barisal. We contacted our own relatives and friends to find plenty of girls who wanted to stay in the hostel to study and used this guarantee of enrollment to persuade the local government to reopen the Barisal girls' hostel that had closed in 1950.

I finally had a place to live and start college. Imad and I were exchanging letters regularly. My world was full of light.

### *My sudden marriage*

In mid-June, Karim Chacha got married in Barisal. At that time, I heard that Imad was coming out of hiding intermittently. His life of hide-and-seek was about to come to an end. But Imad hadn't told me about it. It hurt me to know that even though he was living freely again, he hadn't come to Barisal. Every night, I cried my eyes out for him in secret. One day, I even sent a one-line letter to Imad at Mohiuddin Chacha's address. I wrote, "Imad, heartfelt congratulations on your free life. Signed, Noorjahan."

All I could do was give him an inkling of the ocean of sorrow and despair in my heart. A few days later, Karim Chacha went to Dhaka. Dada, Baba, and I went to Katakhali with Karim Chacha's new wife, Anisa. Our house was full of excitement and festivity and bustling with relatives who had come for Karim Chacha's wedding. We were all eagerly counting the hours until Karim Chacha's return. Then suddenly Dada died of a massive stroke. Karim Chacha heard the news and came home. Instead of merriment, sadness spread over the whole village.

For the first time in my young life, the specter of death struck close to home. I realized how frightening death is. But I never imagined then that in just nine months another death would shatter the very foundations of my life.

After Dada died, we spent our days in a kind of daze. I stayed on at Dada's house because of his death and to take care of Karim Chacha's new wife. We had all grown up in that house.

One afternoon, feeling tired and gloomy, I went over to my parents' house. I started cooking some good food. Ma gave me a hand. We both thought we needed to lighten the atmosphere in the house. Karim Chacha's new wife had arrived at a sad moment. That evening, I was absorbed in cooking, even though my mind was a thousand miles away. A thought came flying in and took hold of my mind: what if, on this stormy night, Imad were to suddenly appear?

After dinner, everyone was ready for bed. Outside, there was storm and rain. Suddenly, I heard my cousin Aziz Bhai's voice outside—"Open the door, you have a guest." Baba quickly opened the door and saw standing in front of him Aziz Bhai, Ali Ashraf, and Imadullah. All of them looked like wet crows. Baba told Kalai to take them to the Kachari Ghar and arrange for bedding and dry clothes. He told me to fix snacks and dinner. The household was aflutter. I was beside myself with delight and surprise.

After they had eaten, our visitors told Baba they had come because they heard the news of Dada's death. I knew very well that city folks never came to this region on stormy days. It didn't take me long to figure out why they were here. I couldn't sleep all night with excitement.

I had known Imad and Ali Ashraf Shaheb for a long time. It would have been natural for me to speak to them. But for some reason nobody called me to talk to them. Custom dictated that I couldn't just go over to the Kachari Ghar to meet them either. Over the next couple of days, I could hear them moving around various rooms and buildings on our compound, laughing and talking. I was feeling very anxious and wondering when I would get to see Imad.

Two days later, Ma and I were sitting and talking on the veranda in the evening. Imadullah and Ali Ashraf Shaheb were resting in the Kachari Ghar. That day, the sky was covered in clouds after the Asharh rains.[10] The rain could come down again any moment. Suddenly, I saw Ali Ashraf Shaheb striding toward us. Stepping up on the veranda, he said to me, "I came to talk to your mother, because I'm leaving tomorrow morning. Noorjahan, why don't you go talk to Lala [Imadullah] for a while? Lala's about to go crazy."

When Ashraf Shaheb said this, I felt like I had the moon in my hands—I had been waiting for this moment for the past two days. When I came to the Kachari Ghar, Imad jumped up from the bed and said again and again, "Darling, it's been so long since I saw you! I'll never leave you again. Believe me, I promise."

I was swept off my feet by his unbridled emotion. As he held me, I felt like I was floating in a sea of happiness. When I came to myself, I saw that his chest was damp from my tears. Who knows how long this would have gone on? But then I heard a few people talking inside the house. Sayyad Bhai from Phelabunia, Hamid Phupha, and Rashid Chacha (my father's third brother) had come to see Imad. I went to make tea and snacks for them.

That evening, everyone ate together, including Karim Chacha. Then everyone left, except Imad and my cousin Sayyad Bhai, because Imad wouldn't let him go. There was a full moon that night, and every corner was flooded with magical moonlight. There was a playful murmur in the air. I was in our building getting ready to go to sleep when Sayyad Bhai brought a note for me. Imad had written, "Tonight I want to spend the whole night talking with you by the pond. Sayyad will be there too."

I couldn't ignore this invitation. After all, I wanted the same thing. So I went out to meet him, taking my younger sister Lutfa with me. For all my fear of the unknown, the promise of happiness was stronger.

Imad and Sayyad Bhai had reached the pond before me and spread out banana leaves to sit on. Lutfa and I went and sat near them and started talking. Our conversation had neither head nor tail to it. We went on saying whatever came into our heads. The earth was still, awash with moonlight. Imad and I were talking and sitting close together. Lutfa was around thirteen years old. After a while, she said she was sleepy and went inside. Now it was just the three of us. At some point, Sayyad Bhai lay down on his banana leaf. Imad and I sat facing each other, talking of all the things we'd never had a chance to talk about. It was almost morning, the roosters were crowing, the birds were chattering, hinting at dawn. The eastern sky had begun to turn blood red. Then I said to Imad, "I have to go now." Sayyad Bhai and Imad didn't object; they went into the Kachari Ghar. I quietly slipped into my room by the back door and lay down. I knew Ma was awake.

The next morning, I was late making tea and snacks. Karim Chacha came over at some point. After that, Imad asked to speak to my parents. Karim Chacha took him into my bedroom. Baba went in there, and Ma stood outside the door. I sat there silently. Imad said to Karim Chacha, "Why is Noorjahan sitting at home when college is in session?"

Karim Chacha said, "It wasn't intentional. Baba died right after my wife came home, and everything got confused. Noorjahan and Pori [the nickname of Chacha's new wife Anisa] will go to Barisal soon."

Imad proposed that we leave for Barisal together the very next day. He said, "It's not right at all for Noorjahan to waste her time here."

But Karim Chacha and Baba rejected this proposal right away. Then Imad said firmly that he wouldn't leave me behind. After a lot of back and forth, it was decided that the new bride Anisa Chachi and I would go with Imad to Barisal the next day. Karim Chacha would follow in a few days. After that, Imad strode off to the outer room like a victorious warrior.

The next day, Karim Chacha and Baba went to Galachipa and helped me and Anisa Chachi board the steamer. Imad the victor was with us. When we got on the steamer, Imad himself made up our beds in the ladies' compartment. Then he sat next to us and started talking up a storm. We talked for a long time. Then he had some food sent to us, went and gulped down his own food in the dining area, and came back to talk to us again. But this time fate was against him. The male guardians of the other ladies in the compartment objected to his presence, so Imad had to leave.

A little later, Imad came back and called me out of the ladies' compartment. He proposed that I come to his compartment to sit on his bed and talk. Suddenly, I noticed my mother's uncle Manik Nana. He was going to Barisal that day too. I saw him watching us with deep distrust. I stopped chatting out of fear. Imad asked me what was wrong. As soon as I told him, he got up and went over to Manik Nana, touched his feet in respectful greeting, and practically carried him in a bear hug over to where I was. Imad sat Nana down beside me and quickly vanished. A little later, he appeared again, bringing Nana every kind of food the steamer ferry's dining room had to offer. Nana was impressed by Imad's care and gave him his blessings; he ate the food Imad had brought and went to sleep. Imad and I spent the whole night talking. I was impressed by Imad's ingenuity.

When the steamer reached Barisal, we set off in two rickshaws: me and Anisa Chachi in one and Imad in another. When we pulled up in front of the girls' hostel, Imad helped Chachi get down. Then he told her very politely, "Please take your things inside. I'm going to take Noorjahan to my house. I'll introduce her to my mother and bring her right back."

Chachi silently agreed, and I set off with Imad for his house. Sitting beside me in the rickshaw, Imad was smiling gently. I couldn't quite figure it out. When the rickshaw stopped in front of the gate and I was about to step down, Imad grasped my hand and said, "Wait a moment. Let them come first, then you get down."

Hearing Imad's calls, everyone came out of the house. When everyone saw me, their eyes widened. Imad's mother said, "What have you done? How did you bring her here?"

Imad answered gravely, "I abducted her."

I was bewildered—what kind of behavior was this? I went back to the hostel after the visit with his family.

The next few days, I was quite nervous because I had to go past their house on my way to and from college. My classmate Laili shared a rickshaw with me, and I had to pick her up and drop her off at the house directly across from Imad's house. Laili's boyfriend Khokon also lived on Bagura Road. Khokon and Imad used to stand right in front of Laili's house when we were coming and going every day. I couldn't look at them from shame and fear. I was worried that Imad might suddenly stop the rickshaw and take me into his house!

I arrived in Barisal not long before 14 August, Pakistan's Independence Day. The morning of the 14th, Imad came to the hostel and took me to his house for the whole day. He asked sulkily why I didn't look at him on my way to college, and why I didn't make some excuse to come and see him at their house. When I had been at his house for a long time already, he asked me to go to the hostel and change into his favorite sari (a yellow one the color of *champa* flowers) and come back. His request was almost like an order. I never met anyone who could disobey his orders. I had to carry out his orders too.

That afternoon when I went to their house again, Imad told his mother he was taking me out. That was the first time I sat beside him in a rickshaw and went out in broad daylight. I was sitting diffidently in the corner of the rickshaw. The streets were crowded for Pakistan's Independence Day. First, we went to the riverbank. Then he took me to a restaurant called Ruchira in Sadar Road. Ruchira was the heart of Barisal, the center of social and political life. Imad went into the restaurant holding my hand. The place was full of his friends and other important people of Barisal. Everyone was looking at us. No one said anything. I think they were amazed that the rumor that had been going around was finally out in the open.

Imad took me to sit in a booth at the back and ordered various dishes. He was expecting his friends to come to congratulate us, but no one came except Nikhil Sen. Imad was disappointed and said to himself, "They're all jealous of my good fortune." The next day, Imad went to Dhaka, and I was able to focus on my studies without anxiety.

But I didn't realize this was the beginning of a storm. It was 27 or 28 August 1955, possibly a Friday. Karim Chacha suddenly came to the hostel and took me to Ali Ashraf's house. When I went in, I saw Imad sitting with Ali Ashraf Shaheb. I didn't know what was going on. Then, out of the blue, Imad said, "Our wedding has been fixed for 8 September." What wedding? Karim Chacha and I were dumbfounded. Imad said more clearly, "Noorjahan and I will be married on 8 September."

Karim Chacha said, "So quickly?! That's impossible. Besides, you have to discuss with everyone before fixing a date."

Imad became agitated and said, "My mother and Shah Shaheb fixed the date; this date can't be changed."

I felt really offended by this and said angrily, "I'm not ready to get married before finishing college. What's the hurry?"

Karim Chacha tried to change Imad's mind, but he could not be swayed. Karim Chacha said, "Noorjahan is the eldest daughter of our family. Everyone will want to attend her wedding. Everyone in the area is expecting the wedding to be held in style in the village house. Besides, you're familiar with the area too. This wedding should happen in Katakhali." He continued, "Lala, in our area we don't let even a cat out of the house in the month of Bhadro.[11] And Noorjahan is everyone's darling."

Hearing this, Imad jumped up and started for the door, saying, "If this wedding happens, it will happen on 8 September, otherwise it will never happen."

Ali Ashraf ran to stop him, took him by the hand, and sat him down, saying, "Calm down, everything's possible if we talk it through."

Karim Chacha was looking suspiciously at me. He thought Imad had talked to me before making this decision. I started crying out of shame, outrage, and sadness.

Seeing this turn of events, Karim Chacha decided he would take me back to the village that very day. He would go tell everyone the news and ask the blessings of all our relatives. As soon as Karim Chacha said this, Imad's face changed completely. He looked very happy and started pressuring Karim Chacha and me to come eat lunch at their house. Karim Chacha got out of lunch by saying he had to get ready for the trip home. But I couldn't escape since it was Friday, a day off. When I went to Imad's house, I found a festive atmosphere. I felt bad that they maneuvered all this with no thought of how my family would feel.

In the evening, I boarded the steamer for Galachipa with Karim Chacha and went to sit in the ladies' compartment. A little later, I looked toward the door and saw Imad standing there smiling. With him was a thin gentleman. Imad introduced him to me. I learned that his name was Swadesh Bose. He had just been released from jail that morning after six months' imprisonment. Seeing his poor health, my heart went out to him. They left after seeing us off, and the steamer set off for Galachipa.

After this quick trip home to Katakhali, we came back to Barisal on 6 September. Imad greeted us with smiles at the steamer dock. He wanted to take me to their house, but Karim Chacha and I objected. When he saw us getting on a rickshaw to go to Abdul Aziz Talukdar's[12] house, he followed us there, ate with us, and talked up a storm. Swadesh Bose came with him too. Toward evening, Karim Chacha made the excuse of having work to do and asked Imad to leave. But he didn't budge, saying he would help with the work. Karim Chacha was still angry with Imad and his family for their selfishness in fixing the wedding date. I felt the same way. It bothered me for a long time afterward that they did this without considering our situation at all.

That day, when Imad was leaving, Karim Chacha said pointedly that tomorrow would be my *gaye holud* or ritual turmeric bath and that Imad should not come.

The next day, I had my *gaye holud* in a small room in A. A. Talukdar's house. Imad's younger sister Bela brought the turmeric paste in a bowl. Just when they were finishing off this ceremony with happy excitement, I was startled to hear Imad's imposing voice. Everyone started shouting, "No, no, you can't see Noorjahan today, not for anything!"

Imad laughed and said, "I can't go twenty-four hours without seeing my beloved!"

That day, Swadesh Bose and many others had been busy since morning decorating the biggest room of A. A. Talukdar's house with colored paper to make it look festive for the wedding. Imad went to the kitchen and told Anisa Chachi he would eat lunch there and help with everything. Karim Chacha became intensely annoyed with all this joking around and finally told Imad to leave. "You're not doing any work, you're just making extra work for us, so why don't you just go home."

That ruined Imad's mood, and he got ready to stomp out of the house. Then everyone realized that Imad was very upset and started telling him never mind, please stay. But the damage was already done, and Imad stormed out. I knew there was no way to bring him back, and I felt extremely angry at his head-strong attitude.

By ten o'clock that night, a rumor had gone around that our wedding the next day, 8 September, had been called off, because Imad had shut himself in his room and was refusing to eat. At this news, a shadow of grief fell over A. A. Talukdar's house. The men started discussing whether they should send someone to his house to try to pacify him. They finally sent Swadesh Bose to his house. I went to bed without eating and silently cried myself to sleep. Late at night, Karim Chacha woke me up and asked me to come talk to Swadesh Bose. Swadesh Bose called me out of my room and asked me to see Imad and talk to him. He said "Noorjahan, this isn't the time to be angry. Think it over calmly, because Imad is waiting for you outside."

I went outside and saw that sure enough, Imad was standing there, leaning against a garden fence a little way off. Even though I could see him in the pale moonlight, I couldn't understand what he was saying. When I went closer, Imad said to me, "My future is in your hands. Suppose your father died today, would you still marry me tomorrow?"

I thought a bit and said, "I know that neither my father nor yours has died, so this question is irrelevant. Besides, I don't know about your household, but what will we say to our guests? We agreed to hold this marriage according to your wishes despite a lot of inconvenience to my family and me. I have only one thing to say today: our wedding will take place at the fixed time tomorrow, 8 September, or else it will never happen." With that, I quickly went into my room and lay down. I sobbed the rest of the night, confused by Imad's volatile behavior and wondering what kind of marriage I was getting into.

The next day, all went according to plan. Swadesh Bose came and lent a hand with everything, and he told Karim Chacha that there would be no more problems. He had gone to visit Imad that morning and found him in a very cheerful mood.

I had sent handwritten invitation cards to my friends. I still remember the wording of those cards:

> On 8 September 1955, I will take the hand of my friend Imadullah and go forth to greet a new world. I greatly desire your presence in this auspicious moment.
>
> Signed, Noorjahan

In the evening, the marriage took place in the sitting room of Imad's house. Someone came and asked me if I agreed to this marriage or not. This is a social custom. I don't know if it has any real value or not.

My friends and relatives began arriving at A. A. Talukdar's house in groups in the afternoon, all dressed up. In the evening, a meal was served. Imad came too with a few of his friends, but no one from his family came. This made Karim Chacha, Anisa Chachi, and everyone else feel a little depressed. At the time of the *shubhodrishti* or auspicious first glance, one of my nanus (my mother's chachi) and Halima pestered me to look up, and I saw Imad's face, bright with love.

We spent the night at A. A. Talukdar's house. The next day, Halima came again. Several of Imad's friends came too. Anisa Chachi, Halima, Janu, and my cousin Shefali were busy cooking. We were all having a good time. In the afternoon, Imad sat down to play cards with Swadesh Bose. I didn't like that at all: he was ignoring his new wife and playing cards!

In the evening, Imad's older brother Kaysar Mia, his wife, and his younger sister Bela came over. Everyone was busy greeting them. When Imad's older brother said to dress me up quickly and get me ready to go, all of us were flabbergasted. This wasn't what we had agreed. We had discussed and agreed that I would stay in this house for a few days after the wedding. When Imad went to work in Dhaka, I would return to the hostel and focus on my studies. Then in the month of Magh or Phalgun, whenever was convenient for everyone, Imad's family would come and bring me to their home. But Imad's older brother Kaysar Shaheb said emphatically that I was the new wife of their household, and they would not leave without me. I looked at Imad to see what he thought. Imad said gravely that he wouldn't go against his brother's wishes. I understood that this decision had been made with his knowledge. This time too, Karim Chacha suspected that I was part of the decision. He thought I knew everything, and that Imad and I were out to humiliate him.

Then Halima quickly dressed me up in a light-green georgette sari. When I was done putting on the sari, Karim Chacha started crying loudly. At Karim Chacha's piercing cries, Imad embraced him and started crying too. I saw them both rolling on the floor crying. I've never seen anything like it. Then, when they were done crying, we took a rickshaw to Imad's house in Bagura Road. His younger brother Khosru was studying electrical engineering. Thanks to his efforts, the whole house was flooded with light to celebrate the wedding. Imad didn't have many relatives in Barisal, but a few neighbors had come and gathered in their sitting room. A meal had been arranged for them too but was finished by the time we arrived. As soon as we entered the room, Khosru started playing a film with a rented movie projector and generator (which was not uncommon as part of wedding festivities in that era).

Seeing all these arrangements, I understood that everyone in this household had planned to bring me here against my family's wishes. They had only given false assurances to my parents and community. At night, when I went into the room they had given us, I saw it was decorated with colored paper. I don't know who had taken care to decorate it, but it made me feel better.

Even though everything happened in a hurry, I felt that I had gained something immense. In my young life of seventeen-and-a-half years, what more could I wish for? I was anxious about the future, but I felt, when love is endless, there's no room for fear.

At night, Imad came into the room, pulled me close to him, and said, "Darling, I know you're angry with me. And with good reason. But when you hear what I have to say, you won't be angry anymore. I demanded a one-month break from the Party. If I don't have you close to me for this one month, I'll go crazy. I'll just die. Darling, I know you won't be angry."

I listened in astonishment to his childish talk and grew concerned as I realized how irrational these hasty decisions had been.

Then the days drew to a close, and even before Imad's one-month break ended, the police started arresting political workers again because of a strike. Many people escaped arrest by going into hiding. One night, Imad too took leave of me to go into hiding.

I had no communication with Imad after that for quite a while. On 27 or 28 November, Bela and I were sitting at home in the evening trying to study for our exams with the door shut. The door to our room suddenly opened and in came a man covered head to foot in a wrap. Startled, we saw that it was Imad. He lifted the wrap from his face and put his finger to his lips, motioning to us to keep quiet. When Bela was about to run inside and tell everyone the news, he stopped her and instructed us not to let anyone know of his coming here except his parents. When Bela went out of the room, Imad stood silently gazing deep into my eyes. Then he said tenderly, "Darling, I've come back for you. I couldn't live without you."

In the meantime, Bela came back with a plateful of rice, dal, vegetables, and *macher jhol*[13] hidden in her *achol*, the end of her sari. At the sight of the food, Imad's eyes gleamed with happiness, as if he hadn't eaten for days! As soon as Bela put the food on the table, Imad started gulping it down. I felt a mixture of delight and pain to see him eat so ravenously, because clearly he was starving. A little later, his parents came running. They seemed both terrified and happy to see him.

Then began a strange honeymoon. No one outside knew that Imad was home, and yet he was home all the time. Bela and I took turns bringing him food in secret. If there were guests to the home, his meals would be irregular, but he put up with it cheerfully. Imad was crazy about his older brother Kaysar's children. He was missing them terribly. Kaysar's five-year-old son Tarek sometimes played in the field in front of our room. Imad would stand on the bed to watch him. Not being able to play with the children made him depressed, so one day I went and told Tarek and his siblings Zebu and Minu, "I'm going to show you a person. You can only call him 'person' and you can't tell anyone about him. This is a secret game. If you tell anyone, that 'person' will go away, and the game will be over."

They were very excited to hear this, especially Tarek. One night, I called them into my room and showed them the person lying under the blanket. Before the three of them could start shouting "Boro Chacha!" I put my finger to my lips and said, "He's not Boro Chacha, this is that 'person' in the game."

They looked around, confused. Then Imad himself explained the reason to them very nicely. After that, the three of them came every evening to play with him for an hour. I was thrilled at being able to take part in this childlike happiness. Watching them, I couldn't help thinking that Imad would make an outstanding father.

*Facing cruel fate*

Around this time, there was an outbreak of smallpox across the country, including Barisal. The municipality's employees were going around door to door vaccinating everyone. They came to Imad's house one day and vaccinated all of us. That day, Imad was reading a book in the north room. Later, I said to him, "There's a serious outbreak of smallpox, but you missed getting vaccinated today."

At that, he smiled gently and didn't bat an eyelid. I said again, "The vaccination team left for today, but I'll go to their office tomorrow morning and bring someone to give you the vaccination."

Imad said nothing. The next day when I was getting ready to go out, Imad suddenly grabbed my hand, pulled me close to him, and said, "You might as well tie me up and turn me over to the police. Did you forget I'm a runaway?"

I stood there bewildered. Then he laughed and said, "You're thinking I missed the vaccination only this year! I've never been vaccinated. This amulet my mother gave me has protected me every time and it will protect me in the future too. Don't worry, darling."

He stroked the amulet that hung on a silver chain around his neck. What he had said really scared me. I tried hard to change his mind, but I couldn't make this wise pandit see reason.

Then in mid-January I started having morning sickness. I couldn't eat. I threw up all day. At first, I kept it a secret, but it wasn't long before everyone realized that I was pregnant. I couldn't even drink water. I became very weak. I was astounded to see how Imad cared for me during this time. I wasn't the only one—everyone was amazed.

Imad's mother and his Nanu gave him 1 rupee a day for cigarettes. Imad saved up that money and sent his cousin Aziz to bring *muri* and then he fed it to me little by little with his own hands. I was afraid of throwing up if I ate too much at once. I couldn't drink water. Imad took tiny spoonfuls of tea from his own teacup and moistened my lips with it like a little child. I couldn't stand the smell of cigarettes, so he practically stopped smoking too. After dinner, he would go outside and smoke just one cigarette, then brush his teeth thoroughly, rinse his mouth, and eat a *paan* before coming to see me.

When I woke up late at night, I would see Imad sitting there reading. When he was absorbed in reading, his eyes would blaze. He had a big collection of books on art, literature, philosophy, history, politics, and social science. Besides these, he read books on many other subjects with deep attention. He also had Dr Benjamin Spock's *Baby and Child Care* in his vast book collection.

Our room got very cold at night. The roof was of tin and the walls of bamboo slats. The walls had big gaps in them. Above the door, there was a gap of almost two handspans. The wind blew in through that gap and chilled me to the bone. Imad made glue out of flour and pasted old newspapers over the fencing. He closed the gap above the door too. Even then it was cold. So he bundled me up in his socks, undershirts, and wraps and slept hugging me to his chest. Sometimes he would lull me to sleep right on top of his warm chest, cover me up with the blanket, and lie there quietly so as not to wake me up! In the morning when I woke up and saw myself like that, I would blush with embarrassment. I felt guilty too. I thought, maybe the poor man can't sleep at all because of me.

Meanwhile, everyone was worried about my incessant vomiting. They sent for their family *kobiraj* or ayurvedic doctor. When the *kobiraj* came, Imad was still in hiding. Imad's father, mother, and Bela were sitting with me. The *kobiraj* looked closely at me and said, "Bouma [daughter-in-law], where is Lala? Did he come here recently?"

I kept quiet. He laughed and took his leave. On the way out, he said, "Nothing to worry about."

Everyone started whispering to each other. Now no one had any doubt that I was pregnant. My heart shrank with fear. I felt like the ground had slipped out from under my feet. How could I take responsibility for another life? Imad looked very worried too.

In February, Imad wrote a letter to Baba asking him to come to Barisal. When Baba heard the news, he came. Imad told Baba, "Noorjahan will go stay with you for a while. When the time comes, I'll go and bring her back myself." In Bengal, it is customary for a woman to go home to her parents for the birth of a child.

Baba came to Barisal to take me home, but Imad's mother said that it would be good if I could stay for a couple of weeks because Imad's brother's wife was expecting a baby any day, and they could use my help with the newborn. Baba happily agreed since this would give him time to see his doctor in town and he could also spend time with his mother. Baba would stay at Karim Chacha's rented home in the Jhautala area of Barisal, where Karim Chacha, Anisa Chachi, and my Dadi (Baba's mother) had been living for several months. Karim Chacha was away in Barobaishdia for his political work. Baba gave me and Imad some money and left for Karim Chacha's house in Jhautala. We were very happy to get this money and to have more time together. Imad and I left for Jhautala as soon as it got dark. Imad only went out at dark since he was in hiding.

Imad and Dadi were very close. They somehow hit it off as soon as they met in Katakhali. Both were fun-loving and down-to-earth with big personalities. Whenever they got together, Imad and Dadi would become immersed in wide-ranging conversation and almost oblivious to the world around them. It made me so happy to see this deep friendship between my grandmother and Imad. When we arrived at Karim Chacha's home, we saw Anisa Chachi was preparing tea and snacks. Baba and Dadi were delighted to see us. Baba decided to go shopping for our dinner, and I knew he would bring back a feast. He came back with two huge bags full of chicken, *galda chingri*,[14] goat meat, *ilish mach*,[15] lots of winter vegetables, and dessert. Chachi was not experienced with such elaborate cooking, so I decided to take over the preparation while Chachi helped. I decided to make chicken korma, *galda chingri malai* curry, fried *ilish*, spicy goat curry, cauliflower *dalna*, and *bhaja mug dal*. Chachi made salad and chutney. Baba sat on a cane *mora* (rounded woven seat) and supervised our cooking. When dinner was ready, Imad sat between Dadi and me, and Chachi served us. Imad ate everything with glee and praised Chachi for the cooking. Baba had brought *mishti doi*, *pantua*, and *roshogolla* for dessert. We ended our feast with my Dadi's extra special *paan*. Imad and I walked back home quite late—no rickshaws were available.

The next day, Imad's niece was born. I became very busy as a mother's helper from dawn until late at night, not coming to Imad until 10 or 11 pm at night. Imad would be sulking and upset, and every night he would tell me not to go help with the baby the next morning. But Imad's mother came looking for me every morning, and it was impossible for me to refuse. The only reason I didn't go home with Baba yet was to help with the new baby. Every afternoon, Imad would say, let's go to Jhautala to see your family. But I had to stay to help with the baby, so he would sulk and not go either. Finally, it was my last night in Barisal, and I would be leaving the next day for Katakhali with Baba. Imad told me to stay with him the next day, to not go help in the kitchen or with the baby. I didn't reply, but when I tried to get up in the morning, I fell to the ground! Imad had tied the end of my sari to the corner of his shirt. He woke up and pulled me to his chest and told me to stay with him that day. Imad's mother was already calling me, and I tried to explain to Imad that I had to go and help. Imad could not understand my predicament. I became angry and left to help his mother. When I came back to our room after lunch, I found Imad lying silently on the empty cot. He had folded my bedding for me to take with me to Katakhali that evening.

I tried to talk to Imad, but he would not answer. By then, some women had arrived to say goodbye to me, and I could hear them outside. I had to rush out to see them before they tried to come inside our room, because Imad was still in hiding. I wanted to talk to Imad before leaving, but it wasn't possible. Baba had arrived early to get me. I rushed back into our bedroom, and Imad jumped up from the bed. His eyes were red from crying. I bent down to touch his feet, and he pulled me up and held me tight. Then Baba came in the room along with Imad's parents. Baba took my bedding and my trunk with personal belongings and put them in the rickshaw. I said goodbye to everyone, and we took off in the rickshaw to Jhautala. From there, we gathered Baba's luggage for the steamer. I told Baba that it was still early and we could go to the steamer later since it departed late at night. I knew that Imad would want to come see me one last time and that he could not leave the house until dark to avoid being seen. But Baba wanted to go early, so we took off for the steamer port in daylight. I later heard from Dadi that Imad showed up in Jhautala in the evening and cried like a baby when he heard I had left.

I got on the steamer with Baba feeling very sad. When I reached home, I learned that Imad had left for Dhaka the very next day. His movements were no longer restricted. This was around the middle of February 1956. I heard rumors that Imad was traveling all over the country organizing for the Jubo League's annual conference. The conference was held at the end of March. From my region, my uncle Benu Mama, Mosharaf Biswas from Lalua, Ratan Mia,[16] and many others went to Dhaka to participate in the conference. When they came back, everyone told me the conference had gone well. They had yet again almost forced Imad to take the post of General Secretary. Imad had apparently told Benu Mama that in a few days, as soon as he could get things in order, he would come straight down to Barobaishdia.

I thought maybe my days of waiting were almost over. A flute of yearning was playing in my mind. Imad might come any day now. Our household was getting ready to greet him with great excitement. The local people were always asking, "When is Boro Jamai [your oldest son-in-law] coming?" Imad was a prominent youth leader. On top of that, he had a law degree. At that time, lawyers were respected almost as much as police inspectors. There was no better profession for a son-in-law.

My family had begun to tidy up and decorate the house. The local boatman Joynal Majhi's boat was waiting at the ghat. As soon as we knew the date, everyone would go to the steamer dock to greet Imad. I was counting the moments. I was afraid maybe Imad would come and surprise me, without telling anyone. This suspicion arose in my mind because he hadn't even sent me a letter—and I was mad at him for not writing. At the same time, I was full of love and longing for Imad. I had no one my age to talk to in the village. My sisters were very young then. I couldn't sleep and was growing anxious. What was taking him so long? The conference was over on 26 March. Suddenly I thought, I hope he's not sick? Why is he so late, why is he tormenting me like this?

On 6 April, I couldn't sleep all night. I must have fallen asleep toward dawn. Moments later, I woke up from a terrible dream. I called my mother and said, "Ma, I had a bad dream. I don't feel good."

Ma stroked my head and body and said, "Don't worry, maybe our *jamai* [son-in-law] will come today."

In the morning, I washed my hands and face, picked up the mirror I had gotten as a wedding gift, and started combing my hair. Suddenly the mirror slipped out of my hand and broke. I felt even more depressed. All day, I wandered sadly around the pond. I felt restless. I was thinking, what happened to Imad? How can he be so late?

On 7 April, I was still restless. In the afternoon, I was sitting on the outer veranda, looking around to see if anyone was coming. Suddenly I saw two policemen in khaki uniforms almost running toward our house. I asked Baba, "Who are they and why are they coming to our house?" Baba ran to meet them. I ran to the doorway of the sitting room. One policeman said to Baba, "We want to see the MLA Shaheb [that is, Karim Chacha].[17] Is Begum Imadullah here? A radiogram has come for her. But I can only give it to the MLA Shaheb."

I ran and practically snatched the radiogram from his hand, took it out of the envelope, and started reading it out loud. It said: "Imadullah is seriously ill. Begum Imadullah should be transferred to the nearest police station immediately. Later she will be taken to Dhaka by helicopter."

I immediately sensed that Imad was not alive. Baba took me in his arms and sent people all over to look for Karim Chacha. When he heard the news, Karim Chacha hurried home. Baba, Chacha, and I got ready within an hour and then, along with those policemen, we walked nearly 2 miles to my Nana's house in Tungibaria. Some people from our village came with us. I didn't know at the time, but apparently many of them had already heard about Imad's death. We left for Galachipa in the police boat. Baba and Karim Chacha were sitting in the boat. They laid me down on the deck of the boat and started stroking me and saying, "Don't worry, we'll take him to Delhi or Kolkata. It's only smallpox, with proper treatment he'll get better."

As soon as I heard the word "smallpox," I burst out crying. "Baba, Imad won't live, he's never had a smallpox vaccine in his life."

When they heard that, both Baba and Karim Chacha fell completely silent.

The boat traveled all night. It was a moonlit night. The water lapped against the bottom of the boat, and the tears flooded our three faces. How could we comfort each other? But even a night of sorrow must come to an end. By the time we reached Galachipa, it was morning. I saw there was a huge crowd waiting for us at the dock. The chief inspector of police was standing there looking grave. Karim Chacha asked him to arrange the helicopter. He said with deep regret, "We just got word from Dhaka that there is no helicopter available. Please go to Patuakhali. The SDO Shaheb will make arrangements for you."

After that, we hurried onto the launch to Patuakhali. The launch moved forward at its own pace, but to me it seemed as if the time didn't want to pass. Baba and Karim Chacha tried to reassure me. Around four hours later—which seemed an eternity—we reached Patuakhali. My schoolteachers and many other acquaintances were standing there. Atul Mastermoshai[18] came forward first, hugged me, and said, "We've arranged for you to stay with Nargis [a school friend of mine who was later elected member of parliament]."

When I heard that, I said in surprise, "But I'm going to Dhaka right away!"

He said, "Why don't you rest and eat a little? Your Karim Chacha is going to see the SDO Shaheb and arrange for the helicopter."

I felt a little calmer and went to Nargis's house.

I took a bath, and Nargis made me eat some food. Then Karim Chacha came and said, "Bad luck, the helicopter can't come because of bad weather. We have to go to Barisal by launch."

We set off again soon after. Before leaving the house, Nargis came and whispered in my ear, "Are you pregnant? How many months?" I looked at her and said, "Four."

Then, surrounded by my dear teachers, friends, and acquaintances, we boarded the launch for Barisal. Everyone was looking at me. Finally, the launch was about to depart. Just then, another launch coming from Barisal drew up next to ours and B. D. Habibullah got off it. He was a well-known lawyer and politician. He came into our room and started to tell Baba and Chacha something, but then he suddenly glanced at me and said to Karim Chacha, "Karim, come outside for a moment. Let's talk." Baba and Karim Chacha followed him outside.

But once they had left, there was no sign of them coming back. The launch didn't leave either. I was restless. I kept thinking, why don't they come back? From time to time, I burst out crying, and then I would steady myself and ask someone to go find Baba and Karim Chacha. I don't know when the launch finally left. There was no sign of Baba and Karim Chacha. The trip from Patuakhali to Barisal was almost four hours. I was alone. Unfamiliar people were dampening my forehead and fanning me. I wanted to have Baba or Karim Chacha near me, but they were so cruel and didn't think of me. They were lost in their own sorrow. I only wished I could become a bird and fly to Imad, that I could touch his face and head lovingly, cure him of his illness with my kisses. That day, I only wished I could hold him in my arms, just one time.

At the end of the evening, the launch reached the ghat. There were a lot of people on the ghat, but I didn't see anyone from Imad's family. Only Abdul Aziz Talukdar Chacha was there. He carried me into the rickshaw and took me to Imad's house. There was a vast crowd of people in front of the house. The whole house was lit up and glittering like a wedding hall. When we got there, someone or some people carried me inside. I heard a murmur, "She's here, she's here!" Suddenly I heard someone say, "Where is that *rakkhoshi*? Because of her I lost my dear son! *Rakkhoshi*! *Rakkhoshi*!"[19] At that, I lost consciousness. When I came to, I felt my dear friend Halima's hand on me. She was holding me in her arms trying to calm my tears. From time to time, she dampened my face and head. Someone tried to make me eat something. Then everyone left without my noticing. I was drowsy from fatigue. When I woke up, I sat up and looked around. I saw everyone lying here and there, fast asleep. Suddenly I remembered everything and felt a sharp pain in my chest. I felt as if someone were stabbing me over and over. I went blue with pain. Then I had a thought that made me feel slightly better.

The fact that Imad was not alive was clear as daylight to me then. But no one had actually told me that he was dead, perhaps because of cultural hesitation to give news of death to a close relative. Somehow, I had an idea in my mind that perhaps they had kept Imad in our bedroom for me to see. I knew that among Muslims, women can't touch their dead husbands, nor men touch their dead wives. But the night was almost over, and everyone was fast asleep. I thought, if I go running and take Imad in my arms, no one will know, they won't be able to stop me. I quietly opened the door and ran alongside the pond to our room. When I pushed open the door to that room and went inside, I saw only the empty cot. What a deep emptiness, what a deep feeling of lament! I had never thought before that a person's life could be lost like this, could end like this. A huge emptiness came and swallowed me. I started screaming and crying. Hearing my heartbreaking cries, people woke up and came running from this house and that. I was screaming, "Why didn't you let me see Imad one last time?"

The same question I asked that day, I still ask myself now. Two people were dearest and most important to Imad: his mother and me. Why didn't anyone think of these two people? Who decided to bury Imad without us? It's unforgivable, the way they deprived us of the chance to say goodbye to Imad. Even today, in this society, important decisions are made every day without mothers, daughters, and wives having any say. I wonder when this will change.

I know it's very hard to let go of someone we love. Even today, I can't help thinking, why, Imad? Why did you have to die so young?

I later learned more about how Imad died. On the last day of the Jubo League conference in Dhaka, Imad told everyone that he was leaving for Barobaishdia that evening and that he would be gone for a while. He had not been feeling well for several days but was not going to let that stop him from going to the Narayanganj Port[20] to take the steamer ferry to Barisal and then onward to Barobaishdia. The ticket master at Narayanganj refused to sell Imad a ticket because Imad looked unwell, with a swollen face and reddish eyes. Unable to board the steamer, Imad came back to the Jubo League office. Nobody knew that

Imad had fallen ill and returned to the Jubo League office. A few days later, a friend of Imad who was a Jubo League member went to the office looking for an important letter and heard a noise in the back room. He opened the door and found Imad curled up on the floor in a shawl and obviously ill. There was no telephone in those days, so this friend had to run and get help and inform Imad's brother. Imad was taken to the hospital, but the hospital refused to admit him, saying the case was not serious enough. Imad was taken back to the Jubo League office even though all his friends were very worried about his condition. Doctors were brought to see him, and they were all quite worried. Just a few months before, Abu Hossain Sarkar had become Chief Minister and formed the government of East Pakistan in Dhaka. He appointed Sheikh Mujibur Rahman[21] as his commerce minister. Hearing the news of Imad's illness, Sheikh Mujib rushed to see Imad and took him to the hospital. Sheikh Mujib said that Imad's family should be informed and a government helicopter should be sent to Barobaishdia to fetch me from the island. Imad apparently talked to his sister Bela (who was in Dhaka) and asked whether I was informed and whether I would be coming soon. But all of this was in vain, because Imad died before I could get there.

PART 3

# STRUGGLE AND RENEWAL

## *An empty life*

About a month after Imadullah's death, the Jubo League invited his mother and me to Dhaka. At that time, the steamer from Barisal stopped at Narayanganj. The day we came, the leaders of the Jubo League and several other parties were there to welcome us at Narayanganj. We stayed at Imad's Khala's house in Gendaria.[1] They had arranged various programs for us: for example, taking us to eat at Imad's friends' houses, assembling at the Jubo League office and garlanding us, and inviting us as guests of honor to political meetings and cultural events on Nazrul Jayanti. I was the guest of honor at a meeting of the Awami League. Sheikh Mujibur Rahman was present at that meeting. He came and sat down next to me and put a garland of flowers around my neck. I was crying the whole time.

I didn't know any of the political leaders in Dhaka. The ones whose names I remember were Mohammad Toyaha, Ali Ahad, Kamaruzzaman, Mohammad Sultan, Sayyad Altaf Hosen, Tajuddin Ahmad, Abdul Motin, Jamiruddin Ahmad, Mahmud Ali, barrister Amir-ul Islam, Abdus Samad Azad, Barisal's

Mohiuddin Ahmad, and Ali Ashraf. The few days we spent in Dhaka, they came every day to check on me and Imad's mother and tried to comfort us.

I remember only a few of the many houses in Dhaka where we ate. I remember Ali Ahad Shaheb's sister's house and Dr Karim's house. The incident at Ali Ahad Shaheb's sister's house was very funny. We were invited to eat lunch there one day. The day of the invitation, it was raining hard all morning. It wasn't possible to get there on time in all that rain. In those days, there weren't telephones in every house, so that we could just call and say we couldn't come. That day, someone had arranged a car for us, but I remember the car didn't come on time. When the car finally came, it was very late. We hurried off to Ali Ahad Shaheb's sister's house. I thought they must have been waiting for us. But when we got there, we found that on this rainy day they had all eaten and gone to sleep. When they heard us calling and woke up, they were startled. When Mohammad Sultan said that we had come for lunch, they were caught off guard. They had thought we wouldn't be able to come in the rain, so they hadn't cooked anything. Everyone started bustling around. We were a group of ten or twelve. There was no time to go to the market, so they cooked whatever they had in the house—*dim bhaja* (fried eggs), dried fish *bharta*, dal, *chachchari*, various kinds of pickles—we all ate happily. Later they served us *luchi*, *porota*, meat, several kinds of sweets, and fruit with tea.[2] When we left, everyone in the household asked us to forgive them. But I enjoyed eating what they gave us that day much more than I would have enjoyed rich, festive dishes like korma, *polao*, or biriyani.

One incident from that trip is etched deeply in my mind. That was the day we were taken to the Azimpur Cemetery.[3] They took us somewhere or other each morning and evening. None of us ever knew beforehand what the plan was. That day too, they took me and Imad's mother in a car. When we got out of the car, we saw quite a few people waiting for us. I saw some beggars there too. Looking around, I instantly understood where we were. Then I suddenly fainted. Later I heard that Mohiuddin Chacha had quickly caught me and laid me down on a table in the office. When I came to, my face and head were all wet. Maybe somebody had splashed water on my face. I saw worried faces all around me. As I slowly began to feel a little better, Mohiuddin Chacha took my hand and led me back to the place. Surrounding me were countless friends of Imad's. Many of them later became famous individuals in Bangladesh. But at the time I just thought, where is the one I came here to see? Where is my Imad? The life of such a lively, humorous, smart, strong, and self-sacrificing person ended in just thirty years!

Later, when they took me back to the car, Sheikh Mujibur Rahman took me by the shoulders, lifted my face and looked into my eyes, and said, "Everyone told me Lala's wife is very young, but I didn't realize you were such a child. Dry your eyes, my dear girl. You'll be fine. Go home and study and raise your child well—that will be your greatest service to your country."

Then he said to everyone present, "I warn you, don't make too much fuss about her or try to make her into a leader."

He took my hand and carefully helped me into the car. I stared at him in wonder. That gaze of his still glows in the depths of my heart like a pearl. His words still ring in my ears. Today, after so many years, I know that it takes a truly wise person to say something like that. I was only eighteen then. I had just passed my matric exam and entered college.

The news of Imad's death and editorials about it were printed in all the newspapers. There were articles about him in the papers for eighteen days after his death. Obituaries were published by various individuals and parties. Many people sent personal letters to me. I especially remember Maulana Bhashani's letter.[4] Another person sent a letter from jail, but not to me—

that letter was addressed to Imad's older brother Obaydullah, whose nickname was Kaysar. The writer was Swadesh Bose. When I read that letter, I felt it was written for me. Later, when I asked Swadesh about the letter, he said, "It might not have been appropriate for a Hindu man to write a letter to a widow belonging to a Muslim family. So I wrote to Kaysar instead. Besides, we were students at BM College together."

I kept many of those letters for a long time. Later I lost all my treasured letters due to various natural and political storms.

After the Jubo League invited me to Dhaka, I felt reassured. If I had so many of Imad's friends, so many talented and knowledgeable people around me, then I had nothing to fear. They all loved Imad, and I was sure they'd never forget me or Imad's child. But still, life was very hard and very scary.

Before he died, Imad had entrusted me to Baba and said he would come for me later. And he had told me that he would have Mohammad Sultan elected as General Secretary of Jubo League in his place and start practicing law with his friend Jamiruddin Shaheb instead. But now what? I was pregnant. No one in Imad's family had an income except his father. He was getting older, and it was time for him to retire. Imad's older brother Obaydullah or Kaysar was unemployed at the time and had several small children. His younger brother Khosru was studying electrical engineering. There were several other members of the family, the children of relatives on Imad's mother's side. It was a wonder his father was managing to support such a big family. And when Imad married me and brought me home, he had only added to his father's burden.

After Imad's unexpected death in 1956, I didn't know what I would do, where I would live, how I would spend my life. Both of us had thought that even after our marriage I would stay in the hostel and finish my studies, and once Imad was established we would make a home and participate in politics together. But his sudden death shattered our dreams. Baba didn't own a house in the city of Barisal, and he couldn't afford to rent a house for me either. My parents had a big family in the village with my four sisters and brother—Fatema, Lutfa, Runu, Taslim, and baby Lina. I couldn't think what to do. I was always sunk in a deep depression. Everything looked dark. One day when I was four months pregnant, the jewel in my womb suddenly woke me up. The child in my womb stirred as if to say, Ma, I'm here. You can't afford to be scared. The two of us will fight for a good life. You and me. You're not alone anymore.

I jumped up and stroked my belly with deep affection. It was wonderful, I felt so happy. Everyone was sleeping. I slept with Imad's mother. It was late at night, but my heart was full of light. I couldn't stay shut in the room anymore. I went and stood outside. The world seemed flooded with light. I was walking back and forth all alone and stroking my belly. Then slowly the day dawned.

I remembered a poem by Rabindranath Tagore: "This morning the sun's rays / touched my heart / the dawn birdsong / touched the dark cave / I don't know why, after so long / my heart awoke."

I felt that I was not alone. I had to live, to stand on my own feet. If not for myself, then for my child. He had only me. After that, I slowly began trying to return to normal. When my friends and relatives came to visit, I talked to them.

Everyone asked, "Aren't you going to take your exam?" I said, "What exam?" My mind was wandering a thousand miles away from any exam. Day followed night, and night followed day. Then my days of waiting were over. At 8 pm on 24 August 1956, filling my world with light, Jaseem was born in a little room, hardly more than a veranda, attached to his Boro Chacha and Chachi's room. This little room was a kind of extension made of bamboo slats with a tin roof. After Jaseem's birth, a wave of tears swept through the house. I cried my heart out too. Everyone felt restless with renewed grief at Imad's death.

Baba had arranged a woman doctor, Dr Hosne Ara, and nurse from the hospital for me beforehand. I went to Dr Hosne Ara for regular checkups. The nurse was my mother's Phuphu and my Nani. Her name was Zobayda. In those times, women from elite households didn't go into nursing, as it was considered a lowly profession. Zobayda Nani was very tall and big-boned and had an overbite. She wore her hair in a bun. If she didn't wear a sari, no one would have guessed she was Bengali. It seems she hadn't gotten along with her husband, so she'd come to Barisal and taken up nursing. She was very cheerful and fun-loving. Wherever she went, fountains of laughter sprang up. Everyone in my in-laws' household liked her.

After Imad's death, my mother-in-law often said Imad had left his child for her. I never paid much attention to this; after all, she was a mother who had lost her son. The day I gave birth, after the doctor and nurse finished their work and left, my mother-in-law finished eating and came to sleep in my room. She told me quite emphatically that a skinny little girl like me could hardly take care of her grandson. Then she took my baby into her arms and lay down with him, and told me to lie at a distance, because I could roll over in my sleep and suffocate him. I silently did as she said. But after five minutes she fell asleep and started snoring. That day, my mother-in-law was exhausted too, so she fell asleep as soon as she lay down. When I could tell she was out cold, I slowly took the baby in my arms. I changed the wet quilts several times in the night and tried to feed the baby breastmilk little by little. My father-in-law came a few times to check on us and smiled sweetly seeing my mother-in-law fast asleep.

The next morning, my nurse-Nani came again to bathe the baby and do her other duties. Boro Bhabi (my sister-in-law,

Kaysar's wife) gave me and Nani a good breakfast of *porota*, eggs, and tea. My mother-in-law was still sleeping. At my Nani's sudden guffaws, she jumped up and saw the room full of people. The baby was sitting in his mother's lap happily drinking breastmilk and looking radiant. Maybe she felt a little embarrassed. Seeing her face, I thought she felt reassured about my abilities. After that, she never considered me incapable of motherhood, or at least that's what I think. She never objected to any of my decisions about Jaseem. There may have been another reason for that. Very few girls in my situation would have decided to stay with their in-laws. I decided to stay with them for two reasons. First, the deep cries of a mother who lost her son echoed in my heart; both of us women were ravaged by the loss of our beloved Imad. Second, Jaseem never met his father, so I wanted him to know his Dada and Dadi. I wanted his little heart to be full of their love.

Just two days after Jaseem was born, Imad's only sister Bela also had a son. We two new mothers spent our days sitting and talking on the same cot in the same room. Two days later, Bela's husband Mohammad Nabi brought two soft toys. One was a dog and the other a tiger. The eyes of the two toys glowed in the dark. Nabi also brought a letter for me from the Communist Party of East Pakistan. In that letter, the Party asked me to name my child Jaseem, because Imad was known as Jaseem among Party members. The letter was worded like this: "We want to know Jaseem's son as Jaseem." But before Jaseem was born, his Dada had already given him a name: Khandakar Mohammad Mohiuddin Saifullah. No one thought that I might have a preference in this matter. I silently gave up my own choice and deferred to theirs.

Later, when I went abroad, the name in Jaseem's passport was Khandakar Mohammad Mohiuddin Saifullah. He enrolled in school at Cambridge under the same name. But Jaseem often asked me to change his name. Even after he came back from Cambridge to Karachi, Jaseem insisted on changing his name. Finally, we did change his name officially to his nickname, Jaseem. Now I think maybe it wasn't right to give in to his wishes and change the name. I didn't like my name either when I was a child, but now I like my name. Bela's son was called Nasim to match with Jaseem. When Nasim was a little older, Bela moved to Dhaka with her husband and son. After that, I lived with Jaseem in the room I used to share with Imad. We had one cot, and my mother-in-law had another small cot in the same room. We two bereaved women spent several years of our lives, full of laughter and tears, in that room!

After Jaseem was born, many people came to Imad's house to see him. Ali Ashraf from Barisal (a journalist with the *Dainik Bangla*) and Abdur Rab Serniyabat[5] came together. Each of them gave 10 taka for my son and said they would come again. Another person came, Mahmud Ali, who was a minister at the time. Since he was on tour in Barisal, he came by for a few minutes with other friends of Imad to see Imadullah's son. We all cried during that visit. Later, I received a registered letter from the East Pakistan government signed by Mahmud Ali stating that I would be given 10 *bighas* (around 3 acres) of land to help me raise my son Jaseem, the son of Imadullah who died prematurely while working for his country. The letter explained: This land is in recognition of the great service given by Imadullah for this country, and we will make all arrangements and prepare legal documents after we hear from you. At the time, I was very sad and distraught but did not want any help from the government. My friends and family thought I had a right to take the land, but I disagreed and sent a reply letter declining the offer.

Within a few months of Jaseem's birth, all the political prisoners were released from jail. That was toward the end of 1956. I heard that Swadesh had been released along with the others. I thought that Swadesh would come to see Imad's son, but he didn't come. I wondered why he never once came to see Jaseem. Swadesh was a very close friend of Imad. Imad invited him secretly to our room almost every evening; he would close the door, and the two of them would carry on hairsplitting discussions of various aspects of Marxism late into the night. Or sometimes they would just do "*adda*" (the famous Bengali institution of hanging out with friends and talking up a storm). Sometimes the three of us would walk down to the riverside and sit on a bench in the Ladies' Park eating peanuts, talking about the same things: when, where, and how the revolution would come, when the people of this country would be free of the curse of hunger and poverty! It was odd to me that Swadesh never came to see how we were doing. I kept thinking, how could the person who sent that letter from jail act so aloof? None of Imad's other friends had written letters like that.

Then one day I took Jaseem to visit Karim Chacha in his house in Jhautala. Karim Chacha lived in a rented room on 2nd Street on the west side of the pond. When I arrived, I found the door open. I went in and saw Swadesh sitting on the bed tutoring Anisa Chachi. Chachi was supposed to take the intermediate exam that year. Swadesh was completely dazed to see me and Jaseem there. He kept quiet for a while and then said, "Noorjahan, it's you! Is this Jaseem?"

He'd never seen me in a widow's white sari and blouse before. Besides, he may have been wondering whether I was that same girl he used to know. It seemed as if that was a thousand years ago. Swadesh also looked different. He was much thinner than before. His eyes were hollow and gleaming. His cheeks were sunken. It looked like he had trouble standing up. But he somehow stood up and reached out to take Jaseem in his arms. I said, "Why don't you sit down first and then take him?" He said, "Don't worry, I won't drop him."

We talked for a while, and I learned that he'd found room and board in Shaula Lodge on Mallik Road. A *jotedar* family from Shaula village in Bauphal had bought an old brick house and some tin rooms across from the Police Club and named the place after their village. I remember thinking it was a miracle that they'd given the place to a convicted Communist straight out of jail.

### *Standing on my own feet: my first job*

After a while, when Jaseem was around ten months old, I began to feel that one way or another, I had to get a job. At the same time, I thought, who is going to give me a job? Finally, after a lot of thought, I decided one day to go and see the head teacher of the Sadar Balika Bidyalay girls' school, Ms Shanti Guha. Shanti-di knew me well, because she was the secretary of the Barisal Women's Hostel, the same hostel I used to live in, which was shut down after the riots of 1950 and reopened again thanks to my own efforts. I'd had to run around and pin down a lot of people to get it done. The old hostel was in A. K. Fazlul Huq Shaheb's mother's house. The new one was on Agarpur Road. A huge lot with two big houses belonging to two famous barrister brothers had been lying empty for a long time. One of the brothers was named Binoy Gupta; I don't remember the other one's name. After 1947, they left this big property in the hands of a caretaker and moved to India.

After the riots, I had asked Shanti-di to open another girls' hostel. A. K. Dutta was Barisal's DC at the time. When I kept asking Shanti-di about the hostel, she took me with her one day to see the DC. Shanti-di gave him a stellar rationale for converting that abandoned house in Agarpur into a girls' hostel. The DC listened carefully to what Shanti-di and I had to say. I informed him that there were six or seven of us students who would live in the hostel. After hearing us out, the DC went to see the house and promptly arranged for it to be converted into a hostel. Within a few days, the girls' hostel opened and Shanti-di was appointed secretary. She lived in her own house and came to the hostel every day. Sometimes she brought guests. I talked to the guests, showed them around the hostel, and tried to answer their questions. Shanti-di was very pleased with me for that.

Both buildings on the hostel property were filled with expensive things: glass and brass plates, glasses, dinner sets, tea sets, and above all a very valuable library. I've never seen so many books in anyone's personal library. The library was a treasure for me, and I devoured the books whenever I could. There was a huge piano too, in the middle of the sitting room. The caretaker of this large property took every opportunity to sell off its valuable items of crystal and glass. I saw this with my own eyes when I lived in the hostel. Later when I took the post of hostel supervisor, it was still going on. I didn't have any way to stop it, but I would always tell Shanti-di what I saw.

Shanti-di had an ancestral house in Barisal too. She lived on the second floor, where there was a big, wide veranda. Her younger sister was always lying in a big cane easy chair on the veranda. This sister had suddenly become paralyzed after completing her BA. They had made special arrangements for her. A woman called Robir Ma looked after her. Robir Ma was a widow; she lived with her children downstairs. I always saw the sister wearing a bright white shirt with an apron over it, because there was always drool coming from her mouth. She always had a book in front of her, and someone would turn the pages for her. When Shanti-di was at home, she lovingly did this task herself.

All the bedrooms were upstairs in Shanti-di's house. There were many rooms downstairs too. I don't know who lived there. Shanti-di's parents had died long ago, and her other siblings had gone to India. Since then, Shanti-di lived in this house alone with her disabled sister. Downstairs, there was a long veranda at the back of the house, the kitchen on the west side, and next to it the *thakurghar* or pujo room. On the other side there were the servants' quarters, and in the courtyard in the middle there was a well. Beyond the outer wall was a cowshed. Every day, they had fresh home-made milk, ghee, and curd. The house was called "Refuge."

In any case, one morning on a holiday I went to Shanti-di's house again, this time for my own sake. I'd been there many times before, so I knew where in the house I would find her. This house of Shanti-di's, built on a large property by the pond, was the pride of Barisal. Shanti-di's father Sharatchandra Guha was a big Congress leader. That day, I went and saw Shanti-di sitting at a huge round table in the hall upstairs looking over some papers and files. That's how I saw her most of the time. The walls of the room were hung with oil paintings of the family. Then there was a huge glass-front cabinet full of rows and rows of bound books. Shanti-di looked up at me and said, "Noorjahan, come in, come in. I've been thinking of you! The last time I saw you was when you came to see me before your wedding. You've been through a lot since then."

Shanti-di sat me down beside her and treated me to tea and snacks. She asked me what I wanted to do now. Then she herself said, "You can't sit around doing nothing now." She asked after my son—how old he was, whom he looked like, and so on. Suddenly I said to her, "Didi, I need a job."

I started crying. She got up from her chair, came over to me, and stroked my head. Then after thinking a little, she said, "Where are you going to get a job? You're so young, and you haven't finished your studies. On top of that, you have a baby son!"

She said this as if talking to herself.

Then she said, "The women's hostel superintendent resigned today due to illness. I need a new hostel super by tomorrow. Can you do this job? Not long ago you were a student there. Some of the girls are very naughty. You know everything."

I had no idea Shanti-di was going to give me such a big responsibility. I stared at her, but no words came out. There was no one in Barisal who didn't fear Shanti-di's eyes. Really, those eyes were like stone. Those who judged Shanti-di by her stern exterior didn't know how soft-hearted she was. Later, she kept in touch with me through letters to her dying day. I got all the Barisal news through those letters. Whenever Swadesh saw a letter from Shanti-di, he'd say, "Here comes Radio Barisal."

That day, Shanti-di put her hand on my head and said, "I know you can do it, Noorjahan. Your salary will be 30 taka a month, plus free room and board. You'll live in the big room downstairs on the east side of the hostel. I'll tell them to clean it and fix it up today. Tomorrow morning you come with your things; I'll be there."

I sat there for a few moments, overcome. Then I suddenly thought, oh my goodness, I didn't even give Shanti-di my *pronam*.[6] I touched her feet with tears in my eyes. Shanti-di touched my head in blessing and said, "May you be happy and successful in life."

Then I practically flew from Shanti-di's house to my in-laws'. I had a job, free room and board, 30 taka a month, and a safe shelter! Apprehensively, I told my father- and mother-in-law the news of my appointment at the girls' hostel. My mother-in-law's face darkened, but my father-in-law was very happy. He enthusiastically supported my decision to take the job. He even said this was the best possible job for me. But my mother-in-law still didn't soften. Later I explained to her, "I'll be living very close by, and I can come and see you every day. Shanti-di said she'll find a good *ayah* [nanny] for Jaseem. The *ayah* will bring Jaseem to see you every day."

Finally, everyone accepted my decision because they had no alternative.

The next day was the first day of my job. I arrived at the hostel at the appointed time. Shanti-di came and told everyone that I was the new superintendent from today on. Then she showed me the account books, how to look after the finances, and all my other duties, and left. A few days later, she arranged for the mother of the girl who worked in her own house to work as Jaseem's *ayah*. The *ayah*'s wages were very high, 10 taka. She had worked as an *ayah* for the officers of the steamer company. Shanti-di said, "Her wages are high, but you can leave your child with her worry-free. She's very trustworthy and loves children."

I followed her advice and hired this *ayah*, even though it was expensive for me. I had no choice. Later, two sisters named Farida and Bedana came to live in the hostel. Their brother was a professor at the agricultural college. He was going to America for higher education, so he entrusted his two sisters to me—including their private tutoring. I was paid 30 taka for tutoring them. There was no happier news for me at the time. Later, when I left the job at the hostel and lived in a rented house, I was still Farida and Bedana's local guardian.

After I joined as hostel superintendent, the girls made a big fuss over Jaseem. They competed over who would pamper him the most. Even though I told them many times not to, the girls kept giving him chocolate and sweets and sharing their meat and fish with him. Then suddenly something happened to Jaseem. He got a high fever and diarrhea, and his stomach got swollen. We called a doctor. First Dr Shamsur Rahman, then Dr A. C. Ray. None of their medicines had any effect. Fever, diarrhea, thirst, swollen stomach, none of these symptoms went away. Jaseem couldn't sleep. Then we called in a couple of other big-name doctors, but without results. Each of them went away looking grave.

This drew a crowd in front of the hostel and a lot of people started saying, "The widow's only son could draw his last breath any minute." I was almost crazy with fear. Suddenly a gentleman named Manoranjan Biswas came out of the crowd and asked to see me. Someone brought him to me. He told me very politely that he wanted to give my son some homeopathic medicine. I had nothing to lose. The big doctors had all left. That day, Swadesh was there with me. He had been sitting with Jaseem for almost twenty-four hours. Then Manoranjan Babu took a rickshaw back to his home to bring the medicine and gave it to Jaseem. Half an hour later, he gave Jaseem another few drops of the medicine. He didn't leave; he stayed there with us. In about an hour, Jaseem fell asleep. He hadn't slept for four days and nights. I kept putting my hand on his mouth and face to check if he was still alive. Within two hours of taking Manoranjan Babu's medicine, his fever and stomach swelling went down.

Manoranjan Babu gave Jaseem one more dose of the medicine and went home. By then, it was midnight or one o'clock. On his way out, he said he would bring more medicine in the morning. Swadesh sat up with me all night. My sisters were there too. Jaseem slept through the night. I kept checking on him anxiously every hour. Every time I went to check on him, I thought, maybe my son is dead. Again and again, I felt his breath, put my ear on his chest to hear his heartbeat. A miracle happened before our eyes. The next morning, Jaseem had no fever and no swollen stomach. He was perfectly normal, and most importantly, the diarrhea had stopped. Jaseem opened his eyes and said, "Ma, I'm hungry."

He was a year old and had just started talking. Nothing as incredible as this has happened to me since. Maybe nothing ever will. I later understood what happened: Jaseem had food poisoning. In those days, the doctors didn't have the right medicines to treat it. At least, the doctors in Barisal didn't know them. This was in the middle of 1957. I still think of Manoranjan Babu often. I am forever grateful to him. Thanks to his good deed, my Jaseem is still alive today.

The job at the girls' hostel was a big responsibility for me. I did my best to handle it well. My college friend Meera Chatterjee was the daughter of an elite family in Jhautala. Meera's younger sister Neera was in seventh or eighth grade at the time. Both sisters were very good-looking. Around this time, a rumor went around that Neera was in love with a good-for-nothing Muslim boy from Kaunia neighborhood. Everyone in Barisal knew that boy. He rode around the city on a horse-cart advertising movies. We heard other things about him too. One day, I heard that Neera had run away with that boy. There was a flurry of discussion all over the city about this thirteen- or fourteen-year-old girl's future. I remember being so worried about my friend's sister.

They were later able to rescue Neera with the help of the then DC, A. K. Dutta. One evening a few days after she ran away, there was a knock on the main gate of the hostel. I opened the gate and saw Shanti-di standing in front of the gate with someone in a burqa. Then she came into my room and told me to close the door. Shanti-di told the girl in the burqa to take it off, and reluctantly she did. I saw she was our Neera. Shanti-di told me, "You have to keep her in the hostel until I can make other arrangements. Be very careful. She might try to run away again, or the boy she ran away with might bring his gang and try to take her away by force. I'm trusting you to do this, Noorjahan. I hope you'll be able to handle it."

Then Shanti-di left. I closed the door and stared at Neera in amazement. Neera told me she had converted to Islam and married that boy. They were living together as husband and wife, in hiding. That day, the police had found her and rescued her on the orders of the DC.

Neera grabbed my hands and feet and begged me to let her go. I tried to explain to her that, if the boy were a good person and if Neera were of age, then no one could say anything, but under the circumstances letting her go was completely out of the question. I told her to eat something and go to sleep. I had a sister and a few close cousins in the hostel and called on these sisters to help. We made Neera a bed in my own room. I told my sisters to be on guard. I called the gatekeeper and told him to sleep in front of the outer door of our room. I didn't tell the other girls in the hostel anything that night. I stayed up all night. Neera cried herself to sleep. In the morning, I told my sisters to stay on guard again and took a rickshaw to Neera's house in Jhautala. I begged her parents to take her back, but they flatly refused. They said that if they took her back, they would have no face in society. Besides, they had to think of the other girls in the family. Neera was dead to them. Seeing there was no way to change their minds, I went to Neera's Mama's house and pleaded with her Mama and Mami. They had no children. They agreed to come talk to Neera in the hostel, but they didn't agree to take responsibility for her.

When I came back to the hostel, I found my room full of people. The girls had heard the news and come running to see her. Everyone was talking. Some of them were saying, "Neera got married according to her own wishes, what's wrong with that? It's great that she's converted to Islam. Everyone involved in this good deed will go to heaven." Some of them suggested we take her back to her husband. Hearing all this, I thought, what a disaster! If the hostel girls want to let her out, how will I stop them? I had to pacify the girls by explaining to them that Neera was a minor and that legally she could neither get married nor change her religion. I hadn't heard any news from Shanti-di, but I couldn't take the risk of leaving the hostel to go see her. So, I kept waiting.

Now, the news that Neera had been rescued and had taken shelter in the girls' hostel spread like wildfire across the city. Hindus and Muslims became divided on the issue. From afternoon onwards, I started seeing a lot of people milling about in front of our hostel gate. In the late afternoon, a government official came to see me. He asked me, "Being a Muslim yourself, why are you out to ruin Muslims?"

I responded, “If your own young daughter wanted to run off with a good-for-nothing boy, would you agree?”

He said, “Forget about me. The girl has become a Muslim and is living with her husband. I heard she wants to go back to her husband. Why are you preventing her from going?”

I said, “The girl is unwell. She’s raving with fever. I can’t listen to her raving and let her go put herself in danger.”

He grew furious, threatened me, and left. I won’t say I wasn’t scared of him. But what did I have to lose? I thought to myself, can I leave this flower-like little girl in the hands of those criminals? No, never.

After that, I somehow got the idea that the hostel might be attacked at night. And that’s what happened. Around midnight, some thugs surrounded the hostel. The hostel building was huge, with many rooms. The girls all lived upstairs. I lived downstairs, and so did the cook. The girls were all asleep. Hearing the noise, I bound Neera’s mouth with a handkerchief and had my sisters help me take her upstairs to the center room. Then I went into every room and woke up all the girls. I told them the hostel was under attack and asked them to go to the center room. Three or four of them sat holding Neera. The thugs stood in front of the gate shouting for Neera to come out. I saw through the slightly open window that they had torches, big axes, spears, and sticks in their hands. The saddest thing was that a girls’ hostel was attacked and none of the neighbors came out to help. The people who lived across from the hostel had a gun; they could have shot a blank and scared the thugs off, but they didn’t. The thugs made a ruckus for two or three hours, then finally left. As they were leaving, they shouted, “We’ll come again.” Those few hours felt like an eternity to us. We were so scared we stayed awake in that room the rest of the night, thinking, what if they come again?

First thing in the morning, I sent the gatekeeper with a letter for Shanti-di. Then I came out and saw the marks of axe- and spear-blows on many of the hostel doors and windows. When she got the letter, Shanti-di hurried over. She said she would solve this problem right away. Then a government car came with police, and they took Neera away. Later I heard that the DC Mr A. K. Dutta had sent Neera to Kolkata to her older sister's house. It comforts me to know that I was able to protect young Neera from a corrupted young man. I wouldn't have been able to do it without the help of all the hostel girls. I don't know where they all are now, but I thank them with all my heart. I never had any contact with Neera's family after that.

*A new start*

I was happy with my job at the hostel, but everyone was pressuring me to continue my education. Studying requires a lot of attention, and I didn't have that kind of environment. At the hostel, new problems cropped up every day. Later I decided myself that I should put my education first, so I left the job and went back to my in-laws' house. I kept doing private tutoring. I also worked as a teacher at the Halima Khatun Balika Bidyalay for a while, with a salary of 50 taka. But I couldn't concentrate on my studies. As long as I was working, I felt fine, but when Jaseem fell asleep and I opened my books to study, old memories would come streaming back to me like scenes in a film, and I felt restless. If Jaseem suddenly woke up and saw me sitting at the table with my books, he would get out of bed and sit on top of them. He was a very unruly boy even with me, and more so with other people. During the day, it was impossible for me to study.

Then my father-in-law did something unusual: suddenly one morning he brought Swadesh to our house. For a man from outside the household to appear in that house in broad daylight, that too a Communist recently released from jail, was unimaginable. My father-in-law said, "I brought Swadesh Babu to help you out a little with your studies."

I couldn't think what to say to my father-in-law, so I kept quiet. I think the letter Swadesh wrote from jail and his staying by my side day and night during Jaseem's near-fatal illness had endeared him to my father-in-law.

Swadesh was ill himself at the time and was preparing for his BA exam at Chakhar College. Chakhar was the hometown of A. K. Fazlul Huq. The place was quite far from Barisal city. I also knew Swadesh did private tutoring to cover his expenses. I thought, how can he tutor me under these circumstances? Besides, I hadn't been able to decide whether I would even take my exam or not.

I told Swadesh, "Now and then, when you're in Barisal anyway, you can come and check on me. If I decide to take the exam, you can help me out then." Swadesh promised to help me, and he kept his promise. I took the exam and passed it. I have to give half the credit for this to my father-in-law Aminullah Shaheb. The other half I give to Swadesh Bose, who is now my husband. For some reason, my son Jaseem also didn't bother me as much while I was studying. I passed my Intermediate Exam in March 1958. Then I enrolled in the BA course at BM College. That year, Swadesh also passed his BA exam and went to do an MA at Dhaka University.

### *My foundation in Barisal: Mashima*

Manorama Basu was called "Mashima" (Aunty) by all. She was a huge influence on my entire life, especially from the time I was twelve until I was twenty-five. After the Language Movement of February 1952, Manorama Mashima and many others were released from jail in April. Manorama Mashima's beloved Matrimandir (Mother Temple) Ashram had been razed, so she also went to stay in the commune in Srinath Chatterjee Lane. She had a lot of people with her, and all responsibility for feeding and taking care of them was on her shoulders. My introduction to Marxist ideals had happened back in Patuakhali. While I was living in Patuakhali, when I came to Barisal during a school break, I stayed at my childhood friend Halima's sister's house, Santosh Bhaban. Halima lived there too. I had nowhere else to stay in Barisal; Santosh Bhaban was my only refuge. There was a street to the right of Bagura Road called Srinath Chatterjee Lane. Santosh Bhaban was on the edge of the pond at the northern end of the lane. Toward the middle in the western corner was Hiren-da's (Hiren Bhattacharya's) two-story tin house, which was known as an unofficial commune. When leftist leaders and workers got out of jail or came out of hiding, they stayed in that house.

I ran over to Hiren-da's house as soon as I heard Mashima was out of jail. I loved her at first sight. There was something magical about that slightly built, dark-skinned woman that always attracted me. With time, a deep and warm friendship developed between me and Mashima that lasted until her death in 1998.

Mashima took me around to all kinds of places in Barisal, from the narrow lanes of slums to the houses of elite people—sometimes to fundraise, sometimes to resolve disputes, sometimes just to visit or to honor an invitation. We rarely went by rickshaw; most of the time we went on foot. Mashima's physical and psychological strength was legendary. Her hands were hard as stone. Writing about her reminds me of another woman with whom I had the opportunity and good fortune of shaking hands: Mother Teresa. Like Mashima, she too was a slightly built woman, except that her skin was white. But the two of them had a lot in common. Her hands were like Mashima's, and her eyes burned like fire.

Manorama Mashima's extraordinary strength of will, selflessness, sacrifice, clear-sightedness, and boundless love and respect for humanity have made her immortal in my eyes. I am also deeply impressed by the immense love and respect that everyone in Barisal had for Mashima, irrespective of caste, religion, and economic status. I remember once Mashima took me to Ismail Choudhuri's house. His was a distinguished and wealthy family of Barisal. At the time, the master of the house was Ismail's son Shahjahan Choudhuri. When we went there, I was elated to see how he and his wife took Manorama Mashima's hand, sat her down, served her with the greatest respect, and paid the donation she came to request. From the small slums to Methorpatti, the sweepers' quarter, doors were open everywhere for Mashima, and for me along with her. Often, we would be out until late in the day, and many people insisted that we eat lunch with them.

Mashima's endurance was extraordinary. After her husband's death in 1954, Mashima became vegetarian and ate only once a day. She was not superstitious—in fact, she usually ate vegetarian anyway. But she was close to many Hindu families and Hindu widows. She told me, "Why make them uncomfortable for no reason? I like eating vegetarian anyway." Of course, when I ate with her, she would always send someone to bring some fish. Mashima's own cooking was sublime, and I still remember the taste of her *tyangra* or *punti macher jhol*.[7] I've tried very hard to cook like her, but her skills are beyond me.

One day, we were forced to sit down to eat in someone's house. They served us biriyani, *mangsher jhol*,[8] and salad. When I saw the food with all that meat, I expected a disaster. I thought, how can Mashima eat this food? Mashima quietly slipped the meat and fish onto my plate and ate just the biriyani rice and salad with satisfaction. No one even noticed. I was amazed. Later when I asked her about it, she laughed sweetly and said, "They served us food with such care and affection, if I didn't eat, they would be hurt."

I never saw her concerned about her own feelings or convenience. One day, we were in the sweepers' quarter until late afternoon. There they gave us *khoi* (puffed rice), *moa*, and bananas on brass plates. We sat side by side on mats and ate. She never gave any importance to caste rules.

It never felt tiring to work with Mashima from morning until night. The word "tired" wasn't in her vocabulary. Of course, despite her ever-present smile, Manorama Mashima's life wasn't always peaceful. But she never complained about it. Mashima worried no end about her youngest daughter Aparna, but she never bothered anyone else about it. She spent a long time in jail, in hiding, or engrossed in organizing. Toward the end of her life, her sons, daughters, and grandchildren tried to bring her to stay with them in Kolkata, but to no avail. Mashima told me, "When I go stay with them, I suffocate. I don't like talking about my own comfort all the time. So I come running back here to Barisal. I love everyone in this country. I don't feel at peace anywhere except my Matrimandir."

Mashima's working life was long and far-reaching. In 1933–4, she opened a hostel for women abandoned by society at Matrimandir. Then she started a school for them. Even when she was a prisoner, she was eager to teach the women prisoners. She didn't have access to slates or paper, but she still taught them the alphabet by drawing with coal on the floor. Mashima's organizational ability was incredible. In each of the country's storms or dark days, especially during political and natural emergencies and during the Muktijuddho (Liberation War), Mashima helped people with her relentless efforts.

In 1948, the untimely death of Mashima's daughter Bashona hit her very hard, especially because Bashona was a believer in her mother's ideals. Mashima's husband Chintaharan Basu also died at an early age in 1954. Despite these losses, Mashima tried to find solace in work. I was close to Mashima's daughter Bhajana, who followed her mother's ideals and spent several years in jail as a political prisoner.

The other people I met at the commune were Sujata Dasgupta, Khuku-di from Patuakhali, Bibha-di, Pinaki Basu, Nikhil Sen,

Maharaj-da, and Khoka-da. Sujata Dasgupta was Maharaj-da's wife. During their long imprisonment, their little son was staying with a relative in Kolkata. Each of these people in the commune endured insufferable separations from their spouses, children, parents, or other loved ones. And yet they kept the candle of love for their country burning bright. Many of them were later forced to leave for West Bengal.

During the Liberation War of 1971, I met Maharaj-da, Khuku-di, Prashanta-da, Khoka-da (Khoka Ray), Juiphul Bose, and many others in Kolkata. All of us had tears in our eyes remembering the old days. We'd gone together so many times around the lanes and offices of Barisal to collect donations! I remember one funny incident—Bhajana-di and I sometimes went around to various offices to collect donations, and people would sit us down and give us tea, sweets, and *shingara*.[9] We would eat quickly and ask for the donation, but then they'd say no. We'd get very angry with them for wasting our time. After that, we stopped going to offices.

Sometimes Bhajana-di and I would sit up talking all night long. Bhajana-di was in love with a revolutionary student leader in Barisal, Prashanta Dasgupta. They were engaged. But even after Bhajana-di was released, Prashanta-da was still in jail. Prashanta-da's younger sister went to school with me. I went to their house a lot. Prashanta-da's mother had somehow become deranged by the separation from her son. I felt bad when I went to their house. I used to read the letters Prashanta-da sent from jail to Bhajana-di. Bhajana-di would cry, and I would feel like crying with her.

Bhajana-di had no fixed address. She often stayed in a house in Kaunia Branch Road. I went there from time to time. She was very sick at the time. In the end, Bhajana-di and Prashanta-da's wedding never happened, because Prashanta-da was released much later. Meanwhile, Bhajana-di grew broken-hearted waiting for him and finally went to stay with her brothers in Kolkata. She was sick for a long time, then eventually married someone else and went to live with her husband in Barrackpur. I never got a chance to see her after that. She is no longer alive. Prashanta-da was released from jail long after Bhajana-di left for Kolkata, and he went to Kolkata too. Mashima loved Swadesh as if he were her own son. She wanted one of her daughters to marry Swadesh, but that wish was not fulfilled.

Manorama Mashima rejected the privilege of her caste and treated everyone equally. Even though she was the daughter of a *jomidar* family, she had no pride and no interest in pleasure and comfort. Above all else, she had unstinting love for people in every walk of life. She was a lot like my mother in some ways. Maybe that's why I loved her at first sight. Both were ordinary-looking, neither of them received much of an education. One was born in a *jomidar* family, the other married into a wealthy *jotedar* family, but both chose a simple life for themselves. In both women, I saw courage, generosity, a soft heart, and when needed, a brilliant spirit and an iron will.

The heartfelt and affectionate relationship I had with Mashima lasted until her death. Even after I left the country, I exchanged letters with her regularly. I wanted badly to be with her in the last days of her life. I felt the same about my own mother. But they say many of our dreams evaporate like bubbles, and that's what happened to my longing to be there with them. Mashima had completely abandoned the idea of staying with her children. In much the same way, my mother too went against all our wishes and remained in the village. My mother drew her last breath in her own house by the sea, and Manorama Mashima in her beloved Matrimandir. I tried to give each of them some solace in their last days, but I couldn't do much from far-away America. This is a sorrow that will be with me until I die. The contribution of these two great women in my life is boundless.

Mashima and I started a school for adults in Barisal. It later shut down for lack of funds. I tried unsuccessfully to reopen the school myself. A few years later, I gave some money to Hiren-da's widow Rani Bhattacharya to reopen Mashima's school for adults in memory of Hiren Bhattacharya. But Rani-di was unable to generate interest in the project. After Mashima's death, I proposed several times that the name of Kaunia Branch Road be changed to Manorama Basu Street. That still hasn't happened. After Independence, Mashima met with Bangabandhu Sheikh Mujibur Rahman and secured government status for her school. Mashima's pride and joy—her Matrimandir and school—are still running. Her Amritanag Library is also still running.

For Jaseem's first birthday, Mashima wrote a beautiful poem in her own hand and framed it for him. I've lost that poem and wish I could remember all the lines.

### *Barisal's intellectuals*

The experienced political scientist Deben-da (Deben Ghosh) was someone we all respected. It's hard to explain to those who don't know this man how self-sacrificing and free of self-interest he was, and how much he loved his country. A lifelong bachelor, he dedicated himself to serving his country, nation, and people. He participated in the anti-British movement as a youth in collaboration with the Anushilan Party. Deben-da spent long years of his life in jail, in the Andamans, and in hiding. No kind of pain or cruelty could make him leave his country. In his old age, he jumped into our Liberation War and was thrilled to see the country gain independence before he died. Neither age nor anything else could sway him in his determination. In his old age, he joined the Awami League.

I saw him for the last time at Manorama Mashima's centenary celebration. He was then 108 years old. Toward the end, he couldn't walk, so a youth from Barisal carried him in his arms like a child to attend the event. That day, Swadesh and I ran and stood at either side of him. Swadesh said, "Deben-da, I'm Swadesh." His eyes lit up with delight. He said, "Swadesh, weren't we in jail together one time?"

When Swadesh said yes, his eyes grew even brighter. I said "Deben-da, I'm Noorjahan."

He recognized me immediately. He said, "Noorjahan, aren't you Swadesh's wife? Do you know what a formidable husband you have?" I laughed and said, "Yes, Deben-da, I know, and I've been measuring just how formidable he is all my life."

Deben-da and everyone around us laughed. I was truly touched by what he said next. Deben-da said, "Noorjahan, you used to like to drink good tea."

A niece of his used to study with me at BM College. When tea came in from Kolkata, Deben-da would let me know. Many a day I've spent at his house drinking tea and talking away. I won't even try to account for all the food I've eaten there. I've been fortunate to have the companionship of a person like Deben-da and hear various stories of his life. I never feel as if Deben-da is gone.

Another person I came to know was Dwijen Sharma, the older brother of my college friend Sandhya. Dwijen-da taught at BM College, possibly botany. I met him and grew close to him when I went with Sandhya to their rented room. Dwijen-da was always busy with plants and flowers. He was also a book lover. I had a keen interest in books too. I borrowed books from Dwijen-da to read, and the day I returned them, we would always spend an hour or so discussing the book in detail over tea he made himself. We all enjoyed Dwijen-da's *addas*. I remember I borrowed the famous book *Spartacus* from him.

I was the matchmaker for Dwijen-da and Debi's marriage. Dwijen-da met Debi in my house on Bagura Road. Later they fell in love. After leaving Barisal, I lost touch with them. After Independence, they went to Moscow, and we went to Washington. After floating around here and there for many years, we ended up back in Dhaka, in Bangladesh, the land of our birth. When we saw Dwijen-da, it was like the same old *adda*.

One time, Swadesh and I went on a cruise with a few friends to Alaska. There we learned that the world-famous salmon swim all the way around the world and come back to die in the same place where they were born. Apparently, the tasty *ilish* of our country—I think there's no tastier fish than *ilish*—does the same thing! Maybe we too were drawn back to Bangladesh by the same invisible birth-cord. Dwijen-da divides his time between Dhaka and Moscow. I too divide my time between Washington and Bangladesh. I want to die in my homeland like the salmon and the *ilish*.

I will end this reminiscence of Barisal by writing about Nikhil-da and Padma-di. I met Nikhil Sen sometime in 1952. In the wake of the Language Movement, the fertile soil of East Pakistan yielded many kinds of thought and consciousness. Many of us were inspired by these thoughts. I met Nikhil Sen and Pinaki Basu[10] at the same time. During the Liberation War, Pinaki Basu couldn't save himself even by converting to Islam. I used to see them in Barisal and talk about all kinds of things, mostly about the country and politics. We also spent a lot of time talking about what books we were reading. At the time, Barobaishdia was a name well known to leftist politicians. Many people thought that this island in the Bay of Bengal, close to the Sundarban, would be the central node of the East Pakistani people's revolution. It was a great place to hide weapons and ideas smuggled from abroad. We knew of many revolutionary leaders and workers who lived in the area for a long time. Their self-sacrifice, selfless love for their country, and open-mindedness touched the students, teachers, farmers, common people, and even the women of the region and sparked a kind of awakening. There was no fundamentalism there. I've never seen a woman in my area wearing a burqa or hijab in the name of religion.

On the other hand, Khepupara, Galachipa, and the surrounding area were completely different from Barobaishdia. Heeralal Dasgupta, Nalini Das, and Patuakhali's Satin Sen were household names. My Chacha Abdul Karim, Saifur Rahman ("Saifu Bhai") from the next village, my Phupha Abdul Hamid Haoladar, Ratan Mia, Lalua, Mosharaf Hosen Biswas, Fakruddin Biswas, Jaseem Biswas, Patuakhali's Abdul Khalek Master, and finally Imadullah created a whole new environment in the area.

Imad came to our house many times and discussed the coming revolution with me. He said that the struggle for East Pakistan's independence would begin soon on the island of Barobaishdia. There was no safer place in East Bengal.

After the election of 1954, Nikhil-da came to our house. That time, Karim Chacha took his friends and Nikhil-da around the village. One day, they were all invited to lunch at our house. Big fish were brought from the pond. Cooking was under way. I don't remember when Nikhil Sen became known as Nikhil-da in our area. Everyone in the village started calling him Nikhil-da, and that's how he's known to this day. That day, the police came suddenly and arrested Karim Chacha while he was bathing in the pond. The villagers came and crowded around on the riverbank. If Karim Chacha had given the command, the villagers would have given their lives to rescue him. There was such hatred toward the Pakistani rulers in everyone's eyes.

A few days before this, Imad had sent a letter informing me that Section 92-A was being enforced and that there would be a military crackdown.[11] There was a spate of arrests and people going into hiding all over the country. In our remote area, nobody had heard of Section 92-A. Then a bomb exploded right in our courtyard. Everyone was shocked. Suddenly my father remembered Nikhil-da, who was taking a bath in the pond with Karim Chacha. Baba brought Nikhil-da into the house, wearing a *lungi*, with a *gamcha* on his shoulder. Baba told me to take him next door and hide him. The police hadn't recognized him, but they could come again any time. I quickly took Nikhil-da next door. Everyone in the household just stood there in bewilderment. After that, we hid Nikhil-da in various buildings during the day and sent food to him secretly. We spent our days in great anxiety.

It was the monsoon, the rainy season. You couldn't go anywhere without a boat or a dinghy. The region was so deep in floodwater, it looked like we were in the middle of the ocean. The houses looked like islands. The villages were cut off from each other. Conditions in the area during the monsoon are still pretty much the same. There are no roads, no electricity. In the evening, aside from the faint glow of a kerosene lamp or hurricane lamp in a few houses, the whole area seemed haunted. I was used to it, but I couldn't bear to look at Nikhil-da. The poor thing had come there to have a good time, and suddenly he was in trouble. Then he fell sick with influenza. Almost everyone in the area had it. Finally, we arranged for Nikhil-da to sleep in our house. I slept with my mother. Our house was built Burmese-style, with a floor of wooden planks. The floor was raised off the ground. It wasn't damp like an earthen house. Suddenly our whole area was deep in flood. The water was almost touching the planks of our house. It could rise above the planking any moment. My parents were keeping track of the wind and water with considerable anxiety. Nikhil-da was lying in my room with a fever. Water everywhere. Baba and I went to sit with him, to give him strength. From the south window, we saw a big snake coming toward the room. Nikhil-da jumped up and shouted, "There's a snake in the room, a snake, what should we do?" I laughed and said, "Nikhil-da, the poor thing is scared and looking for a safe place, just like us. If we don't hurt it, it won't hurt anybody." But Nikhil-da looked very frightened.

Luckily, I had brought some books from the Nirmalendu Library in Patuakhali. I spent the long days and nights reading. Sometimes Hamid Phupha and Said Bhai came from Phelabunia and helped relieve our boredom, filling a few days with laughter and fun. Sometimes they took Nikhil-da to Phelabunia or Tungibaria to my Mama's house. Our Benu Mama, the brother-in-law of "Taloi" Talukdar who lived in that house, was a Marxist like us. Almost three months went by in this way. The results of my matric exam came out. After that, I had to go to Barisal to figure out where I would stay when I enrolled at BM College.

When I wasn't there, no one was ready to take responsibility for Nikhil-da. Finally, he was sent to Lalua Biswas's house. After that, he was arrested. Even though it was unfortunate, at least Nikhil-da got to see his friends in jail—better than nothing, I suppose.

The kinship that arose between Nikhil-da and me kept going until we were both elderly. Nikhil-da married Padma-di, whom I knew already. When I was a first-year student at BM College, Padma-di was in her fourth year. She had a lovely slim figure and a very sweet face, with big eyes. When Padma-di went around by the college women's lounge (our lounge was a floating structure in the middle of a pond!), with a mass of curly hair spread over her back, she looked to me like a swan floating around with her own thoughts. This Padma-di married Nikhil-da and became my Padma Boudi (sister-in-law). I was so happy. Later we taught together at the Barisal Sadar Balika Bidyalay (now the Barisal Government Higher Secondary School).

Nikhil-da and Padma Boudi treated me like a member of the family. Their two daughters Bulu and Nanda and their son Sujoy know me as their only aunt. I sewed little shirts, pants, and quilts for Bulu and Nanda when they were newborns, something I've never done for anyone else. Nikhil Sen is Nikhil-da to everyone in Barisal, irrespective of caste, religion, color, and political ideology. Everyone loves and respects him. I don't know what magic helped him gain the love, respect, and devotion of so many. Several thousand residents of Barisal attended the wedding of their son Sujoy—with or without invitation. Nikhil-da said, how do I decide whom to include and whom to leave out? Nikhil-da passed away on 25 February 2019, but I remain close to his daughter Nanda who lives in Kentucky.

I still go to Barisal. If I don't, I feel like something's missing in my life. This land of Barisal gave birth to Aswini Kumar Dutta,[12] poets like *Charan Kobi* Mukunda Das,[13] Jibanananda Das,[14] and Sufia Kamal, beloved leaders like A. K. Fazlul Huq, prominent academics like Amiya Dasgupta and Tapan Raychaudhuri, and so many other accomplished people who grew up with the colors, tastes, and scents of Barisal. I knew and grew close to many of them. I feel fortunate to be a daughter of this beautiful, talented Barisal. They say the poet Nazrul visited Barisal and was so impressed that he called it "Bengal's Venice."

### *The legendary Heeralal Dasgupta and a destructive storm*

When I was in school, I heard a lot of stories about the revolutionary Heeralal Das. I never thought I'd get a chance to meet him. During British rule, he worked tirelessly in secret among the ordinary farmers and working people in the villages of Aamtoli, Khepupara, Kuakata, and Galachipa in the south of Patuakhali district. He shouldered the responsibility of teaching them how to form an organized movement against poverty and injustice.

When military rule was enforced in 1958, I was informed that I might be arrested. Jaseem was only two years old then. The Party sent word to me to take Jaseem and go back to the village immediately. It was the rainy season. I never went to the village at that time of year, but this time I had no choice. I secretly went to the village, and I learned that Heera-da was the head teacher at the high school there. I was thrilled, thinking now I would get a chance to meet him. I meant to go to the school to meet him, but before I had a chance, he came to see me himself with a big ripe papaya from a tree he'd planted. A tall, fair, impeccable man, he stood at our door, his face radiating tranquility. Unconsciously, I reached down to touch his feet. I felt as if I must have done good deeds in many lives to have the good fortune of meeting such a person. Within moments, we were talking about the state of the village as if I'd known him for ages. We kept talking into the night. Ma invited Heera-da to eat with us, and he did so with pleasure. Jaseem had already occupied his lap. As he was leaving, Heera-da invited me to eat at his house the next day.

The next day, I went with Jaseem to the school in the afternoon. I saw that in his hands the school had taken on a completely new appearance. He had planted flowers and vegetables all around it. The papaya trees were full of big papayas. Some boys were rehearsing for a play. Their presence filled the place with happiness. I was delighted to see this. Later the three of us sat down to eat coarse rice and papaya *ghonto*,[15] and *dim bhaji* for Jaseem. It was a simple meal, but Heera-da's face was full of satisfaction. We ate our fill, and the food tasted heavenly.

While I was there, Heera-da came by our house almost every evening. Sometimes I went to the school. The day of the play, I was in charge of dressing the boys in saris. At that time in the villages, girls didn't act with boys. Now of course things have changed. It's been a long time since then. I went to Katakhali recently and saw that hundreds of girls and boys hold a rally together for International Women's Day. There was co-ed theater in the afternoon. Some mullahs and other village leaders were critical of this. If Heera-da was alive, he would be overjoyed to see it. He had a big hand in these changes. In the few years he was in Katakhali, he touched the lives of every person in one way or another.

One morning while I was in the village, I went with Jaseem in our family boat across the channel to the Burmese neighborhood of Katakhali. Joynal Majhi took us there. When I arrived, a wave of euphoria spread through the neighborhood. I had to go visit every house. People gave whatever they had to Jaseem—coconuts, sugarcane, homemade *chire* (flattened rice), *binni* rice (sticky rice), chickens, ducks, money. We quickly went back home with a boatful of gifts.

That day, the weather had been humid since morning, and the sky had a reddish tinge. All day, the sky was covered with dark clouds. Just after we returned home, gusts of wind and drizzle began. Heera-da sent word to be careful. The wind and rain grew progressively stronger. Fear started to take hold in my mind. At some point, I told Baba we should go to the old house. Baba was a very stubborn person. He thought that leaving his own house during the storm would mean admitting defeat, and he would never do that. So I packed Jaseem's clothes, candles, matches, biscuits, jaggery, *chire*, and *muri* in a big trunk, along with my treasured copy of Rabindranath's *Sanchayita*.

Baba slaughtered a goat and prepared to cook on a makeshift stove inside the house. After eating, Baba got up on the roof of the house and started tying down the thatch to the roof-posts with a thick rope, singing at the top of his lungs. Sometimes he said to the storm, "Come on down, dear, come on down, I'll see to you." I knew Baba was scared, but he wouldn't show it for anything. After some time, water began to rise and come into the house. We couldn't see anything anywhere; we could only hear the howling wind. Hearing that sound, the fear sitting tight in my chest kept growing. In the afternoon, the room started to flood. The rain and wind grew even stronger. I was looking around, terrified, hoping someone would come to rescue us.

This house of ours was relatively new. There weren't many trees, and the foundation was low. It wasn't fit to withstand the destructive dance of flood or storm. I could see trees and houses being swept away by the storm. Ma was asking Baba, why hadn't we taken the children, especially Jaseem, and gone to take shelter in a safe place while we still had time? Just then, we suddenly saw a boat coming toward our house. We all started shouting. When the boat came close, we saw it was my Choto Chacha, Abdur Rab. Without thinking of his own safety, he had come with some of his people to rescue us. We all got into the boat. I took my trunk with me. But Baba refused to leave the house, and Ma wouldn't leave without him. No matter how hard we tried to make them see reason, it was no good. Jaseem's *ayah* Robir Ma was with us too. Robir Ma grew up in the city. She was beside herself with terror seeing this storm. She was constantly calling out to Jesus and crying. After we got into the boat, the raindrops were pricking my skin like thorns. Ma put a mattress and blanket on our heads to protect us from flying branches and debris from broken houses. It was normally a five-minute trip from our house to the old house. This time, Choto Chacha and his people had to fight for almost an hour to get us there. Somehow, we managed to get into Choto Chacha's house. If Choto Chacha hadn't taken us to the old house that day, we might not have survived.

Evening was falling. The power of the storm and the force of the water were increasing steadily. I felt like Choto Chacha's house might fly away at any moment. We decided to take shelter in Dada's brick building. The courtyard was completely flooded. Choto Chacha and his people covered the children with blankets and swam with them one by one to the building. Choto Chacha and I went last of all. I didn't forget to bring my trunk with me. I thought, if we live, we'll need the things inside. When I reached the building, I took a towel out of the trunk, dried off Jaseem and the other small children, and dressed them in dry clothes. The rest of the family came to the brick building too. Everyone was shivering with cold from being wet all day. There was some dry wood in the building, so we put it in the middle of the room and lit a fire. I sat on top of my trunk. Jaseem was only two then. He fell asleep in my lap. My little sister Lina sat huddled in my lap in fear. Eleven-year-old Runu and seven-year-old Taslim sat up against me, shivering. Eventually they fell asleep too. Jaseem's *ayah* Robir Ma also leaned her head on my back and fell asleep. As if I was everyone's safe place.

I kept checking with Choto Chacha and the others about the force of the storm and the height of the water. It was extremely important to know how many steps of the building the water had risen, because about 100 years before there had been a storm and flood exactly like this. At that time, only my mother's Mama's house in Chalitabunia had a brick building. On the night of the storm, people came from three or four villages to take shelter there. None of them paid attention to how high the water had risen. Suddenly the building collapsed under the force of the water, and most of them died. A few people managed to get out and somehow survived by clinging to trees. I had heard that story when I was small and seen the ruins of that building. So, we decided that as soon as the water started to enter the building, we would jump outside.

We took turns checking how high the water had risen. I was worried sick about my parents. I was thinking, even if we somehow survive, my parents might not. I felt as if the world might come to an end that night. Everyone around me was saying "Allah, Allah," some were praying or reciting the call to prayer. Many of the women were crying. It was a waste of breath to try to calm them. Sometime during the night, Choto Chacha opened the door and came running in to tell us the storm was losing force and the water was going down. We all started crying out with excitement. I felt relieved too that in the end, we didn't have to jump out into the water. How would I have survived with such a small child! Everyone knew it would have been hopeless, even though no one let it on to me. I kept thinking about my parents. I broke down and cried, thinking they must be dead. Why didn't I make Baba come with me? Because of my father's stubbornness, I lost my mother too!

Slowly, morning came. A little later, I went outside and saw a terrible sight. The dead bodies of human beings, cows, buffaloes, and other animals and birds were scattered all around. As far as the eye could see, there were only ruins of trees and houses. The air was heavy with the cries of wounded people. A sound came floating from the south building. Choto Chacha struggled over to that room and shouted with exuberance, saying, "Bura Ma [Choto Chacha and I were around the same age, and he called me "Bura Ma" or "Old Mother"]! Come over here quick. Nanu and Nunu [that's what he called my parents] are here. They seem to be alive." I struggled over there too and saw my parents lying there, almost unconscious. I asked someone to bring a few burning sticks from the fire in the other room. My parents' jaws were locked from cold. There were signs of injury on their heads, arms, and legs. There were countless coconuts lying around in that room. Someone broke one open and fed my parents the coconut water. Then they slowly opened their eyes and started crying their hearts out. My parents both thought we were all dead. One by one, Runu, Taslim, Lina, and Jaseem came and crowded around them. What a reunion!

The sky was clear the next morning, and the wind was still. It seemed hard to believe the incredible tempest of the night before. But there was destruction all around. I told people to cut away the fallen branches and clear the area, because the debris made it hard to get out of the house. It looked like a warzone. I stood on the edge of the pond on the west side of the old house and saw there was no sign of our new house. All the buildings of the old house were still standing. Ma and Baba had come to the old house when they were unable to withstand the storm.

Then suddenly I caught sight of Heera-da. He had come to check on us, with deep anxiety in his eyes. Before he came, I was thinking of sending someone to check on him, but he beat me to it! Heera-da and I discussed how to begin the rescue work. The most important thing was to clear away the debris and dispose of the dead bodies. We also had to find drinking water. The saltwater had contaminated all the ponds and wells. I suggested that for now everyone should drink coconut water and eat coconut meat.

At the same time, I had to think of my own family. Ma endured Baba's tyranny her whole life, and yet she had always done the needful with a level head. That day after the storm began, she had filled big containers with rice, dal, salt, turmeric, and chili powder, put them in jute sacks, bound them tightly shut, and immersed them in the water. There was also a grinding stone and some pots in there. She stored unhusked rice in the water in the same way. After the storm, she had those lifted out of the pond, cooked rice and dal with coconut water, and fed us. Heera-da ate with us too and praised my mother highly for her foresight in storing the necessities this way.

For three or four days after the storm, I went around the nearby villages with Heera-da to make a list of the damages and the number of cows, buffaloes, and people still alive. We somehow gathered whatever anyone could come up with to make some small huts for people to live in. When they saw everyone working together, people slowly regained their confidence. Heera-da's tireless efforts and organizational abilities impressed not only me, but all the village people. Heera-da and I went to every house in the villages and tried to console people. Maybe we couldn't give much consolation to those who had lost everything. But maybe they saw a ray of hope at least. The storm took the highest toll on small children and old people. A few young boys and girls were also swept away or died.

I still remember one heartbreaking incident. A young man of seventeen or eighteen from the Biswas family of Nishanbaria had gone to his Phuphu's house in Tungibaria (where my mamas lived) and died in the cyclone. His dead body was found two days later in the big pond outside our old house. His name was Jalal. He was a strong, healthy young man, almost 6 feet tall, and a good soccer player. When people began to get over their bewilderment after the storm, they went looking for their relatives. They looked like prehistoric human beings. Half-naked people with mud-caked bodies, searching for the dead bodies of their loved ones. Some were searching for their most needed things, like pots and pans, clothes, or wood and tin for rebuilding their houses. Everyone asked each other on first sight who had lost their houses and how many relatives they had lost in that immensely destructive storm and flood.

Five or six days later, Heera-da sent people all over to find a boat. The boat was to take me and Jaseem to Patuakhali. Before we left, I wrote a petition to present to the Patuakhali SDO with an account of the damages. I wrote it sitting on the high school veranda. The roof and outer wall of the school had been blown away in the storm. People came there to put their signature or thumbprint on the petition. I didn't want to leave everyone in that state, but I had to go. Heera-da assured me he would do the needful in my absence. He told me to submit the petition to the SDO in Patuakhali and go to Barisal. Finally, I set off with Jaseem. The villagers, my family, and Heera-da saw us off with tears in their eyes.

I never saw Heera-da again, but we kept in touch through letters. He was a true friend of farmers, laborers, and working people. In 1971, he was in Patuakhali trying to organize the people of Patuakhali against the brutality of the Pakistanis. Later the Pakbahini arrested him,[16] tortured him, and stabbed him to death with their bayonets.

*Another terrible storm*

In 1961, I was in Barisal, teaching at the Barisal Girls' School. I was also involved in politics. I remember on 9 May of that year there was a terrible cyclone and tidal wave in our area. When I heard the news, I was extremely anxious for my family. But after the cyclone, communications with that area were completely cut off. One day, I heard that a government launch or small ship was going to go to the coastal area. I went to the house of the Barisal DC to find out if I could go in that boat. Standing on the upper veranda of his bungalow, he told me the SDO Goni Shaheb had been given all responsibilities for this trip, and he sent me to talk to him. Then I went to the SDO Goni Shaheb's house with Lutfa's husband Fakruddin Biswas. At first, he didn't want to pay any attention to me, and when he kept using the informal "tumi" with me, I objected immediately. That flustered him a little. Then I introduced myself. When he learned who I was and who my father and uncle were, he started talking to me more politely. I asked to go with him to the south. He said legally he could not take me with him. He expressed his regret and said that if I gave him the names and addresses of my relatives, he would find out how they were and inform me. I gave him my village address and said, "We might meet again on the way there."

After that, I worked hard all day. I collected cholera vaccines, medicines, bandages, water purification tablets from the municipality office, and money and clothes from my friends. I was ready to leave as soon as the launches or steamers started running again. I arranged to leave my mischievous four-year-old son Jaseem with his Dada, Dadi, and Chachi. I couldn't take him into that town of death. I thought, there's no guarantee even I will return alive and well. That's why I left him behind. When the launch started running, I boarded it with my boxes and bundles. Fakruddin Biswas was with me. This launch only went to Patuakhali. We would have to stay there for one night and then take the next launch to Khepupara. Karim Chacha lived there. His wife, my Anisa Chachi, was a teacher at the Khepupara Girls' School. I had taught there myself two years before, but, being a widow, I couldn't stay long in that job because of sexual harassment.

When we reached the Patuakhali ghat early that evening, I saw Atul Mastermoshai and some other friends standing there. Mastermoshai told me, "Come to our house now. You can sleep at Indumoti Barui's house." Mastermoshai was unmarried. He was wary of getting a bad name if I stayed the night at his house.

I heard that the SDO Goni Shaheb was in Patuakhali and was going to hold a meeting in his launch that evening for the important people of the area. I went there to find out what they were discussing at the meeting. I saw that all the important people of Patuakhali—lawyers, doctors, teachers, government officers, wealthy people, and businessmen—were present there. Everyone was astounded to see me. They all stared at me in curiosity. Of course, I wasn't completely unknown to them.

They asked me to take a seat. They were all having drinks—*sharbat*, tea, coffee, and so on. The SDO asked if I wanted anything. I said no. He gestured toward me and said, "Most of you must know her."

Almost everyone said yes. He looked at me and said, "I have brought news of everyone you asked me to check on. I saw your Chacha Karim Shaheb; he and his family are well. Your mother, father, and siblings are all alive. Your mother had been swept away to Chor Kajal. She is home now. On the way back, your other Chacha Rashid Mia stopped my launch in the middle of the Agunmukha and asked me to tell you he is alive. I saw countless dead bodies. Houses are in ruins. What are you going to do there? Do you still want to go there even after hearing the state of things?"

I thanked him for bringing news of my family and told him that yes, I must go to that area. He asked me what I was carrying with me.

I told him I had cholera vaccines and gave him a list of everything I had. When I mentioned water, he asked, "What if someone steals the water from you, what will you do then?"

I laughed and said, "At least that person will quench their thirst." The gentleman was a bit taken aback. He said, "We need a woman like you to go."

I left Patuakhali for Khepupara the very next day. Before boarding the launch, some of my friends gave me a few things to distribute among the needy. After the launch departed, I looked around with a thumping heart. Up until Galachipa, I didn't see much damage. After we entered the Agunmukha, there were signs of destruction all around. I thought, can there be anyone alive in this wreckage? People came running to the riverbank at the sound of the launch. Not just "people"—they looked like neolithic people. Naked, half-naked, trying to cover their bodies with tattered cloth. Broken vessels in their hands. It looked like they needed food or water. Seeing the crowd, the *sareng* (*serang* or boatswain) and other people on the boat got nervous. There were a few drums of water and some food on the launch. Some people said the crowd of needy people at the ghat would try to loot these things, so they decided not to steer the launch to the riverbank. I was very pained by this decision. I thought, four or five days after the event, even the light of hope of a little help is fading before their eyes.

I went to talk to the *sareng* myself. I told him: "These are innocent people, they don't want to rob us. Their faces show only despair, not anger or rebellion. Please, steer the launch to the bank. I take personal responsibility for giving each person one mugful of water."

Finally, they listened to me, and the launch pulled up along the shore. I got down immediately and said with joined palms, "Please stand in line. I have only a little water with me. Everyone will get one mugful. More launches will come with help. Please be patient."

Those helpless people who had lost everything stood in line just as I asked. Each of them took one mugful of water and left without a word. I noticed in astonishment that many of them took a sip of the water, then carried the rest away with great care to give to the other members of their families. If I hadn't seen it with my own eyes, I wouldn't have believed it. When thousands of people are desperate for water in one region, those in other parts of the country are leading normal lives. I had seen myself that in Barisal, schools, colleges, and other institutions were operating normally. So were cinemas, theaters, and other forms of entertainment. Another staggering thing was that there was water, water everywhere, but that water was unfit to drink. The influx of salty seawater into the rivers and ponds and the decomposing corpses of humans and animals floating in them had contaminated the water.

On the way to Khepupara, we stopped in a few other places and distributed water in the same way. When we reached Khepupara, I saw Karim Chacha come running along with many others. He had heard I was coming. He said to me, "Why did you come to this town of death? Why did you leave Jaseem alone? Who'll look after him?" I didn't know what to say. I took what little I had and went to his house. I gave a glass of water to the person who carried my things. Gladness and satisfaction showed clearly on his face. I gave him some clothes for his wife and children too. I didn't have much to give, even though I wanted to give more.

I heard from Karim Chacha how they had fought the storm and survived. Karim Chacha's daughter Nupur was only a year old. They had gone up and sat on the loft of the home with her. My middle sister had gone to visit the Biswas family before the storm. She hadn't come back yet, and no one had news of her. That night, I stayed in Khepupara. The next day, despite Karim Chacha's strong objections, I boarded a *goynar nouka* (large boat for carrying goods) and traveled to Barobaishdia. My fellow passengers were just a few men. There were no other women or girls; I was the only one. People stared at me in surprise. Of course, they treated me with due respect. I sat in the boat watching countless dead bodies of humans and animals go by. They had already started to rot and stink.

The boat stopped at Tungibaria, where my Nana's house is. Everyone came running to the ghat to see me and started crying. I learned that my own Nana and Nani, their daughter Rekha, and my beloved Mariyam Khala had all died in the catastrophic cyclone. Mariyam Khala was pregnant when she died. One by one, I learned of the deaths of many more loved ones. Our Katakhali village is about a mile and a half away from Tungibaria. I got ready to go to the village before evening. Everyone objected. How could I cross the river in the evening, through all these dead bodies? I didn't listen to anyone. Saju Bhai came forward to accompany me. I still had some water left, so I gave everyone there a little bit of water. The last little bit I took with me for my parents and siblings. I walked through the ruins. My mind and body were exhausted. I wondered what I would see when I reached home. I had heard from the SDO in Patuakhali that they were alive, but was it true? Even if they were alive, how were they living? Was the house there, or not? Where were they sleeping?

Evening fell. I had almost reached Katakhali. Our house was right across the river. The man who was carrying my few things and the pot of water went across the river ahead of me. Then Saju Bhai went forward and shoved aside the swollen dead bodies of humans and animals to clear a path for me. I closed my nose and tried to cross the river, almost swimming. Finally, I made it. When I got up on the bank, I saw no sign of life around me. I walked behind Saju Bhai to our house. When I saw the state it was in, my hands and feet went cold from fear. There was no sign of the house. It was dark everywhere.

Saju Bhai took my hand and led me onward. There was a guava tree at the southwest corner of the pond. There I could see the faint glow of a small fire coming from a tiny hut made of coconut leaves and branches. I went there and saw my parents, Runu, Taslim, and Lina lying there. Nearby, they were trying to make a fire with some branches. They all started sobbing when they saw me. Ma hugged me to her chest and cried. I learned my youngest brother had been swept away in the cyclone.

Ma was still breast-feeding my brother, who was around eighteen months old, and she held onto him throughout the cyclone, even while floating in water. Ma was swept away to another island called Char Kajal. She woke up from unconsciousness and realized the baby in her arms was dead and that blood was coming from his nose. Fearful that the stray dogs would eat the corpse, she found a floating pillow nearby and placed baby Mahim on it and floated his body away. Then she lost consciousness again. The next day, local villagers came near her and asked who she was. She had lost her sari and was wearing only her blouse and petticoat. She was worried about being raped or trafficked and immediately said, "Take me to your village chairman. I am a daughter of Mia Bari and wife in Munshi Bari." The villagers brought her a sari and took her to the Char Kajol chairman's house. One of Ma's cousins, Rosu, was married in that household and came out and hugged Ma. Ma was safely brought home later that day. Even though she was battered by the cyclone and had lost her son, she kept her calm and was able to astutely protect herself and get home to Barobaishdia Island.

After seeing me, Ma started crying bitterly for her dead son. When she calmed down a little, I said, "Ma, look around you—all of us could have been killed. So many families have lost everything."

She didn't know yet that her own parents and siblings had died. That night, everyone ate the *muri*, jaggery, biscuits, and water I had brought with me, and we lay down to sleep, hugging each other, under the open sky. That was the first time in my life that I spent the night on a bed of straw under the open sky. I thought, what's going to happen tomorrow? How can we bring back their normal life? What could I do? But even the saddest night comes to an end. In the morning, I saw everyone in my family had injuries. Especially my brother Taslim, whose body was torn all over by date thorns. Some of the thorns were still embedded in his body. Runu, Lina, and Baba were also covered with injuries. Ma was almost mad with grief for her one-and-a-half-year-old son. Losing all her possessions was nothing to her. We all understood how she felt, but what could we do?

The specter of death had visited every house in Katakhali. As the day progressed, the village people started running over to tell me their sad stories. Each of them told me how many members of their families had been swept away. Many people had died in their relatives' arms. Houses, cows, rams, goats, ducks, chickens, in other words, a farmer's all—they told such sad stories of losing these. I decided what I had to do. Nobody had started the work of disposing of the dead bodies. Many people's relatives had been swept away, so they were searching only for their bodies. Meanwhile, the bodies of unknown people and animals were lying scattered all over and starting to rot. Conditions were ripe for an outbreak of epidemics like cholera, diarrhea, and dysentery.

I told everyone, "Let's gather up whatever tools we can find and bury these dead bodies immediately. If we sit around like this, none of us will survive." There were dead bodies in many of the ponds too. We buried those first. I tucked my sari in at the waist and joined in along with the others. It was hard work to supervise. I felt like crying over and over as I tried to direct these hungry, grief-stricken people to do this difficult work. If this area had been considered a part of civilized society, the government, non-governmental organizations, and the military would already have come in to take part in this work. But the government or local administration of the time didn't take any initiative. At least, I didn't see any sign of that. Later I distributed whatever clothing, medicines, and money I had brought with me among the villagers, even though it wasn't much.

After that, I tried to devise a better shelter for my parents and siblings. Some people pitched in to help recover some of the scattered tin, posts, or pieces of wood from our ruined house. I told them, "Let's leave it for today, you're all very tired. We'll start the work tomorrow."

But nobody listened to me. They ate the *muri*, jaggery, and biscuits I had brought along with some coconuts they found lying around, and within two or three hours they built a small building on the site of our old house. A few years before, Baba had left his ancestral homestead and built a house of his own in the open land to the west. I never liked this idea. I was born in Dada's brick house, and we all grew up there together. After we left that house for the new house, I felt like we were living on a far-off island. This time, I again brought my family back to the old house. I told my parents, "In times of danger, it's not right to live separately like that. I won't leave you in this swamp." They didn't protest.

I couldn't stay there very long, because I'd left my son Jaseem in Barisal. Besides, I had a job there. But how could I leave them like this? At first, I thought I'd take them all back with me, but I knew my parents would never go. Besides, where would they stay? I lived in Imadullah's father's house, in a small room. Jaseem and his Dadi lived in the same room with me. Even forgetting the financial problem, we were five siblings plus Jaseem. There was no way so many people could stay in that house. I felt very depressed thinking of all this.

Finally, one day I left for Barisal with Runu, Taslim, and Lina. We took a dinghy to Galachipa and spent the night at my Boro Mama's house. That night, there was another storm. I started crying bitterly for my family back home. Boro Mama started saying loudly, "Aha-re, my sister came back from the jaws of death, who knows if she'll survive this time!"

In the morning, we got news that this second storm hadn't caused any significant damage. Then we boarded a launch for Barisal. I was worried about Jaseem. How was my restless son managing without his mother? I came back to Barisal after about a week. When I got home, I saw a bandage on Jaseem's head. The blood in my chest froze in fear. I hugged him and asked what happened. Jaseem said, "I fell down jumping off the pillow, it didn't hurt much, Ma."

I soon arranged for my siblings to stay in that same little room in my in-laws' house. Imad's parents welcomed them warmly. I will never forget their kindness. I started looking for another place to stay. At the same time, I took a few private tutoring jobs. At first, I found a place that belonged to a distant relative of ours.

Later I found a big tin house in College Road with several rooms for 30 taka a month. It was an airy place, with a playing field in front and a big pond next to it with a cement ghat. In those days, it was unthinkable not only in Barisal but anywhere in Bangladesh for a twenty-three-year-old widow to live alone with her young siblings. It gave me courage to know that the respected Husamuddin Shaheb (a professor of Arabic at BM College) and Abdul Gafur Chacha (a high school teacher and friend of Karim Chacha) and his wife Beena lived nearby. So it was a secure environment for me. After moving to College Road, I enrolled my siblings in school. Taslim still had date thorns stuck in his body. We had to cut the skin and remove them. I tried to do everything with a smiling face, but I couldn't sleep at night from anxiety because I couldn't afford to feed everyone. Later I brought our domestic help Afsar from Katakhali. He did the grocery shopping, brought water, and helped with other basic chores. My siblings split household tasks among themselves. Before going to work at the school, I cooked breakfast, and we all ate together. Then they went to school. Only Lutfa studied at home.

At the time, my salary was 120 taka. I'd gotten a raise just a few months before. After the Sadar Balika Bidyalay gained government status, my salary went up from 60 to 120 taka. I was overjoyed. But now my household wasn't just me and Jaseem. Even my new salary wasn't enough to feed a family of six or seven.

Swadesh was working at the PIDE (Pakistan Institute of Development Economics) in Karachi then. When he heard the news of the cyclone, he sent some money for me at my friend Jhantu's house. People started talking about it, but without that money I couldn't have supported my siblings. No one else came to help me. No one came to ask how I was managing with so many siblings. And yet these same people were all too ready to cook up juicy stories about me.

### *Standing up to my molesting uncle*

After Imad's death, the uncle who had sexually assaulted me when I was a child tried to get his paws on me again. But he was unsuccessful. One time, he came over to my in-laws' home and said that Jaseem and I should go and live with him and his wife. He kept saying, why are you staying here when Imad is gone? We can take better care of you. I knew that he was dangerous and wanted to sexually use me, so I steadfastly refused. After I moved to the house in College Road, this uncle suddenly rented a room and moved in right next door. His wife would be out most of the day, and he would constantly be coming over to visit or would call me or my younger sisters to help him with this or that. He would say he wasn't feeling well and needed my sisters to come over. I became increasingly worried that he was molesting my sisters or planning to do so. I had to go to work and to my classes, so I couldn't constantly watch over the situation.

One day, my uncle was moaning and groaning from his nearby room, crying out that he wasn't feeling well and needed help. I decided to take action. I grabbed a huge cutting knife or *da* and went over there. I found him lying alone on the bed. I said, "Get up, you son of Satan! What the hell are you doing? Why are you here?! You destroyed my life! And now you are after my sisters? If you *ever* touch them, I will kill you. Maybe you already did touch them, but if you ever do it again then I will chop you to pieces with this knife and kill you and go to jail. I don't care if I go to jail but I swear I will kill you. I will kill you. I want you out."

He didn't say anything but looked shaken. I went home with my knife. That very night, my uncle and his wife left that room. For many years, I had no contact with that uncle.

It was such a relief to finally be able to confront my uncle and express my anger and rage. I had to do it to protect my sisters. I couldn't believe that I was able to do it, to stand up to this criminal. He never tried to touch me or my sisters again. I felt a kind of release after threatening to kill my uncle, but my nightmares, trauma, and constant reliving of the sexual abuse continue to this day. I never got the chance to tell Imad about my uncle's criminal acts because Imad suddenly died just a few months after our marriage. If I had told Imad, he probably would have killed my uncle.

*My relationship with Swadesh*

I learned Swadesh's story from Karim Chacha and Manorama Mashima. He was born in January 1928 in Barisal. In 1948, he was supposed to take the BA exam and then go to India. His siblings had all gone to India after the Partition in 1947. Only Swadesh had stayed behind to take his exam. But in March 1948 the Language Movement began. The faction of the East Pakistan Students' League that supported Sheikh Mujib and the Tamaddun Majlish[17] called for a strike on 11 March to demand freedom of language. In Barisal, Swadesh, Mozammel Haq, Abdul Khalek, and Kazi Bahauddin printed pamphlets in support of the movement. On 10 March 1948, Swadesh was arrested along with his friends and was released and rearrested many times until he was finally released in September 1956. The Pakistani government had told him he would be released from jail if he agreed to move to India, but he had refused. Once he got out of jail, he had no one to call his own in Barisal. He was in love with a girl in 1948, but while he was in jail, that girl married someone else and moved to Kolkata. Swadesh had no communication with his family after his arrest. Swadesh was released from jail in 1956 in very poor health, with fever, dysentery, and eczema on his hands and feet. There was also a rampant influenza epidemic in Barisal at the time.

After Swadesh was released from jail, I saw him once at Karim Chacha's house, then didn't see him for a long time. One day, I heard he had the flu. I took my sister-in-law Bela with me and went to see him. Tears came to my eyes at the sight of him. After that, I heard no news of him. About a month and a half later, I took Jaseem and went to see Swadesh by myself. The house where he lived, Shaula Lodge, was walking distance from us. Swadesh lived in a tin room on the south side of the house. When I went there and entered the room, I found Swadesh moaning with pain inside the mosquito net. The room was incredibly dirty. It looked like no one had swept it for many days. The bedding, pillows, and mosquito net were grimy. When Swadesh saw me, he tried to sit up. Then he said, "Take Jaseem home right now. I have typhoid. Why did you come here? Who told you?"

I quickly took Jaseem home and went back to Shaula Lodge. I found out Swadesh had been bedridden for a month. I brought a broom from the house and swept the room. I brought a bucket of water, poured water from a mug and washed Swadesh's head, brought warm water, and washed his body. Just then, Manorama Mashima came and said, "You've heard the news! Now I won't worry."

I asked her, "Mashima, why didn't you tell me before?"

She said, "You're a widow of a Muslim family. How could I call you just like that?"

Swadesh was skin and bones. He was so weak and sick, yet there was no one even to give him water. Besides, it wasn't in Swadesh's nature to ask anyone for anything. I left Mashima with him and went back to our house again to get someone to buy barley. I boiled barley and fed it to him little by little from a bowl. I tried to go see Swadesh every day until he recovered. His illness affected me deeply. It brought home to me how alone and helpless a person can be.

After that, I felt a deep affection for Swadesh. Not long after, Swadesh finished his BA and went to do his MA in Dhaka. Due to family complications, I also had to take a new teaching job in Khepupara, far to the south. I spent one year there. During that time, Swadesh wrote me three or four letters, and I answered them. There were no declarations of love in those letters. Neither of us was that stupid. Still, the letters certainly showed affection or compassion between the two of us. But just the fact of exchanging letters was enough to spread rumors about a young widow, and if the man belongs to a different faith and a leftist political party, it fuels even more rumors. People started talking with great gusto all over Khepupara about the letters coming to the post office in my name. So after one year, I had to go back to Barisal and start a new job in Didi's school at 60 taka a month. I lived at my in-laws'. In the meantime, Swadesh finished his MA and got a job in Karachi in West Pakistan. He came to see me before leaving.

Even after Swadesh went to Karachi, he sent me a couple of letters. I answered them as before. Suddenly one morning, before Sabita-di's school started, she called me into her room. As soon as I came in, she shut the door and asked if Swadesh was writing letters to me! I was startled and said, "Yes."

Sabita-di said, "Everyone knows about your letters. It seems someone is opening them."

Anyone would have been confounded to hear this, but I wasn't. It was a repeat of Khepupara. That day, I was thinking, how did Sabita-di find out? Later I learned that the district magistrate of Barisal had told her.

After that, I stopped writing to Swadesh, but I never would have expected what happened after that. Every time I went out in the street, the good-for-nothing boys of the neighborhood would recite sections of my letters out loud. There was nothing I could do but helplessly swallow this humiliation.

That same year, Swadesh took leave from work and came to Barisal. A few days after he arrived, he came to my rented house in College Road. He talked with Jaseem for a while and gave him some presents.

Swadesh was staying at Manorama Mashima's house in Kaunia. Then one day Sabita-di sent for me again. Again, as soon as I went in, she shut the door and looked at me keenly. Then she said, "Where is Swadesh?"

I told her, "Swadesh has come to Barisal on holiday. He's staying at Manorama Mashima's place."

Didi told me, "A rumor has spread all over Barisal that the two of you got married last night. The city is in turmoil over it. Go home right now and tell Swadesh to leave immediately."

I refused to go home. She said, "The girls are all leaving their classes to come and see you. Will you be able to teach them like this?"

I said, "Yes, I will."

With that, I left Sabita-di's room and went straight to my classroom to teach. Even though I kept looking straight ahead of me, I could tell Sabita-di was right. The girls were standing outside all the classrooms to gawk at me like they were watching a circus.

I kept my mouth shut and taught my class all day. When school let out, I didn't go home but went to Karim Chacha's house, which was nearby. Karim Chacha lived in his friend Barkatullah Shaheb's house. When I arrived, I found Mohiuddin Chacha there. The two of them looked at me and said, "We were just thinking of you." Karim Chacha added, "The city is in a bad state. Swadesh is leaving this evening."

I said, "Why, what's happened?"

Karim Chacha said, "Last night some thugs ganged up with sticks, surrounded Manorama Mashima's house, and made a ruckus all night. They've spread a rumor that you two are married. The city is on the verge of a riot."

I stared at Karim Chacha in astonishment and said, "You people are so scared you're going to banish Swadesh without even letting me see him once! I won't let that happen. I'm going to see him right now."

They both told me, "That's absolutely out of the question."

I said, "Then the thugs are winning. This is what they want. I won't bend my head for them. You find a way to bring Swadesh here. Otherwise I'm going to Manorama Mashima's house."

So Karim Chacha was compelled to go and bring Swadesh. The two of us sat facing each other in the next room. Karim Chacha and Mohiuddin Chacha sat in the other room looking concerned. For the first time, Swadesh and I talked openly, face to face, about our feelings and our future. Swadesh described the previous night's incident to me. He confirmed that a crowd of people had surrounded Mashima's house with sticks and threatened him all night. They dared Swadesh to come out of the house and slung unspeakable insults at him. Some of them later entered Mashima's house and searched for me all over, even in the loft. They told Swadesh to come out because they had important things to say to him. Manorama Mashima was home too. After hearing everything Swadesh told me, I said, "That's why you got scared and planned to run away without telling me?"

Swadesh shook his head and said, "No. I want to marry you, but I'm not getting permission from the Party. Besides, we have to think of Jaseem first."

Finally, we decided not to communicate anymore. We would live our separate lives. Swadesh would leave Barisal.

When Swadesh and I finished talking, I took a rickshaw back home. When I got there, I found my mother waiting anxiously for me. She was living with me at the time. I'd never been so late getting home before. I thought maybe that's why Ma looked worried. But when I went up to her, she said, "Did you marry Swadesh?"

I was aghast. I had thought maybe Ma didn't know about this rumor. Now I saw that the news had reached her too! I kept quiet for a moment. Then I said, "Could I do something like that without telling you? No, Ma, I haven't married him. But if I did, would you object?"

Ma thought for a minute. Then she said calmly, "I've never seen a finer young man than Swadesh. I have yet to find a Muslim boy his equal. No, I have no objection."

I sat still and silent, tears streaming from my eyes. A few minutes earlier, I had sacrificed everything beautiful, pure, and joyful in fear of society, on Party orders.

My mother was religious, but not bigoted. Ma never missed *namaz* without reason. No one could break her fasts. No one outside our family ever heard her voice. Her head was always covered past the hairline. When I heard what she said, I thought, what has my mother just told me? Of course, I had never thought of marrying Swadesh earlier, that is, until just before this incident. Sometimes it did occur to me that if things were to go that far, my father and uncles might not object. Besides, I didn't care if they objected. But Ma lived in a different world. That same Ma had just spoken these words.

Swadesh left that very night. The next day, I was getting ready to go to school as usual. Just then, a rickshaw driver came with a little note from Karim Chacha. He had written, "Several hundred people are standing outside my house shouting. They want to know if you have married Swadesh or not. Come to my house right away and tell them what you will." I understood that Karim Chacha was scared and so he called me instead of talking to them himself.

Reading this letter, I felt furious. I thought, after being in politics all his life, in the end my Karim Chacha turned out to be a coward! On the back of his letter, I wrote, "I'm not going to justify to anyone, not even my own father, whom I marry or don't marry and when. To marry or not marry is entirely my personal matter. Please read out my letter to those who are concerned for my future. It will take me some time to get there, but I am getting ready to go to your house." I sent the letter with the same rickshaw driver back to Karim Chacha. Then about twenty or twenty-five minutes later, I took a rickshaw to Karim Chacha's house and saw there was no one there. Karim Chacha said, "As soon as I read out your letter, everyone left."

Without getting down from the rickshaw, I said, "This is your politics! You have so little courage, yet you claim you want to change the country and society! Not in a thousand years, Chacha!"

After that, the Party instructed me not to maintain any kind of relationship with Swadesh. My life went on at its own pace.

I was getting ready to take my BA exam. One day, Baba came from the village to see me. He brought me some rice. Not long before this, a cyclone had destroyed our cows, buffaloes, ducks, chickens, and buildings. The influx of saltwater had damaged the crops too. After the cyclone, the rest of the family had come to stay with me. Since then, we had been getting by one day at a time. I was always worrying about what all these people would eat the next day. Swadesh used to send me money from time to time, but now I told him not to send money. I had made a vow that I would stand on my own feet.

### *One strange night*

Swadesh completed his MA in economics from Dhaka University in 1960. He knew he would not be hired by Dhaka University because of his time in prison, so he took a job at PIDE in Karachi. Before leaving for Karachi, he came to Barisal to see Mashima and all his friends.

One year after this, he was supposed to come to Barisal on holiday. The day he was scheduled to arrive, a telegram came stating that, for reasons beyond his control, he could not come to Barisal and that I should come to Dhaka to see him, or else I might never see him again. He sent his address too. I was panic-stricken. What should I do? Dhaka University was in turmoil with the Students' Movement, which had spread all over the country. Things were tense everywhere. How could I go to Dhaka now? I'd never been to Dhaka alone either. I didn't know my way around. Where could I leave Jaseem? I had no money in hand. It was hard to make ends meet.

Still, I decided to go to Dhaka. I left Jaseem with his Dada and Dadi, borrowed 50 taka from Gafur Chacha, and boarded the steamer to Dhaka one evening. My hands and feet were cold with fear. If anyone saw me, I'd have to face thousands of questions. When I went into the ladies' compartment, I saw Nurul Islam Manzur of the Peskar family (a relative of my in-laws) sitting there with his family. He was astonished to see me and started asking questions, where am I going, why am I going, where am I going to stay, and why don't I have Jaseem with me, etc. I gave minimal answers. I had to eat something with them. My throat was dry as wood with anxiety.

The next day, the steamer stopped in Narayanganj as usual. I quickly got off and took a taxi to the address Swadesh had sent me, somewhere in Tantibazar or Shakharibazar, I don't remember the name. After riding around for a while, I finally found that address and got out of the taxi. I had never thought I would have to come to a place like this. After I knocked for a long time, a woman opened the door with a look of irritation and stared at me in surprise. I said, "My cousin's come here from Karachi. I came from Barisal to see him." Lamp in hand, the woman led me into her room and sat me down. It was a three- or four-story building. Very dark. It seemed like light and air had never entered this house. The woman said she was fasting that day for some pujo or other, so she was free of the hassle of cooking. Before taking a bath and sitting down for the pujo, she told me that the gentleman from Karachi had gone to the cinema with a seven- or eight-year-old boy named Rana who lived upstairs. He would be back late. I was in a terrible state. Just when I felt like I was getting cramps in my hands and legs from sitting still, I was called upstairs.

When I went into the room indicated, I saw Swadesh and his friend Saroj Babu standing there. I hadn't seen Swadesh in a year. Saroj Babu said, "Come, let's eat first." I was starving, and we went to eat at a small restaurant nearby. We sat on *piri* on the floor. There was a mountain of rice on each huge metal plate. Next to it a fistful of salt, a green chili, and a slice of lime. A bowl of very thin dal and another bowl with a single piece of *ilish mach* drowned in a thin *jhol*. Following their example, I poured the dal into the rice. After a few bites, I poured the *macher jhol*. I had a hard time managing the dal and *jhol* on that huge plate. Besides, I was anxious. I somehow ate a little and got up. Back at the house, Saroj Babu put up a mosquito net over one of the beds for me (there were two single beds in the room, maybe someone else lived there) and left. Finally, the two of us were alone. Neither of us knew what to say or do. Feelings bottled up for so long were making us restless, but we just stared at each other in surprise, unable to speak. I don't know how long. Suddenly Swadesh said, "We don't have much time. I shouldn't have dragged you here. I've made a big mistake. I might be arrested any moment. The police are patrolling the house. I couldn't tell from Karachi what things were like here. The Students' Movement is going on. The police think I've come to lead the movement, so they're following me." He quickly opened his suitcase and took out some clothes, chocolates, and fruit for Jaseem and a shawl for me. He gave them to me and said: "Put them in your bag. I thought I would go to Barisal to see Mashima and you and Jaseem, but everything's turned upside down. Now what should I do?" I said, "Things will take their course, what's the use of worrying? Sit down here with me." Suddenly he said, "You're still being formal with me?" I said, "What's wrong with that? It's an old habit." I took his hands and felt they were ice cold and shivering. With fear or exuberance?

We were startled by a loud thump on the door downstairs. Swadesh got up and told me, "Get out of here quickly and hide in the bathroom or somewhere. They've come to arrest me."

Bewildered, I ran out of the room and stood behind the stairs. Fifteen or twenty minutes later, when I didn't hear anything, I went in the room and saw he was standing there all packed and ready. I went to the window and saw a man standing like a wooden doll with his face toward the window. Rickshaws, push-carts, and a couple of jeeps were zooming by, shaking the whole house. It was incredibly loud. And every twenty or twenty-five minutes there was a huge thump on the door, and I would run out and come back in again. I got scared every time I heard a car stop in front of the door, thinking it must be the police coming to arrest Swadesh. Morning came. I was hardly able to stand from worry and exhaustion.

The evening before, Rana had come and invited me to eat breakfast in their room. He came bright and early in the morning. I washed my hands and face and went to eat. While I was talking to Rana's mother and father, I accidentally referred to Manorama Mashima as "Mashima," and everyone stared at me. I realized I'd made a big mistake. Swadesh had told them I was Mashima's daughter. When I came back to the room, I said, "I won't see them ever again." And it's true, I never saw Rana or his parents again.

When I was eating breakfast in Rana's room, I heard that the building had a lot of rooms. Most families rent one or two rooms. There was no system of distributing keys for the front door. Many of the tenants worked until late at night. There was no way to open the door except to knock loudly. If I'd known that before, maybe I wouldn't have been so scared that night. Anyway, it was over now.

Swadesh wanted to go and buy a few important things. I found I was burning with fever and had aches and pains all over. I didn't tell him, though. We went to a market by rickshaw. I didn't recognize where we were. After stopping at a couple of shops, Swadesh suddenly said, terrified, "Take the rickshaw and go home right now. Plainclothes policemen have surrounded us. If I don't come back this evening, take the steamer back to

Barisal today. Why did I bring you into this mess? It was so stupid of me."

I went home and fell asleep. I don't know when Swadesh came back. I woke up when a hand touched my forehead. He said, "Oh! You've got a high fever. Your eyes are red. How will you get back to Barisal by yourself?" I said, "Don't worry, I've taken the *goynar nouka* from Katakhali to Patuakhali many times with a fever like this."

If I could just get a taxi to Narayanganj and get on the steamer, problem solved. Swadesh said, "It's already afternoon, you have to get up now." My head and body were both hurting, but I had to get up. The taxi stand was quite far away. When I got in the taxi, Swadesh said, "They're following me again. I don't know what's going on. They're not arresting me, but they won't stop following me."

He helped me lie down in the women's compartment of the steamer and said to the only other woman passenger, "She has a high fever, please keep an eye on her during the night." Swadesh left quickly, saying he would leave for Karachi the next day. After he left, some police in disguise came and asked me a lot of questions. I don't remember what they said. The next day, I reached Barisal and took a rickshaw home. Ma said, "Oma, you're covered in chicken pox!" Then I understood why I was in such pain. Jaseem was at his Dada's house. My younger sister Runu went and brought him home. The funniest thing is that I sent Runu to that house with some fruits (the ones Swadesh had given me for Jaseem). Everyone in that house was already worried because I'd left so suddenly, and now they thought what they would. I didn't think about it at all. The truth is, I was too simple, and I still am. I can't lie, I don't know how. And I've been paying for it all my life.

Meanwhile, I was anxious to know what happened to Swadesh. Since I didn't see any news in the papers about his arrest, I thought he must have reached Karachi safely. Two weeks later, I got a note from him. I felt less worried. It took a while for me to recover from chicken pox. After me, Jaseem, Runu, Lina, Lutfa, Taslim, and finally even Ma got the chicken pox. It didn't take long for the little ones to fight it off, but it had me, Lutfa, and Ma really fatigued.

That night half a century ago could have been a night of romantic encounter, but I still remember it like a bad dream because of what was going on. The police could have arrested us at any time. I can't imagine what would have happened then. Now I think we were so foolish. Foolish, but romantic.

*A telegram from Swadesh*

In 1962, I passed the BA exam. Suddenly a telegram came from Swadesh. He had sent it to Karim Chacha, not to me. In the telegram, Swadesh had asked Karim Chacha to enroll me on an MA course. I didn't know what to do. I thought Swadesh must have a plan in his head. I was thinking, what is his plan? Karim Chacha was also concerned.

Then something unexpected happened: my younger sister, who was preparing for her Intermediate Exam, suddenly started a mismatched love affair. The gentleman was a relative of ours with a wife and two children. I tried very hard to dissuade my sister, but she was very stubborn. She wouldn't listen to anyone; she'd do whatever she'd set her mind on. When I couldn't stop the wedding, I told her, "Then your future husband should divorce his first wife." They didn't agree to that either. This incident shattered me. I worked so hard to help raise my brothers and sisters, and this is how they turn out? I kept thinking, my own sister is going to deprive another woman of her husband, and two children of their father.

None of my efforts were successful. My sister ignored all my protests, got married, and went off with her husband. It broke my heart. At the same time, I was having problems with Jaseem. After enrolling him in a good school in Barisal, I had fixed a rickshaw for him. Every day, I fed and dressed Jaseem and sent him to school, and after school he went to his Dada and Dadi's house. When my school let out, I would bring Jaseem back from their house. The year ended. When I went to the school to get his exam results, I found out Jaseem hadn't even taken the exam. His attendance was also poor. And I knew nothing of this. Jaseem had spent all this time being pampered at his Dada's house. I was even more astounded to think that such a little boy hid such a big thing from me. Not to mention other things. After that, I had only one thought on my mind, that if I stayed in Barisal, I wouldn't be able to bring up Jaseem the way I wanted. I felt this truth in my bones.

Just at this time, Swadesh's telegram came asking me to join an MA program, which was only available in Dhaka. But I had a job and was living in my own residence with my siblings. I was wondering whether I should give all this up to pursue my education. I went to ask Shanti-di's advice. She said, "Swadesh isn't asking you to take such a big step for no reason. Take a study leave and go to Dhaka. I'll try to hold your job for a while." Karim Chacha also agreed.

Even then, there were a lot of problems to solve. I had brought all my siblings from the village to Barisal and enrolled them in school. If I went to Dhaka, where would they go? Besides, where would I stay in Dhaka? I would have Jaseem with me. I talked to my mother. She said to think of my own future and Jaseem's future first. She also told me they would all go back to the village, and Runu, Taslim, and Lina would study in the village school. There was nothing wrong with that. But I felt terrible to dash their hopes.

One day, I wrote to Mohiuddin Chacha to find out if I could stay at his house if I got into the MA course. I assumed that it wouldn't work, and so I would be relieved of the burden of taking this step. But Mohiuddin sent a telegram right away saying that it would be no trouble to them at all and that I should come to Dhaka immediately. He also said university admissions were already open.

Of all the decisions I have made in my life, this was the most important. It was a difficult decision on the one hand, and exciting on the other. In any case, I let Baba know that I would be going to Dhaka to try to get my MA. When he came, I packed everything up and saw everyone onto the steamer, then came back to my empty house and burst out crying. The next day, Jaseem and I took a few belongings and set out for an unknown future. Little by little, I had set up this small household in Barisal. Whatever little I had, it was all bought with my own earnings, from the bookcase of jackfruit wood to the broom I used to sweep the floor.

That day, I wondered how I would begin my new life in Dhaka. Mohiuddin Chacha had loved me like one of his own children since I was small. He maintained that relationship with me until his death. I was worried about how his wife, my Moji Apa, and their children would take to me and Jaseem. After all, Jaseem was very naughty and energetic. Since he had no father, everyone spoiled him. I was the only one who disciplined him. He spent all day with his Dada and Dadi. Who knew how he would manage in a new place with new people? I would have to find a school for him in Dhaka.

I sat thinking all this on the steamer all night long. In the morning, the steamer reached Narayanganj. I took a taxi from there to Mohiuddin Chacha's house in Nababpur, Dhaka. The two of us, Jaseem and I, were a lot like orphans that day. We had with us the same trunk I had bought when I first came to Barisal. I was eleven years old when I bought it, and I still had it then. I also had a mattress, two pillows, a sheet, and a *kantha* (quilt)[18] tied up in a carpet. My mother had made the *kantha* with her own hands. It amazes me now that I was so happy and comfortable with so little.

Besides these, I had with me four white machine-woven saris; each cost around 8 taka. There were four white blouses, three petticoats, and a pair of sandals. I used to wash and starch the saris by hand, dry them, fold them neatly, and keep them under my pillow to wear to school the next morning. In Dhaka too, I wore those same saris to university and various meetings and associations.

The building where Mohiuddin Chacha lived had a lot of other tenants, and the landlord had a lot of relatives. Most of the families lived in one-room apartments, but Mohiuddin Chacha had three big rooms on the upper floor of the building. Mohiuddin Chacha and Moji Apa lived with their children Bobi, Nona, and Bula in the biggest room on the north side. Bobi and Jaseem were only fourteen days apart. The cooking and eating were done on one side of the middle room. The room by the stairs was the sitting room, and it had a bed in it since it doubled as a guest room. After all, politicians have certain responsibilities. They arranged for me and Jaseem to stay in that room. I will forever be grateful to them for this generosity.

## *Life in Dhaka*

In 1963, I had to leave Barisal to answer the call of education and the wider world. Soon after I moved to Dhaka, I began my life as a student at Dhaka University. At first, I took Jaseem with me to class, but I couldn't do that for long. Jaseem was almost six years old then, so I enrolled him at a government primary school in Azimpur. I dropped him off at school on the way to the university and picked him up on my way back. I often had to miss classes to pick him up. After he started school, not seeing him with me in class, Munir Sir once asked me, "Where's your little brother? Is he alright?"

I laughed and said, "He's my son!"

I went back to Barisal during my first break from university. This was a new experience for me. I didn't have a home in Barisal anymore. The house I had rented in College Road was now rented by Karim Chacha. I stayed with him and visited friends and family during the day. Suddenly I got a letter from Mohiuddin Chacha saying they had left their house in Nababganj and taken a nice house in Azimpur, but they wouldn't have room for me there. This was a disaster for me. I couldn't find a new place by sitting around in Barisal. Imad's older brother Kaysar lived in a rented house in Old Dhaka with his wife and several small children. I thought I might as well go stay with them when I got back to Dhaka, and then start looking for a new place to live.

I went back to Dhaka with Jaseem and stayed at Kaysar's house but started house-hunting immediately. They had only one room, so there was no question of staying there long term. Karim Chacha had given me some money when I left for Dhaka. I had to find a place quickly. While I was house-hunting, I went to Mohiuddin Chacha's old place in Nababganj and found their part of the building still empty. I had an idea. I thought, if I contributed something on top of what Kaysar Mia was paying for his place, we could rent those three rooms. I was a woman alone in Dhaka with a small child. No one was going to rent to me. As soon as I proposed this to Kaysar Mia, he agreed. We lived together in Nababganj. The biggest problem in that place was the bathroom. There was a long veranda in front of all three rooms. In the corner on the north side, they had fenced off a room for bathing with bamboo slats, but the toilet was disgusting. Yet there was no point thinking about that. After all, Mohiuddin Chacha and his family had lived in this place for years. By that time, I had learned to take life as it comes. Jaseem was still going to school in Azimpur, and I was taking my MA classes.

Professor Anisuzzaman learned who I was and asked me to come talk to him one day. He told me he had been close to Imad. I am great friends with him today. My other close friend from that period was my fellow student Neelima-di. The friendship that grew between us while we were university students lasted until her death. Even when I moved to Washington, Neelima-di went and found me there and ate a meal at my house. We also exchanged letters from time to time. When I came to Dhaka, I'd go to see her, or if we met at some meeting or other, she would always say, "Noorjahan, where have you been all this time!"

After Independence, Neelima-di said to me, "You and Swadesh won't be able to live in peace in this country. You'll be better off abroad." I wanted to work in my home country, especially to stand with the oppressed women of my country and make myself useful. But does everyone get what they want?

There is a world of difference between the Dhaka of today and the Dhaka I lived in. We would all sit around talking in the women's common room. When the teacher came to the classroom, an *ayah* came to take us to class. We would cover our heads, file slowly into the classroom, and sit in the very front row. We weren't allowed to look around. When the class was over, we left the room along with the teacher. Talking or hanging around with the male students was completely out of the question.

Only on the day of the annual Bangla department picnic did all the students, men and women, enjoy a day together. Jaseem and Munir Sir's son Bhashan were the same age. Munir Sir told me to bring Jaseem with me that day and said he would bring Bhashan. The two of them played together all day. It was so thoughtful of him to invite Jaseem, because otherwise I could not have come.

I have one regret about that picnic. A student had managed to borrow a camera. We were all very excited and took a lot of pictures. We agreed that each of us would take the negatives and get the pictures printed at our own expense. I was the first to get the negatives. But I never had a chance to give back the negatives. I still have a few of the pictures, but whenever I look at them, I feel guilty. The pictures were precious to everyone. I still remember the names of some of my classmates. Saleha, Siddiqa, and Fatema. Saleha and Siddiqa were small in stature like me. Fatema was tall and fair. I don't remember any of the boys' names. The one with the camera was named Abul Hosen, I think. Eight of us girls went to the picnic. Neelima-di, Munir Sir, and five or six other teachers were with us. We went to Joydebpur and spent the whole day laughing, playing, wandering around the woods, and singing songs.

*My marriage to Swadesh*

What happened after the picnic was very theatrical. My life was dragging on slowly then. I had no home, no house, no job, no purpose. I often wondered what kind of life I had chosen for myself and Jaseem. I couldn't go on like this much longer. I had to decide my own future, and soon. Swadesh had not been in touch after his telegram to Karim Chacha insisting that I enroll in an MA program. I decided to write a letter to Swadesh in Karachi. I thought this would be my last letter to him. I wrote: "Let us not think of each other anymore. Let us each take our future in our own hands. Let our relationship end here." I breathed a sigh of liberation and relief after I put the letter in the mail. But in truth, I was still holding onto hope.

A week after I sent the letter, I came home from classes and saw Swadesh sitting in my room. He looked unwell and exhausted. But I was very happy to see him. I asked him, "Would you like something to eat, should I make some tea or Horlicks?"

He said no and asked me to sit down. Jaseem had already jumped into his lap, yelling "Kaku [Uncle]!"

Swadesh told me he had telegrammed Karim Chacha to come to Dhaka. I didn't understand why he wanted Karim Chacha. Then Swadesh suddenly said, "Noorjahan, I want to marry you. If you don't accept my proposal right here and now, I won't even take a sip of water. If I can't take you back with me within a week, I won't go back to my job in Karachi. I know I've delayed this too long. I've thought a lot about Jaseem. I promise you I will treat him with the utmost love and care. Please say yes."

He was out of breath after saying all this. I couldn't believe my ears. Then I made a glass of Horlicks for him and said, "Drink this first."

He refused to drink the Horlicks. I tried to make him understand the social conditions we were in. I told him, "How can we live naturally together in this environment?"

Swadesh said, "We'll go to Karachi right after the wedding. No one knows us there."

He also said he was all ready to go to England within six months. It would be no trouble at all to take me and Jaseem there. He had enrolled at Cambridge University to do a PhD in economics. He had a fellowship from the Ford Foundation.

Swadesh's proposal that day bewildered me. He didn't give me a chance to think it through calmly. Swadesh was so weak that I thought he could faint at any moment. Jaseem was close by. I don't know if he understood anything of what was going on, but he kept saying, "Kaku, drink this, it's my Horlicks, it's really sweet."

I couldn't break Swadesh's resolve. Finally, I said, "All right, fine."

I couldn't think. When Swadesh was drinking the Horlicks, I could see his hands were shaking; he could hardly hold the glass. I had to help him. A little later, he got ready to leave. Jaseem and I came outside and stood on the street waiting for a rickshaw. I saw an intelligence branch official dressed in white standing there. Both of us noticed him. I told Swadesh that it wouldn't be a good idea for him to come to this house again until Karim Chacha was here.

Swadesh told me he was staying at his close friend Dr Aminul Islam's father's house. Later Aminul Islam worked for many years at the Asian Development Bank.

After seeing Swadesh off, I was thinking that if I was going to get married in Dhaka, it was very important for Mohiuddin Chacha to be there. I didn't know where in Azimpur Mohiuddin Chacha's new house was, so I went to his older sister-in-law Setara's mother's house to find out his address. She lived in Azimpur's China Building. When I went there, I learned that Mohiuddin Chacha and his wife and children had gone on a trip to Cox's Bazaar. She didn't know when they were coming back or what their address and phone number were.

Luckily, Karim Chacha arrived quickly. After I told him everything, he looked quite worried. First Karim Chacha asked Swadesh to come to my house and tried to reason with him. He said this interfaith wedding would cause a lot of trouble here. He asked Swadesh to go ahead and enroll at Cambridge and promised to send me there later. But Swadesh wouldn't agree. He didn't believe that if he left, they would send me to him. He thought they might force me to marry someone else against my will. Karim Chacha said, "None of us is capable of forcing Noorjahan to marry anyone."

Finally, Karim Chacha took Swadesh to see the economist Akhlaqur Rahman. He left Swadesh there and went to Barisal. Before leaving, Karim Chacha said Akhlaqur Rahman would take care of everything. If Karim Chacha stayed, it could cause trouble. The fact is Karim Chacha didn't want to be present at our wedding out of fear that it would entangle him in social problems in Barisal. I still think his presence would have been very important and helpful. Akhlaq Bhai and his wife were enthusiastic about this wedding but insisted that the only way to do this quietly was through an Islamic ceremony. We were told it was the only way do it. Swadesh and I had misgivings about this, but interfaith marriage was rare and very complicated and could have led to further trouble.[19] Due to circumstances, we had no choice but to go through with a nominal Muslim ceremony even though we were leftist nonbelievers. Swadesh did not believe in any religion or rituals and never considered himself Hindu or Muslim. Our marriage took place on 28 March 1963. I told my brother-in-law Kaysar that I was marrying Swadesh, and he gladly attended and met up with Swadesh and Akhlaqur Rahman. I wasn't even there for the so-called ceremony. Everything was done quietly to avoid setting off riots. I had tried to reach my sister-in-law Bela to invite her, but she was very ill with chicken pox. I sent her a letter instead.

The morning of our marriage, Swadesh gave me some money and asked me to buy nice clothes for myself and Jaseem. I went to a store I knew in New Market and bought some good quality pants and shirts for Jaseem. But the problem was with my sari. I was dressed in widow's white, so they started showing me white saris. I couldn't bring myself to tell them that I wanted a colorful sari—that today was my wedding. I bought two high-quality white saris there. One of them had a white *zari* border and cost 30 taka. The other had a black border and cost 28 taka.

After the marriage was done, Swadesh came to our place in Nababganj with Kaysar. I learned that we were leaving for Karachi that same night. We were basically running away to avoid any scandal or riots. My belongings consisted of a green trunk, some books, some bedding, and a mosquito net. I thought, I can't take these things with me. Someone brought me a suitcase, and I packed my and Jaseem's few clothes in it. The green trunk had been my companion since 1948. It made me sad to leave it behind. I left some of my precious things in it—some of Imad's notebooks (full of his handwriting) and clothes: a green *lungi*, some shirts he had worn, baggy salwar, an old shawl, a torn *sherwani*. On the night of our wedding, Imad had been wearing that *sherwani* and it tore in the back when he bent over to make a salaam. A lot of people had seen it as a bad omen. There were also a few of my books. I told my sister-in-law to keep them safely for Jaseem. He had never seen his father or any of his father's things. I thought I would give them to him later. But I never found out what happened to that trunk.

Swadesh didn't have any extra money on hand, so Akhlaq Bhai and other friends covered the cost of my and Jaseem's plane tickets to Karachi as a wedding present. Someone took us to the airport in their car. I don't remember who came with us to the airport. This is how we ran away to Karachi to save our own heads and prevent social unrest. We came back only many years later.

## PART 4

# LEAVING BENGAL

*A brief move to Karachi*

In those days, the plane from Dhaka to Karachi left at midnight. It was my first plane trip, and of course Jaseem's too. The plane left on time. I was sitting by the window. Swadesh was in the middle, and Jaseem next to him. Jaseem was amazed that day—his Kaku had suddenly shown up and whisked him and me away to Karachi. Nobody had explained things to him clearly. Even I didn't know how a mother could talk about her wedding with her six-and-a-half-year-old son! Jaseem had never seen me interacting closely with a man.

I had never thought I would marry Swadesh. I still feel amazed when I think about it. Even on our wedding day, I wore a white sari (the new one with gold border). Widows normally wear white, but brides wear red. Seeing me in the white sari, Swadesh was dismayed and said, "Even today you wore a white sari!"

I said, "You didn't buy me a colorful sari. When I went to the shop and asked for a sari, they pulled out these white ones. Then I was embarrassed to ask for a colorful one."

At that, Swadesh stared at my face for a while and said, "You look beautiful in this."

A little later, he took my hands in his and said, "I can't even afford to buy you a ring."

I said, "I don't need anything."

We arrived in Karachi late at night and took a room in the Faruq Hotel. We spent the rest of the night there. In the morning, Swadesh went straight from the hotel to his workplace. Jaseem and I stayed in the hotel room. Quite a while later, Swadesh came back to the hotel with Nuruddin Chowdhury and Azizur Rahman Khan and introduced them to me. I felt like they were both stunned to see me. Neither of them knew the slightest thing about our relationship. Swadesh had suddenly shown up with not only a wife but also a six-year-old son! Later they discussed where we could stay. Nuruddin Shaheb had two children. The son was about Jaseem's age, and the daughter was older. But they didn't have enough room for us to stay in their place.

Finally, it was decided we would stay in Azizur Rahman Khan's house. He called a taxi and took us there. When we got to the house, he introduced us to his wife Mahua. She was also astounded to see us! We ate lunch there and talked for a while. After dinner, they gave us their bedroom and made up their own bed in the sitting room. I objected strongly to this, but to no effect. Their bed was only big enough for two people, so I made up a bed for Jaseem on the floor. Swadesh was lying on the bed smoking incessantly. Jaseem just wouldn't sleep that night. He must have gotten scared seeing Swadesh suddenly in our bedroom, or I don't know what he was thinking. I tried hard to persuade him to sleep, but it was no use. Then Jaseem started screaming and crying. He cried himself to sleep. And Swadesh filled the room with cigarette smoke.

That was our wedding night.

In any case, we stayed in Azizur Rahman's house for seven days. In the meantime, a nearby flat became available. We rented it and moved in. I'll never forget the hospitality that Mahua and Azizur Rahman Khan showed us in that week. Mahua helped me in many ways later too: she showed me where to buy fish, rice, and dal, where to get good meat and vegetables. Having suddenly landed up in a new place, I was very lucky to find a friend like her.

Our flat had a big bedroom and sitting room. There was a small walled courtyard in the back, a kitchen on one side, and a bathroom attached to that. It was a great place for three. Swadesh couldn't afford to buy or make new furniture, so we rented a bedframe for the bedroom and a dining table and chairs for the sitting room. Swadesh had an old iron bedframe and mattress, so we put that on one side of our room for Jaseem.

I bought the necessary dishes, glasses, and pots and pans from the market. We also bought a small kerosene stove. I didn't know how to use it, so I learned from Mahua. The first day in the new house, they came over to eat with us. Swadesh and I had gone around and done all the shopping. I was so happy that day, that we were really setting up our household together as husband and wife, and that we had invited friends to dinner. We'd bought more vegetables and meat than we needed. I put my heart into the cooking. I'd cooked a few things before from time to time, but this was something else.

It was a holiday. I finished cooking, took a bath, and sat down to eat with the guests. They were eating plenty, but Swadesh started finding fault with every dish I had cooked. I was so embarrassed and disappointed I couldn't eat at all. But Azizur Rahman Khan and Mahua kept saying the food was excellent. Swadesh and I have been fighting about cooking for over ten years. If Swadesh ate and then said the food wasn't good, maybe I wouldn't feel so bad. But when he threw it away without even tasting it, I felt terrible. He acted a lot like my father. Baba also used to find fault with food and throw it out. It was a normal thing in our household for Baba to break plates and dishes. I suffered the same fate as my mother in this respect.

That night, I tucked Jaseem into his new bed. Jaseem had never slept alone before. He kept looking at Swadesh. His eyes were asking, why is Kaku going to sleep with Ma?! He couldn't understand it. He'd never seen a husband and wife sleeping in the same bed, so he was constantly restless. I felt sorry for them both. Jaseem had never learned to share his mother with anyone else. And Swadesh had never thought that he wouldn't have his wife to himself even at night. Our days in the new house in Karachi were going by like this. Sometimes in the middle of the night I would wake up and see Jaseem standing by our bed, staring at us in amazement. Later, I succeeded somewhat in explaining things to Jaseem and put his bed in the next room. There was one thing that made it easier to do this. We were supposed to go to England with Swadesh in September. I explained to Jaseem that in England, children slept in their own rooms. Jaseem would have his own room there and would have to sleep there.

I enrolled Jaseem in a good English-medium school in Karachi. For the first time, he had a chance to study uninterrupted. Before this, I had enrolled him in several schools but could never get him to focus. I had helped Jaseem learn the Bangla and English letters at home and taught him math as well. I breathed a sigh of relief when I was able to settle him in a good school in Karachi, because I felt terrible for tearing Jaseem away from the whole world he had known. I didn't know what would come of it. He had lost his father before he was even born. Then he had been close to his Dada/Dadi, Nana/Nani, Chacha/Chachi, their children, and my family. I was worried about taking him away from these close relationships. On the other hand, I really wanted to know what he thought about it.

Ever since he was small, Jaseem was incredibly naughty. Since he didn't have a father, everyone pampered him, and no one disciplined him. I worried about it. When I came home from a day at work, I'd hear stories of his mischief. If I tried to discipline him, everyone objected and scolded me. I just thought, what a mess! How am I going to raise him to be a good person? I realize one thing now: if I had stayed in Barisal, he wouldn't have gotten an education. Jaseem himself says, "Ma, if we stayed in Barisal, I might have become a *gunda* [gangster]."

After moving to Karachi, that rambunctious child became completely calm and started doing well in school. But this sudden change in him worried me too. I thought, is this a good thing, or a bad omen? I didn't like Karachi either. I felt like I'd left my parents, relatives, and friends and gone into exile. I thought, isn't this a big sacrifice just to have one person? Will this be good for me? In one jump, I'd toppled the world I had built slowly over these twenty-five years and come flying who knew where. What would my future hold? I'd struggled hard to get my education. I had a good job and a decent place in political and social life. And then what had I done? I wasn't the kind of girl to be satisfied with just cooking rice, looking after the house, wearing saris and jewelry. Then what was the use of leaving Katakhali at age ten or eleven and crossing the Agunmukha? All these thoughts ran through my head day and night.

Soon after I moved to Karachi, Amartya Sen[1] came there on a visit. A party was arranged in his honor at the house of the director of PIDE, Mark Leiserson. We were invited too. That day, I left Jaseem at Nuruddin Shaheb's house and got ready to go to the party. Mahua brought some colorful saris and jewelry for me, thinking it wouldn't look good if I went as a new wife in my white sari. I thanked her, but in the end, I wore my white sari to the party. Swadesh left me in one place and went off to talk to everyone. He's always like that. What else could I do? I found an empty chair in a corner and sat there. I didn't know anyone, and this kind of party was new to me.

Suddenly, I saw a good-looking young man striding toward me. He came up to me and said, "You must be Noorjahan, Swadesh's wife? I'm Amartya Sen." I looked at him in surprise and said, "How did you guess who I am?"

He said, "I heard Swadesh got married recently. When I saw you sitting quietly here by yourself, I thought you must be the new wife."

After so many years, I still wonder how he recognized me.

*In Europe on the way to Cambridge*

In September, we moved to Cambridge. Mahua and Azizur Rahman were also going, so we all went together. Swadesh and Azizur Rahman both wanted to study in the United States and had even got admitted to Harvard, but at the last minute, US immigration canceled their visas because they had been involved in student politics. Swadesh had also spent eight years in jail. Then the Ford Foundation gave them scholarships and asked the PIDE authorities to let them go to England.

Before leaving, we sold the few household things we had. The landlord's wife came and bought them at a nominal price. Swadesh bought me a Chinese silk sari with a small flower print for 50 rupees and a blue half-silk sari. I wore the blue sari for the journey. Jaseem was excited—we were off to England, after all! I was feeling excited too—that dreamland, England, the England of Rabi Tagore's *Jibansmriti* (Memoirs), Bernard Shaw's England, Bertrand Russell's England, Shakespeare's England.

I'd read about this dreamland. My own dream was to find an opportunity to take some classes or training while Swadesh was getting his PhD. That day, no one came to see us off at the airport, except Mahua and Azizur Rahman's relatives. It was a long plane ride. We were supposed to stop over in Rome and Frankfurt for two days each. I found it very romantic. I thought, how many women are as lucky as me?

On the other hand, I've had motion sickness since I was small. As soon as I got on a boat, my head would spin, and I would throw up. The same thing happened on the plane. I threw up the whole way and even ruined my sari. When we got to Rome, we stayed three nights in a *pensione* and spent the days wandering around. Ruins of old Rome are scattered throughout the new city. The weather was beautiful. We saw many fountains, the Roman Pantheon, and the Colosseum. I don't remember very well what else we saw. I only remember a couple of things—for example, once we happened to glance at a restaurant window and saw tomatoes stuffed with rice. All three of us were overcome with a longing for rice. Without thinking, we ordered a few rice-stuffed tomatoes and sat down to eat. When the bill came, we understood "how much paddy it takes to make rice!" Similarly, another day we saw people sitting outside a restaurant eating. We sat down too and ate sandwiches, cake, and all kinds of things. When Swadesh went to pay the bill, he was crestfallen. We were on a limited budget.

We did a lot of sightseeing with other tourists. In one place, we hit it off with another group. They were very interested to see me wearing a sari. I was talking to them in my broken English. Someone asked me about Swadesh, and when I said he was my husband, they didn't believe me, because I didn't have a ring. In the Western world, the ring is an essential part of marriage. Not having a ring got me in trouble several other times too. The month after we arrived in Cambridge, I became pregnant. I felt sick, I couldn't eat anything, couldn't even drink water. The doctor sent me to the hospital several times. The nurses would look at me and say among themselves, "Here is another unwed mother!" One day, my doctor was there. He overheard them and commented, "No, no, she is very much married to a graduate student." Then they laughed sheepishly. I've had to explain my lack of a ring many times.

I did get a ring, but only five years after our marriage. In 1968, Swadesh went to Kandy in Sri Lanka for an international economics conference. This was after Anita was born. Swadesh saved up some of his daily stipend and bought a ruby ring for me. That was not only my first ring, but my first piece of jewelry. I liked to live simply. I was used to living the same way I saw my mother live. I never bothered much about saris and jewelry.

We were in Rome for three days, then went to Frankfurt. Both families stayed in a small cottage that had been booked in advance. When I saw the airport, I couldn't believe that this country had suffered extensive damage in a war just a few years ago. There was no sign of it anywhere. Everything was clean, neat, and shiny. It seemed like a city of wonder. In any case, we reached the place we were going to stay in the evening. It was a small one-story house. The beds had bright white bedclothes on them. Our room was a little bigger, with two beds. Swadesh and Aziz Shaheb dropped us off and went to look for food. Mahua and I went to take a bath in the attached bathroom, but we couldn't understand how to turn on the hot water, so we bathed quickly in cold water and got under the covers, shivering with cold. A little later, Swadesh and Aziz Shaheb brought some food: bread, cake, and Germany's famous sausage or Frankfurters. It was all cold. We weren't used to eating that kind of food, but we were so hungry that we ate it and went to sleep.

In the morning, we got dressed and went out for breakfast right away. It was a very sunny day. Swadesh and Aziz Shaheb were planning to buy a camera, so we went around to a lot of shops. We two women bought some stockings for the cold. These transparent stockings reached to just below the waist and had to be attached with a kind of garter. We bought those too.

Now they've thought a lot harder about women's convenience and made much better clothes. You don't have to wear garters anymore, the stockings go up to the waist and you wear them like pants, or some of them only go to the knee. They're much easier to wear.

That afternoon was our flight to London. We reached the London airport before evening. I felt like I'd arrived in a dreamland. What amazed me the most was how clean and quiet it was. There were a lot of people, but no noise; everyone went about their work quietly. The three of us went to the hotel we had booked, and Mahua and Aziz Shaheb went to stay at a friend's house.

On the way to the hotel, I looked around at the houses. They were all practically identical. Only the house numbers were different. I thought, it would be so easy to mix up the numbers at night and wander into the wrong house. A funny incident many years later in my house in Washington proved to me that it was indeed possible. We lived at 6209 Redwing Court in Washington for almost thirty years. There were ten identical houses on three sides of the road. The house to the left of ours had the same design. A divorced woman named Sandy lived there. Her sons had grown up and moved out, so she rented out a few rooms of her house.

One night, we were all fast asleep. Suddenly, a sound woke me up. After lying quietly for a long time, I realized the sound wasn't stopping. It sounded like someone trying to open the door with a key. I quickly got up and said to Swadesh, "Get up, there's a thief in the house."

But what's the use of calling him! He never gets up. When I turned on the light and went out of the bedroom myself, I saw a young man trying to open the door to my older daughter's bedroom with a key. I shouted, "Who are you? Why are you trying to open my daughter's room?"

He said, embarrassed, “This is my room, I just rented it this morning.”

Then I dragged him downstairs and sat him on the sofa to interrogate him. He said he had rented a room from Sandy, and since the houses looked exactly alike, he’d accidentally come into our house.

I ran to the phone and found out from Sandy that the young man had really rented a room from her that day.

I also found out that the keys to the front door of all the houses were the same. I’d been living there for so long and didn’t know this. Sandy came and apologized and took her tenant home. The next day, I called a locksmith and changed the lock on our front door. The funniest thing was, Swadesh watched all this from upstairs. He never came down. Swadesh is always like that—he shrinks back at the first sign of danger. He told me a story about this himself: when he was living with some friends in Karachi, one night a thief came into their room. He noticed but pulled the blankets over his head and pretended to be asleep. Only after the thief took all he had and left did he get up and tell the others.

We were in London for two days and went to see the British Museum, Trafalgar Square, Buckingham Palace, and St James’s Park. Jaseem enjoyed the trip very much. He was seven years old then. Even though he was having a lot of fun, there was one thing he couldn’t understand, which was the way girls and boys stood and sat very close together in the streets and parks and everywhere else. He’d never seen this before, and neither had I. Jaseem kept staring at them. We didn’t try to explain it to him because we thought he’d figure things out himself. After two days in London, we went to Cambridge. It was a three-hour trip, and I thoroughly enjoyed the view along the way. On the way to Cambridge, we saw several English villages. There were pretty little houses, each with a flower garden in front. Almost all the villages had a school and church tower at the center. We saw cows too, and people farming with small tractors, and apple groves. We took a taxi from the station to our flat.

*Another life: Cambridge*

Swadesh was enrolled in the PhD program at Churchill College at Cambridge University. This was a new college, so it was a little far from town. Construction was still in progress for the graduate student housing, so they gave us a flat in the teachers' housing. When we saw the house, we were amazed. It was nothing like what we'd heard from friends or read about the houses in this country. Just inside the house was a corridor or veranda. On the left, a huge sitting and dining room. To the right, at the end of the corridor, a small but very nice bathroom with a bathtub. West of the corridor were two beautiful bedrooms. One room had two single beds put together, and the other had a single bed and a study desk and chair. The walls were full of big windows. Next to that room was a big kitchen, with a table and chairs for everyday meals, a big refrigerator, and all the necessities for eating and cooking. In other words, everything we needed to start a household was already there. When we opened the refrigerator, we saw bread, butter, milk, tea, oil, sugar, eggs, cake, and everything. We thought they must have stocked everything since we were coming from a faraway country and didn't know where to find things. I felt full of gratitude. We washed our hands and faces and had tea and bread and butter. When I went to fry some eggs, I saw there was no salt.

The next day, we went out to explore. I thought maybe we'd find a shop somewhere and buy salt. But it was a Sunday, and I didn't know that all the shops are closed on Sundays in that country.

It was a beautiful area, very green. It was September, so it was a little cold, but not freezing yet. The trees and grass were still green. As we walked straight down the road toward Churchill College, we saw a few Bengali graduate students coming toward us. They greeted us enthusiastically. One of them was Nripen Ray, whom Swadesh knew already. They had been in Jagannath Hall at Dhaka University together. Nripen was thrilled to see me and my child with Swadesh. Then he swept us off to his place. He was a PhD student in physics at Churchill College. Later some students from Kolkata and Dhaka gathered in his house, including Gopal Dutta, Lutfar Rahman, and Modasser Hosen. We all had tea together. I asked Nripen where to get salt, and he gave me some salt along with some rice, dal, turmeric, and chilies in a little bundle. He told me where I could get more of these things.

We were thrilled to find people from home in this unfamiliar place. That day, we invited everyone to our place. When we came home, I quickly made some *khichuri* and stir-fried eggs, and we ate and went to sleep, feeling very happy. I didn't have to tell Jaseem anything about the sleeping arrangement. He went into his room and fell asleep by himself. That was his room from then on.

The next morning, Swadesh went to the college. Then the three of us went walking into town. The university campus was built on both banks of the River Cam, and the town is connected by several bridges. Hence the name Cambridge. Every university has its own heritage and beauty. Later we got a chance to explore everything.

A few days later, I found Adam's Shop, which the Bengalis called "Aadamer Dokan." I bought rice, several kinds of dal, turmeric, red and green chilies, and some other necessities there. Then I bought fish from Mac Fisheries and chicken and meat from Sainsbury's. The fish was a small variety called "sprats," a lot like our *parshe mach*. I fried some of them crispy, and the rest of them I cooked with chopped onions and green chilies. I made some cabbage too, and of course dal. So began my monotonous life of eating and cooking, cooking and eating.

The flat we lived in at Churchill was on a hill to the north of campus. There were ten modern buildings there, each with two flats upstairs and two downstairs. About twenty families of students and teachers lived there. The students' flats were across from ours. We were very lucky to get such a nice place—the rent was high, but the flat was very comfortable. Every flat had central heating; we didn't have to use coal to heat the room. There were hot water pipes all around the rooms, which kept the house nice and warm. In the front and back of the building, there were walled spaces a lot like our courtyards. Flowers growing along the walls. I planted some coriander in one corner of the backyard. The gardener who came to take care of the garden gave me a kind of vegetable like little cabbages, called brussels sprouts. Maybe he gave them to everybody. You could go from one courtyard to the other.

All around the flat buildings was a pretty little road. The children rode their bicycles there. To the west was a huge playing field. That green expanse stretched from the college past our flat to the north. There was a high hillock in the north with a playground, sandbox, slide, and swings. After Mini was born, as soon as she could walk a little, she would play there all day. Later they built a chapel on that hillock. Next to it was a common laundry room with washing machines and driers. That's where I first met other women who had come there with their husbands from faraway places just like me. All of them had small children. Some of them had children after coming there. But all of them were shut up in the house. Eilene from America, Sheila from Canada, Francisca from Ireland, Carole, Penny, and Anne from New Zealand and Australia, and Sonoko from Japan. This Noorjahan from Bangladesh was in the same state. There were also professors' wives, whose status was different from ours. There were some well-known professors there, like Kenneth Arrow, George Steiner—his son David and daughter Debra were Jaseem's playmates; Prof. Eeles's son John and daughter Emily played with Jaseem all day too; and there was Prof. Wzaye from Japan.

We arrived in Cambridge in September 1963. In October, I became pregnant and started having terrible nausea. This happened before I got to know the new place very well. I had a lot of hopes, but this changed everything. I spent nine months vomiting. I couldn't eat anything. I spent the days lying in bed alone. Jaseem made friends quickly and started school. He was doing well. Swadesh went off on his bicycle to the economics faculty in the morning and came back late. He didn't know how to cook. I couldn't trust Swadesh and Jaseem in the kitchen after the mess they made of things the couple of days they tried to cook. One day, the two of them put on some rice and eggs to boil, went off somewhere, and forgot about it. The rice and eggs were burnt to coal, and the whole house was full of smoke and a burnt smell. I couldn't stand the smell of rice, fish, or meat in those days, but I still had to cook. I'd crawl into the kitchen and put on the rice and dal, then go back to the bedroom. I'd watch the clock, cover my nose with my sari, and go turn the stove off. When Swadesh came home, he would cry in secret to see me in this state, but he never asked anyone to help me—even though there were arrangements for help in that country. Social workers can help sick people and even do housework.

The milkman left milk on the doorstep every morning. One day, he saw me and said, "Are you pregnant, Mrs Bose? Why did you not tell me? From now on, I will leave an extra bottle of milk for you." Not only that, he also informed the local social workers. They started to come to my house regularly with orange juice and vitamins. When my health took a turn for the worse, they had to inform Dr Swan. There was a doctor for each family there. The doctor came to see me right away and immediately called an ambulance to take me to the hospital. I don't remember the first time I was in the hospital for a few days.

After that, I had to go back to the hospital from time to time. Dr Swan arranged everything. I was already underweight, and I was supposed to be gaining weight during pregnancy, but I lost weight instead.

While I was pregnant, I remember we traveled to London at Christmas time to see the world-famous Russian ballet *Swan Lake* at the Royal Albert Hall. Jaseem went with us too. Swadesh's friend from Barisal, Abdur Rab, went to London to study law and spent a long time there. He was there at the time, and Swadesh wrote a letter asking him to book us a room and get tickets for *Swan Lake*. He sent a letter back saying he had arranged everything. We went to London on the day of the show. When we arrived, we were very hungry. We went to a restaurant and ate our fill of French fries, hamburgers, and coffee or tea. When we got to Rab's house, we found out he had cooked chicken, beef, *dal bharta*, and vegetables for us with his own hands. And we couldn't eat any of it! I felt terrible. On the way to see *Swan Lake*, we dropped by the hotel to see the room. We saw two beds, a double and a single, covered with clean white sheets. It looked nice. But that same night, we realized that you can't tell everything at first sight.

Rab went with us to see *Swan Lake*. Not everyone is lucky enough to see something like that. I was full of happiness. When we got back to the hotel, it was past midnight, and we were starving. On the way there, we were thinking that if Rab offered even once, we would be very happy to go to his place and eat the food he had cooked. But he didn't realize what we were thinking. He said goodbye along the way and went home. The three of us hungry souls silently went back to the hotel. We didn't see any restaurants open, and we didn't know London very well. That neighborhood didn't look very safe to us either.

Because I was pregnant, it was very hard for me to withstand hunger. But we got ready to go to bed without eating and saw that there was a hole as big as a boat in the middle of the bed. When we lay down, we kept rolling on top of each other. On top of that, it was extremely cold that night, and the blankets on the beds were hardly worth the name. All three of us were shivering with cold. The room was like ice. If you put twenty-five pennies in the heater, the room warmed up a bit, but only for five minutes. We bundled up in our clothes, socks, sweaters, even overcoats, and huddled together trying to sleep. But it was impossible. In the December cold, everything was covered in a blanket of white. Swadesh kept putting twenty-five pennies in the heater as long as his cash lasted.

In the morning when we left the place, I noticed a very pretty sign on the wall that said: We will be delighted if you let us know how you have enjoyed your stay in this guesthouse. Thank you! When I saw that, I wanted to scream, "Shut up, you thieves!" Rab had been in London for many years, so I still don't understand how he could choose a place like that for us. From then on, whenever I had to stay in a hotel or motel, I would take a good look first before booking. That time on our way back from London to Cambridge, we had breakfast at the station and bought bread, eggs, and salt there before heading home. It was Boxing Day, and we knew that all the stores in Cambridge would be closed. When we got home, we had our fill of *khichuri* and *dim bhaji*. This is a meal I've eaten many times in my life, but I don't think it's ever tasted so good as on that day.

As winter continued, things weren't going very well with the pregnancy. I was always vomiting. The same thing had happened to me when I was pregnant with Jaseem. I was very sick and depressed before he was born because I had lost Imad. With this second pregnancy, I was in an unfamiliar place with no one to talk to. There was no one to feed me what I liked. And then the severe cold set in, and I couldn't leave the house.

One day, it suddenly started snowing. It was our first experience of snow! That day, Jaseem's school let out early, and he was already home. I was watching the snow for the first time out the window. The flats were on high ground, and I could see Swadesh riding his bicycle through the snow. He was having trouble with the bicycle in the snow. He wasn't supposed to be home at that time. I asked him, "What happened?"

Swadesh came in and said, breathing hard, "I left work early so I could come see snow falling for the first time with you."

I felt so happy. I quickly made some tea for Swadesh. Then the three of us sat watching the snow through the window. Light, fluffy snow fell through the night. It was a wonderful sight! The next morning, we woke up to find everything white. The fields, the houses, the cars, everything was covered in white snow. I felt like we were in the North Pole, in the country of Santa Claus.

Then there was a break from school and college. We spent the days at home. Swadesh bundled me and Jaseem up in coats and took a few pictures of us in the snow. I was craving dried shrimp and cucumbers. These things were very expensive there in the winter, but Swadesh still bought them for me. This was an expensive luxury for a graduate student. Toward the end of my pregnancy, I washed my cooked rice in water to get rid of the smell and tried to eat it with chilies and dried shrimp. I chewed the cucumbers to get hydrated. I couldn't drink water, milk, or juice at all. This was a very hard time for me. The whole big world seemed tasteless. Thanks to Dr Swan's care, I survived. Mini was due on 4 July, America's Independence Day. But she was born on the first of July at 12:15 am in the Cambridge Maternity Hospital. Aziz and Mahua Khan came during visiting hours. Swadesh came, but just for five minutes. When I asked him about Jaseem, he said he hadn't shown any enthusiasm about his little sister.

The next day, Swadesh came to take me home. We reached home around noon. The baby cot had been set up in Jaseem's room. I had bought the baby cot, pram, and a lot of clothes from a neighbor for cheap. Clothes and other things were sold at low prices among the students and teachers.

When I reached home, Jaseem wasn't there. He came home in the evening. I said to Jaseem, "Don't you want to see your little sister?"

He didn't show much interest. I understood he had a lot of questions in his head. Neither of us had enough experience to explain things properly to Jaseem. The next day, Mahua did some shopping and cooked for us. It's rare to have such a good friend far from home. Mahua shopped and cooked for me regularly for seven days. She kept me company. Later when Mahua's son Abhik was born, I thought I would get a chance to help her in the same way. But Aziz Shaheb didn't let me. After Abhik was born, I did some shopping and took two buses to go to their house with Mini, but when I arrived, I found the cooking done and the house clean. Instead of me feeding Mahua, Aziz Shaheb fed us instead. I had told him the day before not to do anything, but he didn't listen. He fixed everything before I arrived. After that, I didn't have the nerve to impose my favors on them.

I'll never forget another friend who helped after Mini was born. Her name was Barbara Reddaway. She was much older than me, but she was like a friend. Professor Brian Reddaway was Swadesh's tutor, and Barbara was his wife. We went to their house for dinner and tea a few times. Both were excellent people. The first day, they sat Jaseem down on the floor to play with their own children's old toys. They were very cheerful people. Their house was full of all kinds of books, from floor to ceiling. It was a wonderful sight. That first day, I was looking hungrily at the books, and Barbara said, "Do you want some books to read? Take some." Both Barbara and Brian rode bicycles. Barbara often brought books and apples from their garden in the basket of her bicycle. Sometimes she carried them over. After Mini was born, she came often to talk to me and help me. My friendship with Barbara lasted all her life. We exchanged letters. They were both sympathetic about issues in Bangladesh.

Barbara was involved all her life with the Centre for the Rehabilitation of the Paralysed (CRP) hospital in Savar, a division of Dhaka district in Bangladesh. She raised funds abroad for the development of this hospital. She always mentioned the hospital in her letters to me. I saw her during a visit to Cambridge a few years after we went back to Bangladesh. I also saw her in Washington, where their oldest son lived for many years. Professor Brian also came to Washington for various invited lectures and so on. He came to see us every time. Before Barbara died, she asked her friends to donate money to the hospital in Bangladesh instead of buying her cards and flowers. In Britain, it is customary to send cards and flowers when someone dies. According to Barbara's wishes, her friends donated money to build a big hall for the hospital, which was named Reddaway Hall. When I later went to see it, I cried. If I hadn't seen it with my own eyes, I wouldn't have believed that anyone could run such a clean, neat, and beautiful institution in Bangladesh. There are fruit trees and flowering plants all around it, a big pond, and huge trees. I was excited to see the cafeteria, where physically handicapped young people were cooking and serving food so gracefully! After successful treatment at the hospital, they stay on to work there. It's such a nice environment that I sat down to eat something even though I wasn't hungry. I placed my order, and the servers brought the hot food. Whether sitting in wheelchairs or walking on crutches, they dream of better lives.

Later in Dhaka I met the director of the CRP Hospital, Ms Valerie Taylor. When she heard I was a friend of Barbara Reddaway, she hugged me. A woman named Mahua works with Valerie. Mahua runs the whole hospital from her wheelchair, working directly under Valerie. Mahua was suffering from paralysis and came to the hospital for treatment, then took a job there and stayed on. She lives with her family in the staff quarters. If Mahua and many others had not come to the hospital, they would have spent their lives lying in bed.

After Mini was born in Cambridge, Barbara Reddaway started coming to our place more often. For me, these visits were like an oasis in the desert. Among the people I met during this time, one was Nabi Baksh from Bangladesh. He had also come for a PhD with his wife and daughter. The daughter was ill. I went to their house sometimes. There were also Pranab and Kalpana Bardhan, both students of economics. Jashodhara and Amiya Bagchi were also there. They had a daughter named Tista. Later I met Professor Das and Mrs Dasgupta, Suhas Chakrabarti, and Kalyan Mukherjee. They were all talented people.

Suhas was doing a PhD in history. He spent a lot of time with us, especially taking Jaseem out and about in Cambridge. He spent time with Mini too. One Christmas when Mini was two years old, she didn't want to come back from her friend's house. When I asked Mini why, she said our house was no fun. Suhas and Swadesh went out right away and came back with a Christmas tree and lights for decorating the tree. Jaseem's and Mini's faces lit up, and we all had a great time.

Kalyan Mukherjee was an interesting character. He was a brilliant student of mathematics and had come to do his undergraduate studies at Churchill College. He came over to our place a lot to play bridge and talk with Swadesh, and my kitchen was of course open to everybody. One day when they were playing together, Kalyan suddenly shouted at Suhas, "Hey, what are you doing! You're playing dirty just like a Muslim."

There was no escape for him then—I started shouting at him, and he had to "rub his nose on the ground" in apology. Then he said, "I don't say such things of my own accord! Before I went abroad, my mother took care to warn me, 'Beware, don't you go and marry some East Bengali Muslim girl! There's no one worse than them in the world.'"

Later he went home during a break, married his mother's choice, the beautiful young Deepa, and brought her back to Cambridge. By then, the construction of the students' flats was finished.

Kalyan brought his new wife to our house. When they got out of the taxi in front of our house, people stared at Deepa in astonishment. She was a real beauty, with a flawless figure and a rosy complexion. I grew close to Deepa, and we're still friends. My children called Deepa "Pink Kakima." Everyone in Cambridge called her the "beautiful Indian girl," and it was the truth. She was only eighteen or so and very sweet-natured as well. Kalyan's father Arun Mukherjee was a judge in the Kolkata High Court, later in the Supreme Court. His father died very young. His mother was a schoolteacher. During the Liberation War, when we were in Kolkata, Kalyan, Deepa, and Kalyan's mother kept in touch with us.

Kalyan did a PhD at Cornell and became a mathematics professor. Deepa was very bright and went on to obtain higher degrees also. Kalyan and Deepa separated, and Kalyan went back to India and joined the Indian Statistical Institute. His second wife Lalita was from Andhra Pradesh. I used to see Kalyan whenever I went to Kolkata, but he is now deceased. Deepa (Sucheta Mazumdar) also did a PhD at UCLA and married Vasant Kaiwar, and they are both professors of history at Duke University in North Carolina.

In 1965, while we were still in Cambridge, we learned that my Dadi and many others had been swept away by the flood during a storm and tidal wave. They were never found. When I heard the news, I was numb with grief for several days. I was very close to Dadi; you could say she raised me.

My Dadi was a small person, dusky-skinned. She wasn't at all what people think of as a beauty. Dadi had a huge overbite, and she had a lot of big moles on her face. Baba and my Chachas always made fun of her for her appearance and her supposed low caste.[2]

It's not hard to understand why Dada, and especially his mother, brought Dadi to their house as a bride. Dadi didn't have any brothers. Dadi's father left his ample wealth to my Dadi, thinking that as an older sister she and her husband would look after her little sisters and surely wouldn't cheat them. They did look after her little sisters, but the sisters' children lived in our house as dependents. Dadi had a lot of property. Her name was Rasooljaan Bibi, and the marriage took place when she was only three years old, with her family giving Dada's family countless buffaloes, cows, and a platterful of silver cash. I heard this story from Dadi herself. She came to live with Dada's family only after she reached puberty, as was the custom at the time.

I've already said my Dadi wasn't beautiful in the traditional sense, but it's beyond the scope of this writing to do justice to all her good qualities. She genuinely didn't distinguish between rich and poor, farmers and barbers, Hindus and Muslims—the doors of our house were always open to everyone, thanks mainly to Dadi. Dadi bathed, fed, and lulled to sleep the babies of her domestic helpers, because their mothers were busy with the household chores. If a woman died in childbirth or when her child was an infant, Dadi would take the child into her own arms and the responsibility of raising him or her onto her own shoulders. Dadi was known as "Kabali gai," the kind of cow who gives milk all year long. Whenever any infant put its mouth to her breasts, they would fill with milk immediately. It's not just a story—even I grew up drinking Dadi's milk, because when I was only a year and a half, my mother had another child. So Dadi raised me—as we say in Bangla, "made me a human," with a mother's care and affection. Eighteen years later, Dadi gave her breastmilk to my son Jaseem to calm him down and help him sleep. Dadi was a wet nurse to many women in the village who had to work the fields and could not feed their babies.

When I was studying social work in the United States in the 1980s, I gave Dadi's example during a discussion about human development and nursing. No one believed me then. But a few years later, considerable research was done on this subject, and it was proven that, with emotional attachment and practice, any mother (adopted or natural) can produce enough breastmilk for a child. My class teacher, Ms Aliyari, later praised me for having talked about my Dadi in class that day.

Dadi was heartbroken when Dada forcibly married the child Hamela. After Hamela had three children, Dada suddenly died, effacing all Dadi's feelings of anger, sadness, and wounded pride. Dadi took on the responsibility of raising Hamela's three children and cared for them like her own children.

In the cyclone of 1965, Hamela was also swept away along with Dadi. Grim death took these two women away to the same place.

We were in Cambridge for three and a half years. Ours was Flat No. 3. Even though I felt terribly lonely there at first, I slowly shook off my depression. When I made friends with the other wives in the laundry room, I saw that they were suffering from loneliness and depression just like me. When Mini was a few months old, I got up the nerve to invite them over for coffee. I told them to bring their friends too. That night, I made *shingara* and cake and felt excited and anxious all night. I wondered, would they really come to my house? And if they came, what would I say to them?

The next morning at 10:30, they all showed up at my house one by one, with their children in tow. My home was full of people. Everyone helped make tea and coffee, and the *shingara* and cake disappeared in no time. Before we knew it, it was one o'clock. The party ended with an invitation to have coffee at another woman's house the next day. We spent the next few days laughing, talking, and having a good time together, and the kids had a great time playing together too.

After that, we decided that every day two mothers would take care of all our children while the other mothers could take a break and do shopping, read a book, watch a movie, or take a nap. This was the beginning of our play group, which created a nice, structured network of friends. Our husbands also got to know each other and become friends. We learned a lot about other languages and cultures at our little tea parties and dinner parties. We began inviting each other over on holidays like Christmas and Eid, coming together in good times and bad, playing cards on Saturday, watching certain TV programs together, and so on. We slowly became one big family. Our loneliness and depression were replaced by a feeling of wellbeing and community. Our children had a fantastic time. Later, this experience at Cambridge served me well in new destinations. Even if it was difficult at first, my efforts to connect with others and create a community have always been successful in the end. I've never lacked good friends. I think that if I hadn't spent decades abroad, I wouldn't have mastered this skill.

There was an association known as "Economists' Wives" at Cambridge that enabled the wives of students and teachers to contact each other, introduce new arrivals to those who had been there longer, and offer various kinds of assistance. In addition, there were monthly lunches and tours of the campus. This was really a big help to me. Later when Swadesh was working for the World Bank, I worked with a similar organization. I met many women at the lunches in Cambridge. One time, I met the well-known economist Joan Robinson. She always wore salwar kameez. She told me once that the best clothing in the world is the salwar kameez and the best food is Chinese. She cooked Chinese food herself. I met her husband Professor Austin

Robinson too. He was very fond of Swadesh. After Bangladesh became independent, he visited Dhaka and came to our place.

When we moved to Cambridge, I didn't have much experience in everyday cooking. I took a class called "Cooking for Brides" and learned all the basics: how to boil an egg, how to cut a chicken and filet fish, how to bake a cake and scones, and kitchen hygiene. The foundation of that course coupled with memories of cooking with my family in Bangladesh gave me the confidence to start cooking simple and complex dishes on my own.

John Cockcroft, a Master at Churchill College who later won the Nobel Prize in Physics, invited all his students and their spouses to a dinner at his house once a year. I went to several of these dinners. The food was very simple: before dinner, some nuts and dried fruits, cheese, crackers, and various drinks (juice and wine). The first course was soup with bread and butter, then rice or potatoes with meat or fish (all of it boiled and without spices, of course) and some boiled vegetables. And finally, cake, pie, or ice cream for dessert. I had never encountered food like that before. It wasn't bad really. But the idea of serving guests such simple food amazed me. This would be unimaginable in our country. For us, having guests means three or four days of shopping and planning, then cooking a day ahead; no one would think of serving a meal without elaborate fish and meat dishes, kebabs, polao, korma, or a special *deshi* roast with many spices. Similarly, Swadesh's tutor at Cambridge, Dr Charles Wroth, invited students to an annual dinner, or rather they called it "high tea." I really enjoyed all these social occasions. They were great opportunities to meet all kinds of people from different countries and societies. Swadesh didn't like these things very much. If he had to go to an event for some reason, he wouldn't want to take me along. I still don't understand why. Every college at Cambridge had a monthly dinner for graduate students and their spouses. Swadesh never took me to the Churchill College dinners. He spent most of his time in the Economics Faculty, but he never took me there. Later I got offended and stopped talking to him about these things.

There's another funny story: every year, the queen holds a special garden party at Buckingham Palace. Important people, teachers, and students are invited along with their spouses. When we lived in Cambridge, Swadesh got an invitation to one of these parties. I knew that in England, invitations were always extended to spouses too, but Swadesh went by himself. When he came back, he said for the first time, "I should have taken you with me. Everyone went with their wives." He was always like that. He felt hesitant to introduce me even to his friends.

Every person has their quirks. Swadesh was no exception. When our children grew up, they were also troubled by this awkward aspect of his personality. He never introduced them to his friends or invited anyone to our house. He never talked about himself, not even to the children. After graduating from Wesleyan University, our older daughter Mini went to study at Santiniketan for a year. Swadesh's friend Sunil Sengupta was there. He was from Barisal. When he heard Mini was Swadesh's daughter, he hurried over and hugged her and started crying and talking about all of Swadesh's escapades. Mini listened in amazement and later wrote a letter to Swadesh asking about his political life. I thought, now there's no escape for him. He'll tell his daughter everything. But he wrote her just a single line about his involvement in student politics.

Life in Cambridge was a huge enrichment to my education and knowledge. I was twenty-five when we moved there. Living in that distant land with two small children, I met so many different people. Over coffee in our little kitchen, I talked with women of many different nationalities, colors, and faiths and learned of their joys and sorrows. Barriers of ethnicity, religion, time, and country are only imposed from outside. In every time, in every place, a woman's only identity is as a woman. She is just an object of consumption. When I was growing up in the village, I thought that it must be only in poorly educated and uneducated rural society that women are objectified and oppressed. When I went to study in the city, I saw that even in educated society, a woman's position is the same. Here too she was oppressed. Then I thought maybe the condition of women is like this only in backward societies like ours, and in more developed societies surely women are given much more respect. But when I went abroad, I saw that women were oppressed in almost every household in those countries too. I kept my eyes and ears open and began to understand the place of women in society worldwide. Many girls are victims of sexual abuse at a very young age in their own homes, mostly at the hands of their own close relatives and family friends. I am personally a survivor of abuse, and at the time I had no way to fight back. This social disease was virulent all around me.

I never slept soundly in Barisal or Dhaka or anywhere in Bangladesh. I could never get on a rickshaw or a boat or a car without being fearful of men. I was a skinny, scrawny girl, but they still went after me. Sometimes I wondered how to escape from the hands of these monsters in the guise of civilized people. Most of all, if the one who protects you is the one who consumes you, then who is going to bring him to justice? As I gathered strength and resolve to protect myself and my younger sisters from this evil, the rage in my heart and mind took the terrifying form of an erupting volcano. My bitterness at society and civilization often made my behavior harsh and unpleasant. I forgot how to speak softly and sweetly. People only saw this outwardly harsh nature of mine. No one will ever know the history of how that flowerlike little girl took on such a fearsome form. From a young age, I always kept a keen eye on the girls and women around me. I understood their pain, their immobility, and their helplessness.

Once I made friends with women in Cambridge, I realized they were as helpless as me in this patriarchal society. Their sorrows and mine flowed together. Instead of suffering alone, I gained strength through my women friends. My life had been crushed, shattered because of my gender. In Cambridge, I slowly started putting the pieces back together. Still, sometimes a shriek would suddenly rise inside me; my body and mind would turn blue with pain. I had no control over my own behavior then. When my son Jaseem was a graduate student, one day he saw me in a terrible rage and said to me, "Ma, why are you so angry? I wouldn't want my daughter or sister to be an angry person like you."

I stared at him in surprise. It's true, I don't want my daughters or granddaughters to be harsh-tempered like me either. I took my son's hands, sat him down beside me, and told him about my life, the reasons for my anger and disgust, my sense of helplessness. I don't know what he thought or what he understood. Now I just think, a happy, innocent girl died one moonlit night on the way from her grandfather's house to Moudubi, in an attack by a depraved monster known as her grandmother's cousin. I've never found that girl again, even after all these years. I don't know if I ever will.

In any case, I had many kinds of experiences in Cambridge. Once we went to eat at an Indian restaurant. Seeing us, one of the waiters suddenly vanished. When I asked the person who came to serve us after that, I learned that the gentleman was a fellow student of mine at Dhaka University. He had left out of shame. With a lot of effort, we finally got the gentleman to come talk to us, and we heard his story. He had finished his MA and come to London to study law. He received money regularly from his family. After the India–Pakistan War of 1965, the money stopped coming. I asked him, "Why don't you go home?"

He said, "If I go home after all these years without being a lawyer, how can I show my face to my parents, brothers and sisters, and friends? My friends must all be well settled by now."

I told him, "But you're ashamed to show your face to anyone here too."

That classmate of mine may still be spending his days ashamed and depressed in Cambridge or London. I've met countless young Bengalis like him during my long years abroad. They came with big dreams of returning home with a foreign degree and lots of money but ended up spending their whole lives toiling in a foreign land. My heart goes out to them.

I also met Jyotirmoy Guhathakurta[3] at Cambridge. He came to our house in Cambridge in 1965. He was doing a PhD in London and knew Swadesh from before. He brought his wife Basanti-di and his daughter Dola. Dola was the same age as Jaseem. They had a friend's daughter and Nikhilesh Chakrabarti with them. We were very happy to have them visit and stay with us. At first, I was a little nervous, but their spontaneity made my doubts evaporate. Then one day, Basanti-di cooked a meal for us. She praised my cooking too. We spent a few days engrossed in eating, going out, and talking late into the night. About 3 miles away from Cambridge, there was a village called Cotton. One day, we all walked there and had a great time over tea and sandwiches in a little restaurant.

One day, we met up with a few Bangladeshi graduate students and took a boat (what they call punting there) to the nearby village of Grantchester. There were tables and chairs set up under the apple trees, and we had a splendid tea with hot scones, fresh butter, and homemade jams and jellies. That was quite an experience. When we came back on the boat, Basanti-di stood up and "punted" the boat herself.

The next year, we went to visit them during summer vacation. We stayed at Nikhilesh's place. Jyotirmoy-da and Basanti-di's place was nearby. We went to their place one day, and Basanti-di cooked a wonderful *labra* (a mixed-vegetable dish), roasted *moong dal*, and chicken. When Swadesh started praising her cooking, Jyotirmoy-da said, "Swadesh, as a husband you're still an amateur. Never praise another woman's beauty or cooking in front of your wife."

After eating, we all went to Kew Gardens and had a lovely day. The next day, Nikhilesh took us to Southend-on-Sea, which has the world's longest pier. We walked the whole length of it. The next time and last time that I saw Jyotirmoy-da was in Dhaka on 23 March 1971. On the night of 25 March, he was shot dead by the Pakistan Army. After three years, our time in Cambridge came to an end. Azizur and Mahua Khan had gone back to Karachi before us. Our other friends were packing their bags one by one. Professor Amiya Dasgupta and his wife had left long before, right after Mini was born. The day I brought Mini home from the hospital, they came to see us, because they were leaving Cambridge the next day. When Mini went to study art at Santiniketan, she got a chance to see Professor Dasgupta, who was spending his retirement there. When I visited Mini in Santiniketan, I also got a chance to see the Dasguptas again. We went for afternoon tea and snacks at their house every day. They wouldn't let us leave without eating *shingara* and *roshogolla*.

Professor Dasgupta was from Barisal, so I knew many of his friends and relatives. I was close to his younger sister Monikuntala Sen, Satu Sen, Sharat Guha and his daughters, Shanti and Manorama Guha (my teachers), and many others. Because of my involvement in politics, I was friendly with everyone in the art, cultural, and political worlds of Barisal. So there was no end to the stories we shared.

When we were in Cambridge, we couldn't go as many places as I wanted. Swadesh was very busy with his studies, and our budget was also very tight. Still, we did go to London several times. We visited Kew Gardens. For the first time, I saw the camellias of Rabindranath Tagore's famous poem[4] and rhododendrons that reminded me of the line in *Shesher Kobita*: "... the clusters of rhododendron flowers crowning the impudent branches."[5] When we bought our first house in Washington, the first things I planted in front of that house were a camellia and a rhododendron. I cared for them myself for a long thirty-two years. They filled the front of my house with flowers, and passersby would stop to look at them. Later when we had to sell that house, I cried my heart out for those flowers—not for anything else.

I didn't want to return home to Bangladesh without seeing Shakespeare's birthplace, Stratford-on-Avon. When I was a student in college, the character Portia from *The Merchant of Venice* had made an impression on me. D. N. C. Sir at BM College taught this text wonderfully. He also acted out each character brilliantly for us.

We settled on a day to see Shakespeare's birthplace. We got on the bus with Jaseem and Mini, feeling very excited. On the way, we saw cornfields, cows, sheep, and pretty little houses. Some barns and farmhouses. There were barns full of wheat and corn everywhere. They don't farm with cows like in our country; here they did everything with machines. I wondered when Bengali farmers would see such good times. They could get a better yield with less work.

Finally, we reached Stratford. Our bus was full of tourists, and the place was teeming with people. It was a holiday, so it was very crowded. Just like us, all the other passengers on the bus were eager to see the town full of memories of the world-famous playwright. We hurried off the bus and went toward the river, where we saw a statue of Falstaff (a comic character from *King Lear*) standing there with his huge potbelly. Mini kept stroking that huge statue's belly and saying, "So soft, so soft!" Jaseem and Mini stopped right there and started playing hide-and-seek. Shakespeare's theater on the bank of the River Avon was a sight to see. Since we hadn't reserved tickets in advance, we couldn't see the play. Anyway, we hadn't tried to buy tickets since Mini was only two. Jaseem and Mini ran around to their hearts' content on the lovely big lawn next to the building. Then we took the tourist bus to the house where Shakespeare was born. It was a small one-room house with a few things in it. I don't know if those things were from that time or not. The beds were very small, and the doorway was low. When I asked the guide, he said people were shorter then. The house was 450 years old.

A mile from there was the house of Shakespeare's wife Anne Hathaway. This house was very beautifully built. If I hadn't seen that house, I wouldn't have known how beautiful a thatched roof could be. In front was a lovely flower garden. It looked to me like Anne's father must have been a rich farmer. Shakespeare, on the other hand, was the son of a common farmer. The guide told us that in those days, when someone came to eat at a common farmer's house, they had to bring their own spoons and forks, because those families couldn't afford to keep extras. Finally, the day came to an end, and we went home full of happy memories.

*Back to Karachi*

Swadesh finished his PhD within the expected time, just three years. The topic of his thesis was: "Regional Cooperation for Development in South Asia: With Special Reference to India and Pakistan." It was considered a very controversial topic, and though Cambridge University Press wanted to publish the thesis as a book, the Pakistani government was strongly against publication. So Swadesh was unable to publish.[6] In 1967, we came back to Karachi, and Swadesh rejoined PIDE. We rented a flat on the top floor of a two-story building in the Kokan Society. At first, the landlord and his family treated us very well, but later they started acting strange. They kept turning off the water and electricity, and whenever they met us, they would turn their faces away. We couldn't understand why. I used to buy rice, dal, oil, and spices at the shop next door. One day, the shop owner advised me to leave that house and go somewhere else. When I asked why, he told me that in the 1947 Hindu–Muslim riots the Hindus had murdered the landlord's father, so they were anti-Hindu. He also said that they might try to do us harm.

This made me afraid. I told Swadesh, and after talking about it we decided to leave that house as soon as possible. I had grown very close to the family next door, so we asked their advice. The husband went with Swadesh the very same day to look for another house and came back shortly with news of a possibility. With the help of those neighbors, we moved to the new house the next day.

The new house was only one story. The area was called Rohail Khand Housing Society. On one side lived the widowed landlady with her son and two daughters, and we lived on the other side. We became friends in no time. Three-year-old Mini spent most of her time with them.

After we came back from Cambridge to Karachi, Jaseem was enrolled at St Patrick's. Swadesh dropped him off at school and picked him up. All the students there had to learn Urdu, although the medium of instruction was English. I went to see the principal and said my son would learn Bangla instead of Urdu. He said that I had to take responsibility for teaching him Bangla myself, so I arranged a Bangla tutor for him. After that, another Bengali friend of mine, Anwara Siddique, also made the same arrangement for her three sons. There was also a Bangla school in Karachi. Mahua Khan taught there.

Later I also put Mini in a nursery school. It was called Mrs Hawkins' Nursery School. A woman from Scotland had started this school. It was a little far from our house. I dropped Mini off there by bus and picked her up. At the time of day when she got out of school, the streets were completely empty.

One day, I was standing on the side of the road waiting for the bus to go pick Mini up from school, when a car suddenly pulled up in front of me. The driver opened the door, got out, and asked me to get into the car. When I said no, he insisted, practically ordering me to get in the car, and I got scared. Just then a bus came, and I jumped on the bus. After that, I took Mini out of that school. Later I enrolled her in a school in our own neighborhood, walking distance from our house.

Right next to our house was Hill Park, which was a little hill, a nice place to walk around. There was a restaurant there that sold samosas, pakoras, *phuchka*, kebabs, *porota*, drinks, and tea. Once Jaseem got terribly sick after eating samosas with tamarind chutney there. Swadesh was out of the country at the time, so I asked our friend Arthur MacEwan, who worked at PIDE, for help. Jaseem was so weak that Arthur had to pick him up and carry him to the car. If I hadn't admitted him to the hospital, he might not have survived. After four or five days of treatment, he recovered and came home. I was very close to Arthur and his wife Phyllis.

There were a few other American families there. We were great friends with Toby and Ann Clark for a long time. Toby and Swadesh wrote a paper together. Ann and Toby's oldest child Elizabeth was the same age as Mini. When their second child Carter was born, Ann went back to the United States for a while. Toby threw quite a few lovely dinner parties then. We went sightseeing with them several times. We went on a boat trip on the Arabian Sea and caught a lot of crabs. I taught Ann's cook how to shell crabs. My father used to make crab *bhaji* and feed it to us children. Ma didn't eat crabs. In Karachi, I learned how to cook crabs myself.

One time, we went with Toby and Ann to the nearby town of Thatta. It's an old town, with a beautiful old mosque. We went around and saw all the sights. There were a lot of tourists, especially foreigners. Ann bought an old iron (it had to be heated with coal) and two iron *bonti-da* (large, curved knives fixed upright in a wooden base) complete with *korani* (coconut scrapers) from the market. Later I went to their house in Washington and saw those things nicely displayed in their living room. In the house of another wealthy friend in Washington I saw a *badana* (pitcher used in the toilet) from our country on display.

We became close friends with Mark and Jean Leiserson soon after we moved to Karachi. Such good friends are rare. They were a lot like family to us. Later it was Mark who persuaded Swadesh to join the World Bank, and we ended up spending a large part of our lives in the United States. We remained friends with Jean and Mark until their death and are still in touch with their wonderful children and grandchildren.

In Karachi, a lot of foreign women came to me to learn how to wear saris. Sometimes we gave cooking lessons at each other's houses. Once, I taught the women how to make *luchi*. After the cooking, everyone would eat and talk together. Our husbands were at their offices, our children were in school, the little ones came with us, everyone had one or more domestic helpers. Sometimes on days off there would be invitations to dinner, lunch, or tea.

Among the Bengali families we knew in Karachi were Hasan Imam and Fozaila. They had one daughter named Shetu. She was good friends with both our girls and is still close to them. Fozaila and Hasan Imam were like family to us. Hasan Imam also worked at PIDE and had done a PhD in economics in England.

In Karachi, I also got to know Akhlaq Bhai and his family, who moved there a year or two after we arrived. Saeedul Haq and Loni were also there. I had met them in England when they lived in London. We also went to their place in London. Akhlaq Bhai and Saeedul Haq worked at United Bank. In return, they got huge furnished houses, big cars, and all kinds of conveniences. When we went to their houses, our children would stare in amazement at all these luxuries. We went for picnics with them. One time, we all went to Haleji Lake. Each family had cooked something. Akhlaq Bhai's wife had asked me to bring my famous (in her opinion) potato salad and cake. Loni brought *khichuri* and roast chicken. We went and ate together. Akhlaq Bhai tried to catch fish but had no luck. On the way back, we bought a huge *rui* (carp) fish. With Akhlaq Bhai and his family, we went to Hawk's Bay, Sound Beach, and a beach near the Defense Colony several times. He was always the life of the party.

Akhlaq Bhai's older daughter Tahmina was younger than Jaseem. Liza was Mini's age, and their son Tapan was younger. They were all playmates. Later Tania, the daughter of Akhlaq Bhai's earlier wife, also came to Karachi. Tania was at a difficult age, maybe fourteen or fifteen. One night, she came over to our house without telling anybody. We didn't have a phone then, so Swadesh went himself that same night to tell Akhlaq Bhai not to worry about Tania. A few days later, we took Tania back home. Akhlaq Bhai was like our guardian in Karachi. He was our protector in all kinds of trouble.

Akhlaq Bhai, Swadesh, and Nuruddin used to play bridge together, sometimes all night. Since we didn't have a phone, I wouldn't know when Swadesh was coming home. I used to argue with Swadesh about it a lot. Later they agreed to play for a fixed amount of time. If he lost the game, Akhlaq Bhai would get very upset and shout. Many people had their complaints about Akhlaq Bhai, but it's hard to find a match for him in compassion and willingness to jump in and help at his own risk.

We were happy in Karachi, but it was extremely difficult for me not to be able to go to see my family and friends in East Pakistan. From the time I married Swadesh and came to Karachi in 1963 until 1967, I didn't see any of my relatives or friends back home. In December of 1967, when Jaseem's school let out, we went to Dhaka. Karim Chacha was living in a one-room apartment in Dhaka's Purana Paltan. The apartment had a veranda, a bathroom, and a setup for cooking. We couldn't stay there because there were four of us. So Karim Chacha rented another room from the same landlord in another building for one month. The advantage of this was we could stay close by without imposing on each other. We spent all day at Karim Chacha's and ate there, then came back to our own place to sleep.

I then headed south to see my family and friends. First, we went to Barisal by steamer and stayed at Lutfa and Fakr's place for a few days. I saw almost all my friends in Barisal and had a great time. One day, I went to Rab Serniyabat Chacha's place and heard that Arju's wedding had been arranged with Sheikh Moni. They had chosen each other. Arju was making her own blouse to match her wedding sari. Her face was shining with happiness.

Later I left Swadesh in Barisal and headed to Barobaishdia with Jaseem and Mini. I was going there after almost five years, so my mind was full of happiness and anticipation. Jaseem and Mini also couldn't contain their excitement, constantly asking when we would arrive at their Nana's house. Mini was a little over three years old then. It was hard to keep her calm. Everything was new to her. The launches, boats, huts, rice fields stretching to the horizon, ponds, and especially the people. In the village were her Nana, Nanu, khalas, mamas, and countless other relatives and friends. Mini was enthralled by the fruits, vegetables, ducks, chickens, cows, and goats at the house. They kept her busy all day. She'd go fetch eggs from the ducks' house, help my sisters pick broad beans and long beans, boil and eat them, run around in the rice fields with her khalas and mamas or Jaseem—she wouldn't leave the cats and dogs alone either. They were in a bad state from all her petting and pampering. There was a cat in our house whose name was also Mini. That made Mini very upset. But Ma had named the cat before Mini was born. Indeed, many cats in Bengal are called Mini.

Then we ran into a problem with Mini. Later we found a good solution. Most homes in the village had rudimentary outhouses.

Mini absolutely refused to use the outhouses. In our region, we used to cook outside in the winter. They would build various kinds of stoves with sticky clay next to the permanent kitchen and cook on those. The women with their creative genius made all kinds of wonderful stoves. In the dry season, it was very convenient to cook outside. You could talk to the neighbors while cooking. My mother made a mud stove and told Mini that this was her toilet. Mini liked this arrangement very much. It looked a lot like her training potty! My mother made a new toilet every day, and my daughter very happily used them. I don't know what Ma did with them after that.

Mini had been begging to get her ears pierced like the big girls. There was a woman in Katakhali called Malekar Ma who used to pierce the ears and noses of little girls in the village. She also made a name for herself sewing quilts and doing other handicrafts. Malekar Ma pierced my daughter Mini's ears during her first visit to Katakhali at age three. My mother also helped by holding Mini and keeping her calm. Malekar Ma had a very interesting story. During the British era, her husband was known as a famous thief. He had been to jail many times. Finally, the British government sent the whole family to the Andaman Islands. This was a thrilling event in our village. After the creation of Pakistan, they came back to the village and were given the status of hero and heroine. Everyone ran over to see them. Actually, no one from the village had ever gone to such a far-off place by train or steamer, and this couple had not only traveled to but had lived for long years and made their home in an unknown, unfamiliar dreamworld. Now everyone addressed that thief's wife as Malekar Ma (Maleka's mother). She was cheerful and pretty. The villagers listened to her stories like fairy tales. This Malekar Ma had brought something new with her: a manual machine for cutting *semai* noodles (thin like vermicelli) for making the dessert *semai*. Everyone crowded around to watch her make *semai* noodles with this machine in wide-eyed wonder. If you made a dough of ground rice and pushed it into one end of the machine while turning the handle with the other hand, beautiful fine *semai* noodles came out. You dried them in the sun, and you were done. Malekar Ma's status in the village rose precipitously. Everyone invited her over with that machine, and she performed this task of making *semai* with great pride. Once, she used to hide in shame as a thief's wife, and later she was so respected.

All too soon, our time in Katakhali was over. Swadesh took Jaseem back to Karachi because his school was starting. Mini and I stayed in Dhaka a little longer. My younger sister Runu was living with Karim Chacha in Dhaka. Everyone was worried about her education and her prospects for marriage. While I was in Dhaka, she got a few proposals, but Swadesh and Karim Chacha didn't like any of them. In the end, Runu came with me to Karachi. Within two months, I realized I was pregnant again. My physical and mental condition were very bad during my first two pregnancies, and this time was no exception. I was always vomiting and couldn't eat anything. In short, I could barely get out of bed. When they heard the news, all my foreigner friends came to see me. At the time, Ann and Toby's work in Karachi was over, and they were about to leave. I bought all the necessary baby gear from Ann: a baby cot, changing table, pram, and many other things. I hadn't brought any of Mini's things from Cambridge, so I had to buy these things again. Later Phyllis MacEwan also left Karachi. My close friend Ingaboke Floystad, who was Norwegian, also left Karachi. They had a son named Gunnar who was three or four and played with Mini.

Before leaving, Ingaboke came to see me in the hospital and gave me a book: *She Came to Stay* by Simone de Beauvoir. After reading this book and *The Second Sex* by the same feminist author, the ideas I had held all my life changed forever. The first change in my thinking came from my exposure to Marxism–Leninism. Now, reading these books by de Beauvoir changed my way of analyzing personal life. I found out the causes of many unknown, ill-understood problems. I understood the history of the ups and downs of my own life from the lens of gender. The relationship between women and men is not the creation of one person in one day. There are a thousand years of well-planned patriarchy behind it. Women are not weak, helpless, or stupid. They have been made that way for men's personal interests and to maintain their dominance in society.

I was in Dhaka for about two months. During this time, there was a big change in Mini's speech. She was born in Cambridge, and we spoke English with her from the start. We thought if we were living there, she needed to know English. Her friends all spoke English. I never thought about the fact that it's no problem at all to teach a child two languages. Mini understood Bangla, but she couldn't speak it. All our relatives and friends in Dhaka spoke Bangla. For the first two or three weeks, Mini didn't speak at all, just listened to everyone. Then suddenly one day she started talking, and that too in Bangla! We silently took notice of this change in her. Even after we went back to Karachi, she continued speaking Bangla. Our landlady asked her in English one day, "Where is your mother?" When Mini kept quiet, she asked in Urdu, "Tumhara Ammi kidhar hai?" Mini answered, "No mother, no Ammi, say 'Ma kothay?'"

Flabbergasted, the woman came and told me what Mini said. I was astounded too. After that, Mini spoke Bangla beautifully with everyone. When our foreign friends came over, she didn't talk, she kept very quiet.

We were in Karachi for three and a half years. I could have learned Urdu if I wanted, but I didn't. Whenever I met West Pakistani neighbors or friends from Swadesh's office, they would start talking to me in Urdu. They never even asked if I knew

Urdu or not; they assumed I must know Urdu. This made me feel angry and offended. They refused to learn Bangla, but they insisted we had to learn Urdu. They thought of themselves as superior to us. A lot of people criticized me for not wearing salwar kameez and for wearing a *teep* (bindi). They told me repeatedly that saris and *teeps* are for Hindus. After my youngest daughter was born, the landlady came to see her. When she heard that her name is Anita, she looked unhappy and said, "That's not a Musalmani name, it's a Hindu name."

I didn't like their bossing me around even about my own daughter's name. "Anita" means unrelenting or unbowed in Bangla. After Anita was born, we also gave Mini a longer name, "Monica," which means small gem in Bangla.[7]

During Ramadan, the neighbors would always ask me whether I was fasting or not. I didn't fast, so I would say no. They would make a face and scold me for it. There were Bengali male domestic helpers in almost all the middle- and upper-class houses. They were very polite and hard-working. On their days off, these Bengali boys would come to see me and talk about their troubles and their families. They told me that in the houses where they worked, hardly anyone fasted, and they cooked three meals a day. But they would always tell outsiders they were fasting and send *iftari*[8] regularly. When we lived in PECHS,[9] I noticed that nobody fasted in the house opposite. We could see for ourselves—since we lived above the garage, we could see what people were doing in their houses whenever we wanted. They cooked three meals a day even during Ramadan. But when they saw me, they would profusely advise me to fast.

In Karachi, my sister Runu took her higher secondary exams. During her exams, we learned that Shanti Babu's wife Bithi was also taking the exams. Shanti Babu was teaching her himself. Then I became very sick. I couldn't eat or even walk. I had to go to the doctor regularly. One day, I noticed that my eyes and my whole body had turned yellowish. I went to the doctor, and he agreed that I had jaundice, which was confirmed by various tests. I had to be admitted to the hospital right away and spent six weeks there. A few days after I recovered and went home, I had to go to the hospital again with labor pain. Anita was born on 30 August 1968 at 1:15 pm at Holy Family Hospital. Anita had a round face and a head full of black hair.

Not long before Anita was born, we had to move again. The same problem cropped up in the Rohilkhand house as well. When the landlady found out that Swadesh was Hindu, she started treating us badly. Swadesh was at a loss trying to find a new house. A gentleman named Dr Ghori had a house in PECHS. Sayyad Manzur Elahi and his wife Nilufar rented a part of this house, and our famous singer Runa Laila's mother lived downstairs with her two daughters Runa and Deena and her young son. Runa was a schoolgirl then. Runa Laila's father was a civil servant. He lived in East Pakistan and came to Karachi from time to time. Runa's mother seemed a bit conceited and didn't mix with Bengalis, but Runa and Deena were very polite and talkative. Finally, we got a flat in that building. We lived in a flat at the back above four garages.

It took a long time to take Mini to nursery school if we walked on the road, so our landlord suggested we could take a shortcut through Runa's family's garden. I went and asked Runa's mother for permission to use the shortcut through her garden, but she didn't agree, so I had to take Mini to school the long way.

Swadesh, Mini, and Ani came down with chicken pox when Ani was around one. Apparently, Swadesh had never had chicken pox before, and he became very ill contracting it as an adult. Jaseem and I had already had chicken pox in Barisal, so we were spared this time. That year, there was also a bad outbreak of the more deadly smallpox. A hospital was designated for smallpox patients. No doctor would make house calls. I called Aziz Khan and all our other Bengali friends from Swadesh's office to let them know that Swadesh had chicken pox. Everyone I called told me to send Swadesh to the hospital, but I absolutely refused because I was afraid he would get smallpox there. I knew one Dr Motaleb in Karachi. Seeing no alternative, I took a taxi to his house. He lived very far away in Nazimabad. When I finally found his house, I learned that he had moved.

Akhlaq Bhai was in Bangladesh then. But I went to his house too and left word that Swadesh was sick. As soon as he returned to Karachi a couple of days later, he drove over with a doctor in the middle of the night. He had told the doctor that the patient was his brother and had to be saved at any cost. No one but Akhlaq Bhai would have said something like that. Swadesh's whole body was swollen, his eyes were blood red, he had a 103 or 104-degree fever, and he was vomiting frequently. The doctor gave him antibiotics and some other medicines right away. He and Akhlaq Bhai spent the rest of the night with me. Toward morning, Swadesh's fever went down, and he fell asleep. When I think what would have happened if Akhlaq Bhai hadn't come that day, my heart still skips a beat. I'll never forget my debt to him.

We had to move one more time in Karachi. This time, we took a house in Tariq Road. The house was big and had a lot of doors. In front was a huge mango tree. We lived downstairs, and the landlord lived upstairs. He was polite and friendly. One of their daughters had married a Bangladeshi. While we were living there, on 7 December 1970, Pakistan had its general elections for the National Assembly. The day before the election, the landlord told us not to go vote for fear of trouble, so we didn't go. When we heard the election results on television, we were overjoyed. A month before the election, Cyclone Bhola killed around 500,000 people in the southern part of East Pakistan, not far from Barobaishdia Island. Everyone noticed the failure of the Pakistani government to prepare for the storm and to provide emergency relief afterwards. Because of this, language tyranny, and other issues, the people of East Pakistan were roaring with rage and despair. They responded with their vote, voting en masse for the Awami League, led by Bangabandhu Sheikh Mujibur Rahman.[10] Swadesh had visited Dhaka just before the election. When Swadesh came back from Dhaka, he said, "East Pakistan might become independent."

In December 1970, PIDE shifted to Dhaka, and we went home soon after. Swadesh and his Bengali colleagues had strategically argued that PIDE should be in East Pakistan because that was where more needed to be spent on development. It would also be safer for them to be in East Pakistan seeing the growing movement toward independence. We happily started making plans for the move. We were going home after so long! It felt so good to think about it—I had been separated from my parents, relatives, siblings, friends, and above all the soil of my homeland. I had the song "My Golden Bengal, I Love You" running through my head day and night. Whatever household items we had accumulated in our three years in Karachi, the Bengali boys I knew came and took them away in a donkey cart. Unburdened, we stretched our limbs and set out for our own country.

PART 5

# WAR AND LIBERATION

*A timely move to Dhaka*

Swadesh was so busy with shifting the PIDE office that he didn't have time to look for a house for us. When we first came to Dhaka, we stayed at our friend Khandakar Nurul Islam's house. Later we rented a single-story house on Road No. 24 in Dhanmondi on the eastern side of Abahani Maath (a playing field). The landlord was Muslim League leader Sabur Khan's[1] older brother Abdul Goni Khan. On the other side of the wall behind our house was Sabur Khan's huge house. In front of our house, there were red poinsettias and hibiscus flowers of many colors all along the wall. The house had large verandas on both sides. It was a perfect place for Ani and Mini to play.

To us, the Abahani Field was like a public thoroughfare. During the days of March 1971, we were witnessing the people's independence movement even sitting at home. Processions of little schoolchildren, of everyone from street people to farmers and laborers, went through this field every day toward Road No. 32 and the house of Bangabandhu Sheikh Mujibur Rahman. Having come home after so long, we shuddered to see the despair and frustration the public were expressing. We felt one with them. Since I had been living abroad for a long time, I felt deprived of a sense of the step-by-step progression of the people's struggle for liberation. Whenever my children and I heard a procession going by, we would go and stand outside, clap our hands, and cheer the marchers on. I took a lot of pictures of the processions too, but sadly, both the pictures and the camera were ruined after sitting idle through the nine months of the Liberation War.

My daughters were then six and two-and-a-half. Imam and Fozaila's daughter Shetu came to play with them almost every day. They would march on our veranda with flags in their hands, shouting slogans. They played this game all day long. On 21 February, I took the children to the Shaheed Minar[2] and saw the real face of the people's movement. We heard quite a few new slogans. When my daughters got home, they started using those slogans too: "Kick Bhutto in the face, free Bangladesh!" They asked me to make a flag.

The last few months in Karachi, Swadesh had worked incredibly hard; he ate and slept irregularly and never gave himself any rest. Right after we moved to Dhaka, he fell sick with a high fever and a pain in his leg bone. We had just come back and didn't know a good doctor. One of our neighbors was a doctor, so I asked him to come over. After examining Swadesh, he advised me to admit him to a hospital. I followed his advice and took Swadesh to Holy Family Hospital. After a lot of tests, they called a bone specialist, who said there was a serious infection in the bone, and without proper treatment it might have to be amputated.

So he started treatment. Everyone told me, "Don't waste your time trying to treat a serious illness like that here. You should send him to get treatment abroad." I made all the arrangements, but Swadesh refused to be separated from the family given the uncertain state of the country.

Meanwhile, the political situation was going from bad to worse. Even though Sheikh Mujib's Awami League had won an absolute majority, the current government was not willing to let him form the government for all of Pakistan. We saw constant protests and marches and the signs of ordinary people's discontent. Discussions were under way between Yahya Khan—Pakistan's President and an Army General—and Bangabandhu in the interest of reaching a compromise. The real problem was, the people had voted for Bangabandhu Sheikh Mujibur Rahman, but the West Pakistani leaders, especially Zulfikar Ali Bhutto, were completely unwilling to admit this fact. They had used religious slogans to create Pakistan and pursued their own ends this way for many years, exploiting East Pakistan all along. Now it was difficult for them to accept that their days in power were numbered. They had never even thought of the common people of East Pakistan as human beings—why would they hand over their power to them!

On 7 March, Bangabandhu called for a non-cooperation movement. There was a tremendous response from the governmental and non-governmental organizations of East Pakistan. Everyone was amazed by this response. The common people also responded to the call. Meanwhile, the government of Pakistan kept up the farce of negotiation while they began secretly transporting soldiers and weapons from West Pakistan. People were saying something like this might be going on, but no one was expecting such a huge betrayal.

The Students' League made announcements several days in a row that on 23 March everyone should fly the Bangladeshi flag from their houses and vehicles. They gave a description of the flag: a red map of Bangladesh on a green background. We were trembling with excitement. My sister Runu was at my house, because an unknown fear had compelled me to bring her home from her dorm room in Rokeya Hall at Dhaka University, where she was now enrolled. On the evening of 22 March, the two of us made two Bangladeshi flags together. That day, Dr Jyotirmoy Guhathakurta, our old friend and now a professor of English at Dhaka University, came to our house with his wife Basanti-di and their daughter Dola. I was very happy to see them. I made tea and Jyotirmoy-da's favorite fried chicken. After we ate, Jyotirmoy-da whispered to me to teach Basanti-di the recipe. When he saw that we were making flags, he warned me, "Noorjahan, you're Swadesh Bose's wife. Don't be too quick to raise the flag. Take a good look around you beforehand."

Then he said, "The rain will come soon. I'll come and help you plant your garden." Sadly, that garden was not to be.

On the morning of 23 March, my children and I walked to Road No. 32. We crossed the bridge and stood near Bangabandhu's house. I saw many different groups of marchers coming and gathering in front of Bangabandhu's house. Suddenly I saw a vast procession led by the Students' League coming that way, flying a huge Bangladeshi flag. Then Bangabandhu came out and stood on the front veranda. The student leaders handed him the flag. Slogans shook the air. My whole body was trembling with excitement. I thought, who can stop this vast ocean of humanity? It felt wonderful to think that I was one of them.

Then we hurried home. There was a spontaneous flag-hoisting competition going on all around. I flew into the house and told Swadesh we were going to raise the flag. We all ran up to the roof, and in that memorable moment, we raised the flag of Bangladesh in our own home. When I saw the flag fluttering in the wind, my chest swelled with pride, and my eyes filled with happy tears.

There was a flood of euphoria all over the city, and yet we were also gripped by fear. I thought, will the Pakistani leaders accept this bold move? Since '66, with the announcement of a six-point "Charter of Survival," Bengalis had been agitating for self-determination for East Pakistan under the leadership of Bangabandhu Sheikh Mujibur Rahman. I thought, let's see "where the water rolls!" On 24 and 25 March, we started hearing news of unrest everywhere. My brother Taslim and a young relative called Sobhan were staying with me then. They went out during the day to bring back the news. There were rumors all around that martial law was about to go into effect.

On 26 March, a huge procession went through the Abahani Field toward Bangabandhu's home on Road No. 32. The marchers came from far-away villages. One procession after another came through the Abahani Field that day. Many marchers were carrying flags. We went out and watched from the veranda, and I took a few pictures. The day went by in great excitement. In the evening, we went to Dr Nurul Islam's house and then to Hasan Imam's house to hear the news, but neither of them was home. When we got back, we heard Bangabandhu's voice roaring on the television—"Whatever you have on hand, use it to fortify your homes. The struggle ahead of us is the struggle for our liberation, it is the struggle for our independence." Right after this snippet of his 7 March speech, the TV shut off. We sank into a strange terror.

We sensed something ominous in the air. I tucked the children into bed with a thumping heart. Eventually we fell asleep, I don't know when. At midnight, a sudden sound woke me up. When I got up and went to the window, I saw a long line of armored vehicles on the main road; I remember there were tanks among them. They were going along Sat Masjid Road toward the EPR (East Pakistan Rifles) headquarters. There were no lights on along the street. The tanks and armored cars were creeping ahead using their own dim lights. Swadesh told me in a low voice, "I think the government of Pakistan has sent in the military." We realized the rumors were true: while the Pakistani government pretended to negotiate, they had been preparing under cover. A few minutes later, we heard the roar of guns and saw flames leaping into the sky. The sound of gunfire was coming from the direction of the EPR headquarters. Later we heard gunfire and saw flames leaping all around us. I hustled the children out of the room by the street and tucked them into bed in the middle room. Swadesh and I spent the whole night by the window. A rite of destruction was going on all around, and we were only silent witnesses. Finally, that black night of 25 March came to an end.

In the morning, I went up to the roof to look around. I saw the military's armored cars in the main road, roving around with guns raised. The government declared a curfew. There were jeeps in Abahani Field with loudspeakers blaring in Urdu that we were ordered to take down the Bangladeshi flag and raise the flag of Pakistan. I watched from the roof and saw that out of fear, many people were taking down their Bangladeshi flags and raising the Pakistani flag. We didn't have a Pakistani flag then. What could I do? In the end, I cut up an old sari to sew a makeshift Pakistani flag and flew it from the roof. When I took down the Bangladeshi flag, I felt like I was cutting out my own liver. Jaseem carefully folded the two Bangladeshi flags and hid them in a plastic bag. Later he went out in the dark and dug a hole in the dirt behind the house and buried them. Jaseem told me, "We'll fly these flags again after Independence." We didn't get a chance to do that, because it was a rented house; we never went back to that house after Independence.

The house right behind ours belonged to the Muslim League leader Sabur Khan. On the night of 25 March, there was a crowd of people in that house, and feasting, music, and noise all night long. During the non-cooperation movement throughout the month of March, this house had been completely quiet. A Pakistani soldier guarded the house. I used to see him sitting silently on the veranda; the poor thing started and looked around in fright whenever he heard a procession going by. When the girls made their play processions on the veranda of our house, flying their flags and shouting slogans, he watched in silence. From the morning of 26 March, he changed completely. I saw him strutting around with a raised gun, looking defiantly at all the neighboring houses.

On the 27th, the curfew was lifted for a little while. Many people came out of their homes to exchange news. The city was full of rumors. Some were saying that Dhaka University had been reduced to ruins, that no students or teachers were left alive, that the Pakistani military had killed a lot of university teachers. They said a lot of politicians were dead too, that the Pakistani military had killed Bangabandhu along with all the top Awami League leaders.

I went up to the roof again to look around. That day too, the military jeeps and trucks were roving the roads, and they had sent out a lot of orders. Some other people were out on their roofs too. Suddenly, one of the military jeeps opened fire. At the sound of gunfire, I dropped to the floor, and then I crept downstairs. I didn't go up to the roof after that. Since the 26th, we had been trying to listen to the news on the radio. On the 28th, Jaseem was sitting at home turning the knob of the radio, and suddenly he shouted, "Ma, come here! Our war of independence has started."

We all ran in and crowded around the radio. The same announcement kept repeating: "This is Major Ziaur Rahman. On behalf of Bangabandhu Sheikh Mujibur Rahman, I hereby declare Bangladesh independent. Our War of Liberation has begun. Wherever you are, please cooperate with us. We are preparing to confront the enemy."

He kept repeating this. From time to time, the radio suddenly shut off; it kept blaring, then shutting off, blaring and shutting off. We had a hope, a desperate hope, that our young men, especially the Bengali soldiers, were not sitting idle. The call had come to prepare to liberate the country, to rise up against the Pakistani government. The preparations had begun.

At the same time, we realized after the violence of 25–6 March that the Pakistani military was killing mostly Hindus, along with leaders and workers of the Awami League and progressive artists, writers, and intellectuals. Even ordinary people were dying at their hands indiscriminately. The people of Dhaka were trying to escape wherever they could. But we didn't know what to do. I thought, where can I go with Swadesh, who will take us in?

One day, I sent Taslim and Sobhan to Karim Chacha's house. When they got there, they found that everyone had left Dhaka even before 25 March. Meanwhile, I needed to refill Swadesh's prescription. I went to Dr Omar's clinic. He looked at me in surprise and said, "You're still in Dhaka! Take Dr Bose and get out of Dhaka any way you can. I'm giving you three months' worth of medicine and a certificate stating that Dr Bose is not fit for work."

Dr Omar helped me a lot that day, but I never got a chance to thank him. His wife was a British citizen, so they both went to London. I never saw them again; I don't know where they are now.

I told Swadesh Dr Omar's advice. Swadesh just looked at me silently; he didn't say anything. A close friend of ours, Aminul Islam, lived in the next street. Our daughters and their daughters were playmates. I thought I would ask Aminul to hide Swadesh in their house, and I would stay home with the children. As soon as this thought occurred to me, I went over to Aminul's house and asked him and his wife to let Swadesh shelter in their house. They agreed. Aminul Islam was a top executive at Lever Brothers. That evening, Aminul Islam came and picked Swadesh up in his car along with some clothes and medicines and took him to their house. I felt a huge weight off my chest.

I think that was 29 or 30 March. After Aminul took Swadesh in, I thought if he was safe there, I had nothing to worry about. Even though it was hard not to have Swadesh with me, I felt relieved. But just two days later, Aminul Islam bought Swadesh back. I said, "What's the matter?"

Aminul Islam told me that their domestic helpers knew Swadesh, so he didn't have the confidence to keep him there anymore.

I was crestfallen. Now what should I do? Then I thought of Khandakar Nurul Islam. He was an old friend of Swadesh's; they used to live together in Karachi. We had stayed at his house in Mogbazar for a month after moving back to Dhaka from Karachi. I thought maybe he could help.

At that time, no one would enter the main road unless they had no choice. Even men wouldn't go out, much less women. But I had no choice. One day, I pulled my sari over my head, got on a rickshaw, and nervously set off from Dhanmondi for Nurul Islam's house in Mogbazar. The streets were hauntingly empty; only the military jeeps and trucks were roaring back and forth, shaking the street. Finally, I reached Nurul Islam's house, but they didn't look happy to see me. The house was full of people, and all the men were wearing caps. The way they were talking made me uncomfortable. Even so, I told Nurul Islam about Swadesh and asked him if he could help me send Swadesh to a safe place. He flatly refused. I set off for home crestfallen.

Later the same day, I went to Lalmatia. Another gentleman lived there who worked at PIDE and knew Swadesh. We used to visit his house in Karachi. I went and told him our problem, but he couldn't help me either. He refused very politely. I thought, what can I do in this state of affairs? Then suddenly I remembered an aunt of my mother's, her Phuphu, who had married in Bikrampur. The name of the village was Noapara. Since she had a yellowish complexion, I used to call her "Holde

Nanu" or "yellow grandma." She had come to visit our village house many times. One of her sons lived in Rampura in Dhaka. His nickname was Bablu. Bablu Mama was very fond of me. When I was studying in Dhaka, he sent his son to invite me to their house. I thought, why don't I get in touch with him? I sent Taslim to Bablu Mama's house with a letter. At that time, the houses in Rampura didn't have house numbers. Taslim went along asking for his house by name, and when he finally found it, he learned that Bablu Mama's whole family had gone back to the village. Taslim slipped my letter under the door and came back in disappointment.

A young couple lived in the house to the right of ours in Dhanmondi, and an older couple lived in the house to the left. We were acquainted with both couples. They both advised us to leave Dhaka, saying, "Get out however you can. It won't be safe for you to stay in Dhaka." Suddenly I remembered another person from Swadesh's office. His name was Anwaruzzaman Choudhuri. I sent word to him through Hasan Imam, asking him to come and see me. But I learned that Anwar was not in Dhaka; he had gone to his village too.

I had an American friend in Dhaka named Daniel Thorner. He came to see us one day. I felt extremely lucky. Daniel also told me to leave Dhaka immediately. He was planning to leave in a few days. I told Daniel, "Help me save Swadesh somehow. Don't worry about the rest of us." Daniel promised me he wouldn't leave Dhaka without Swadesh and told me to keep in touch with him wherever we were. After that, each day felt like a month. The time just dragged on. Worry kept me from sleeping at night; I would just sit up all night.

I knew Anwar's sister lived in Old Dhaka. She was married to Abdul Latif from Bauphal. One day, I went to their house and told Latif and Anwar's sister everything. They reassured me and said, "Don't worry, we'll send Anwar to you as soon as he comes back to Dhaka."

I was waiting for Anwar. When no one else was willing or able to help me, I settled on Anwar as my last hope. For some reason, I felt that only Anwar could get us out of Dhaka now. I thought if Anwar could get us to Munshiganj, I could find my way to Holde Nani's house and take refuge there.

Finally, Anwar came back to Dhaka. The day he arrived, he came to talk to me, and we decided that we would travel to Munshiganj the very next morning. Before Anwar arrived, I had sent Taslim and Sobhan to bring the latest news. They informed me that people were leaving the city by way of Jinjira, across the Buriganga River from Dhaka. Thousands of people were going that way every day. After talking to Anwar, I sent them again to see the river crossing with their own eyes and to find out if boats were available or what other arrangements could be made. But they came back with bad news: thousands of people had been going to Jinjira by boat just that morning. Among them were Hamidullah Shaheb's wife and son. Then the military came in speedboats and shot countless people dead including Hamidullah's wife. Hamidullah later became the governor of Bangladesh Bank.

That must have been 3 or 4 April. We were supposed to travel by way of Jinjira the very next day, but just then we learned that thousands of people had been killed by the army and the whole area was under army control. This meant we couldn't travel that way; we had to change our plans. Taslim and Sobhan went looking for a new route. While we were trying to solve this problem, a new problem cropped up. Swadesh refused to leave the house. He kept saying, "I'll die respectably in my own home, but I don't want to die on the street like a cat or dog." I understood how he felt, but how could I sit in that city of death without even trying to escape?

### *War: fleeing from the city to the villages*

Every day, we heard people screaming and saw flames leaping in every direction. Hearing the news of killing and rape, we spent every moment of the day and night in terror. We were constantly thinking, now they're coming to finish us off. If they kill us, that's the end of it. But if they torture us? Whenever an army car or jeep stopped in front of our house, the blood froze in my chest. Every day, I wondered, how long will we have to live like this? Meanwhile, Taslim and Sobhan brought news that people were leaving the city by way of Narayanganj. That was the only route open. If we tried, we might be able to leave through Narayanganj. With this news, I reached out to Anwar and Hasan Imam again.

We had 8,000 taka in the bank. Hasan Imam risked his own life to bring us the whole sum from the bank. I'll never forget Hasan Imam's help. The day we were supposed to leave, Anwar came very early in the morning. Hasan Imam took us to the Motijheel taxi stand in his car. There were ten of us: our children Jaseem, Mini, and Ani, my sister Runu, my brother Taslim, Sobhan, and our domestic helper, a girl named Toru, then Swadesh and me. Anwar was our guide.

For the first time since the conflict started, we all went out together. We had a few clothes with us, and we divided the money between us—who knew which of us was going to survive? That day too, we found the streets desolate. Only a few rickshaws and baby taxis[3] were operating, and the military jeeps were rushing by. My heart was beating fast, thinking, now they're going to stop us, now the army is going to shoot us dead. My two girls had closed their eyes and buried their faces in my chest. Swadesh was visibly annoyed and muttering at me under his breath. He was angry at me for dragging him out like this!

At one place on the way, we saw people walking with their bags and bundles to some uncertain destination. We saw the military trucks taking some people away. I don't know where they were taking them, but the fear of death was clear in their eyes. Taslim said, "The army will put them to work somewhere first, and then they'll be shot." Apparently, that was the norm then: the army would put people to work and then shoot them. I heard that after killing teachers and students at Dhaka University on the night of 25 March, the army had seized people from nearby areas and forced them to bury all the bodies in one grave. Then they made them dig another grave next to it, stood them up there, shot them all into the hole, and covered them with earth.

Hasan Imam took us to the Motijheel taxi stand and hired a taxi for us at an exorbitant rate. A few drivers were still risking their lives to drive around the city. If they'd had food at home, they probably wouldn't have been out there. In the taxi on our way to Narayanganj, we felt like the journey would never end. When we reached there and got out of the taxi, we saw that instead of going toward Narayanganj, everyone was going the other way, so we also went the way everyone else was going. We were all walking through the bushes. Swadesh kept muttering at me, but I kept quiet, pretending not to hear. Finally, we reached the riverbank. There were various sizes of boats there. The army boats were patrolling the river, but in the distance. They were opening fire from time to time. We got on a boat and left. Once we were on the boat, we tried to act normal, but in truth we were all shaking with fear.

We had almost crossed the river when we saw an army boat coming toward us. Everyone started screaming, "The military's coming, the military's coming!" We were in a terrible state. Anwar said, "Don't be scared. We'll reach the bank before they get here."

The boat reached the bank just then. We all scrambled out. Anwar helped Swadesh out of the boat. I told everyone in our group, "Beware: don't look back and don't run."

We all had the fear of death in our hearts then. People were getting off the boats and hurrying off wherever they could. There were some rickshaws on the riverbank. We took several rickshaws to Anwar's house. When we reached the house, we found it empty! Everyone had run away when they heard the military was coming. Only Anwar's sister, that is, Latif's wife, was sitting there crying. She was pregnant, so she hadn't been able to run. I hugged her and said, "Don't be scared, we're here with you."

Anwar's sister was about to have her baby any day. Anyway, the others came back a little later. In the end, the military didn't come that way. Everyone knew we were coming, so they came back quickly.

Swadesh had a high-ranking position in Anwar's office, so the family treated us respectfully. We weren't the only ones who had taken refuge there; other people had also come from Dhaka. Anwar's family treated us with care. Even at that dangerous time, they got busy cooking a feast for us. We weren't expecting this at all—we were there for sheer survival, and they were showing us hospitality! I felt bad. There were so many of us. I didn't know what to do. For a group of nine people to stay and eat in another family's house! On top of that, they knew Swadesh was Hindu.

Two days later, Anwar's father suddenly said to me, "What's your plan?"

Even though his question threw me off at first, I thought to myself, we do need to plan. We can't stay indefinitely at someone else's house. I told him, "One of my mother's phuphus married in Bikrampur. If I can get in touch with her, we'll go there." I told him the name of the village. I remembered that this Nana, that is, my mother's phuphu's husband, was nicknamed Sona Mia. As soon as I uttered the name, Anwar's father jumped up and said "Areee, he's a very well-known person. He's president of the local Muslim League. You'll be better off there. You should start right away."

When I saw his haste, I understood that he was unwilling to keep us in his house a moment longer. I asked him to get us a rickshaw. They went and got a rickshaw and told the driver to drop us off at the ferry ghat. We set out again with thumping hearts. On the way, we saw countless people walking to the ferry ghat. We got down from the rickshaw and joined them. We also saw people had come out of their houses along the way and were standing there with *ruti* and jaggery for the tired, hungry travelers. I was touched by this, and thought, who can stop a people as brave and kind as this?

When we got to the ferry ghat, we found hundreds of people there. At last, we crossed the river. When we reached the other side, I asked the boatman, "How far is Noapara from here?"

He said, "That's very far. You can't walk there. It's several miles."

I knew there was another village called Dampara close to Noapara. One of my mother's cousins, the daughter of her chacha, had married there. Holde Nanu's daughter Kohinur Khala had married in the same area. Kohinur Khala had visited our house, and we had played together a lot as children, but I hadn't seen her after her marriage. As we walked, I was thinking that if we could find Dampara we could take shelter there too. At the same time, I wondered, does Kohinur Khala even remember me? And there are so many of us!

We were walking through rice fields. The ground was uneven. We were all having trouble walking. Anita was just two and a half. We took turns carrying her. Swadesh was having trouble too; he couldn't walk too far at a stretch. I held his arm and helped him move forward slowly. On the way, we passed a couple of houses, and people came out to meet us. When I asked them how far it was to Noapara and Dampara's Miyabari, they said, "Oh, that's right nearby. Just walk a little farther and you'll be there." But it seemed to us the road would never end. Two or three times, Swadesh sat down in the middle of the path and said he couldn't walk one more step.

Suddenly I saw a big compound with several large houses. There were a lot of people standing on the high bank of the pond. I thought, that must be the Miyabari. We started walking toward it. A few people came up to us and asked where we were going, who we wanted, which house? Somehow, I had a feeling this was the right place; I asked, "Is there anyone named Kohinur here?"

Soon a woman came around from the back of the house. She was in poor health and looked older. I couldn't recognize her. She came close, and as soon as I introduced myself as Noorjahan from Barobaishdia, she took me in her arms and started crying. I realized she was Kohinur Khala after all.

Then the family made a fuss about us; they took us all into the house and started bustling around looking after our needs. Many of them knew about me through Kohinur Khala. One of the young men in the family was studying at Dhaka Medical College (or, at a medical college in Dhaka) and was a Students' League leader. When I saw they were getting ready to cook a lot of dishes, I said, "We're hungry, we'll eat whatever you already have."

But they wouldn't listen. They'd never thought that we, especially Swadesh, would come to their house. They knew about Swadesh's political reputation too. We had tea and snacks, and then they cleared out a big room for us. Swadesh and the children went straight to bed. A crowd gathered around me to hear stories of Dhaka.

This was the first time since 25 March that I felt relatively calm. I was thinking, now we can take things as they come. At least we got out of Dhaka! It would be easy to get to Holde Nani's house from there, because Holde Nani was Kohinur Khala's mother. We stayed at Kohinur Khala's house for about twelve days, happy and well taken care of. We heard that Barisal was still a free area, and the launch had started running from Munshiganj to Barisal. One day, I sent Toru, Taslim, and Sobhan to Barisal. When we had been at Kohinur Khala's house for ten or eleven days, an uncle of mine called Dulu Mama arrived. He was surprised to see us. He said that Bablu Mama had come back to his house in Rampura and found the letter I had sent Taslim to deliver, but when Bablu Mama went to my house, we weren't there. I knew that Bablu Mama would try to find us if he knew. I asked Dulu Mama to tell another uncle of mine called Badal Mama to send a boat. When Badal Mama came with the boat to pick us up, everyone in Kohinur Khala's family was disappointed. They said, "Did we do anything wrong?"

I said, "Of course not!" I had to work hard to persuade them to let us go to Holde Nani's house

Ma's father, that is, my Nana, was Holde Nani's older brother. When I was small, Holde Nani came with her children to her father's house every year. We would go see them there. I had eight Nanas (my own Nana and his seven brothers) and five Nanis. Holde Nani would spend a month at my *nanabari*, then go back to her husband's house by boat with a lot of gifts. When my sister Fatema got married, Holde Nani came to our house with her children. The day of the wedding, she cooked all night, making all sorts of dishes with the help of the women of our family. Kohinur Khala, Ruzi Khala, Mariyam, Momtaz, and Shaheda were the life of the party, dancing and singing with the other women. Ma's Chacha, Manik Nana, was there that day too. He didn't usually come to our house except on special occasions.

That day, Manik Nana took charge of cooking the *shahi* biriyani. They dug a pit oven on one side of the courtyard and cooked the biriyani in a big copper pot according to Manik Nana's instructions. Nana sat there and supervised the whole thing. But no one in Fatema's husband's family ate the *shahi* biriyani they cooked with such fanfare. They thought we had cooked everything together and served it to them to make them look silly—because they'd never eaten biriyani before! Fatema was married in 1953. I didn't see Holde Nani or Kohinur Khala for a long time after that. I was seeing them now after sixteen or seventeen years.

We were at Holde Nani's house for about two months. Her house was also teeming with people from the city. They cleared a small room for us, and we all slept together in a big bed. The women of the family got busy cooking very early in the morning. There was a market in front of the house. Nana kept sending my mamas (his sons) to the market to get the necessary fish and vegetables. There were about 100 people in the house—everyone had fled from the city to the village.

While we were living there, we heard the Pakistani military had ordered everyone to go back to work. After that, we saw that people with government jobs were all mentally preparing themselves to go back to work. Quite a few of the city people who had taken shelter there had government jobs. A lot of them went back to Dhaka to keep their jobs, but only the men—the women and children of these families stayed behind in the village. Many of them went to Dhaka by launch in the morning and came back at night; they couldn't find the nerve to spend the night in Dhaka. Badal Mama also had a government job in Dhaka and commuted every day. When he got back, we would crowd around him to get the latest Dhaka news. Everyone besides Swadesh had gone back to work, so people started to talk, wondering why Swadesh hadn't gone to work. I told everyone about Swadesh's illness, but he was much better then, so I began to feel it wouldn't be safe to stay there much longer with Swadesh.

I did one other thing then. I thought, if Swadesh has to go back to Dhaka, I need to teach him a few things about Islam. I taught Swadesh some suras of the Koran. I thought, if Swadesh gets caught by the Pakistani Army, this education might just be his talisman for survival. I made him repeat these things over and over until he memorized them. I also taught him how to do *namaz*. In the meantime, Daniel sent word from Dhaka through

Badal Mama that Swadesh should go back to Dhaka. Swadesh got ready to go back, but I didn't want to let him go. I was afraid—what if he didn't come back? What if he fell into the hands of the Pakistani Army on his way to Dhaka? Then it would all be over. I later learned that Daniel along with economists Austin Robinson and Keith Griffin had formed a group to try to save the Bengali intellectuals and economists in East Pakistan from the Pakistani Army. They reached out to Archer Blood, the US Consul General to Dhaka, to alert him to the situation. Archer Blood is famous for the "Blood Telegram" he sent to the US government protesting against the atrocities committed by the Pakistani government during the Liberation War. Jaseem had brought our radio with him. We listened quietly in our room to various radio stations, especially Swadhin Bangla Betar (Independent Bangladesh Radio). As we listened to the news, our bodies trembled with excitement, even though we were in constant fear that the military would suddenly attack the village. One day, I sent Jaseem to Dhaka with Badal Mama. I had promised to keep in touch with Daniel Thorner, so I sent Jaseem with a letter for Daniel letting him know where we were. I was extremely anxious until he came back; I was watching the road all afternoon. In the end, he came home safely. Meanwhile, two of Boro Mama's sons and some other young men in the village were trying to figure out how to support the Liberation War in the village. My Nana was connected to the Muslim League. Even so, they had his complete approval. There were quite a few Hindu families and Awami League supporters in the village. Suddenly one day a speedboat full of military personnel and their Bengali accomplices showed up at the village market. Nana went running to meet them. On his way out, he told me to be ready with Swadesh so that at a sign from him we could hide with the women in the jungle at the back of the house.

I took my two daughters Ani and Mini by the hand and stood by the door with Swadesh and Jaseem. The women of the house all started reciting the Doa-Darood (a prayer) out loud. But no sign came from Nana to run away. Two hours later, he came back himself. I looked at him expectantly. Nana said the military had ordered some people to loot the houses of the Hindus and Awami League leaders and workers. After that, they set fire to those houses and a few storehouses full of potatoes and rushed off on their speedboat. They didn't stay long.

As soon as the army left, Nana told the villagers to put out the fire, and they did. Nana told the people who had looted the houses, "Go and give back everything you took." I later heard that most of them did follow Nana's order and return the things. This was at the beginning of May.

After the army attack on the village, the local young men started to search for a way to get to India. Meanwhile, I was worried by the news that a peace committee had been set up through the efforts of the Muslim League supporters in the village. Nana reassured me, saying "Trust me, I won't let any harm come to you or Swadesh as long as I'm here."

But my worries grew because of another person—my Dulu Mama. I heard Dulu Mama shouting as he went by our room, "I'll make sure the enemies of the nation get caught!"

In other words, we were enemies of the nation. Dulu Mama kept saying out loud for me to hear, "I'm going to go to Munshiganj and inform the military about the enemy."

Munshiganj was then under military control, so this threat made me stiff with fear.

I also knew that Dulu Mama was involved in the Bhashani NAP party. People were saying that one of their factions supported Pakistan. Maybe he was one of them, I don't know. It could also be that he did this for money. Dulu Mama's wife was Ma's cousin, her Chacha's daughter Dolly. When I saw how Dulu Mama was behaving, I called Dolly over and slipped her a 500 taka note to give to Dulu Mama—that is, to shut him up. It worked, but only for a few days. Then. again, Dulu Mama started showing the same attitude, shouting the same words. I gave him money several times. Then I started thinking, how long am I going to put up with this?

*Moving around to escape death*

Around this time, Badal Mama brought a final letter from Daniel. He had written that I should send Swadesh back to Dhaka without fail. Daniel was working hard to try to get Swadesh and Hasan Imam out of Bangladesh. Daniel couldn't stay in Dhaka much longer. I later learned that Archer Blood told Daniel that Swadesh and Hasan Imam should try to leave Pakistan immediately. With Dulu Mama's antics on the one hand and the villagers' suspicion around Swadesh not going to work like everyone else on the other, I thought that if Daniel left, Swadesh's escape route out of the country would be blocked. So I sent Swadesh to Dhaka with Badal Mama.

Then the days went by one after the other; a month went by without any news from Swadesh. Wondering what was happening, I took Anita with me to Badal Mama's house in Rampura, Dhaka, in early June 1971. That day, the Mukti Bahini[4] set off grenades in front of Dhaka's Intercontinental Hotel, now a Sheraton Hotel, to make their presence known to foreigners. I learned about this only later. That afternoon, I was sitting on the veranda of Mama's house when I suddenly saw a tall young man of around twenty striding in my direction. He came straight up to me and asked, "Do you know where Ms Bose lives?"

Startled, I asked him, "Who are you? Where did you get this address?"

The young man took a piece of paper out of his fist and showed it to me. I was even more puzzled and said again, "Where did you get this address?"

He said, "From Swadesh-da."

At that, I quickly took him into the house. I had given Swadesh this address to contact me. I felt extremely lucky and thought, if I had been in Noapara today, this young man wouldn't have been able to find me!

The young man's name was A. K. M. Rahmatullah (Rahmat). He's a big businessman now. In 1996, he was elected MP on the Awami League ticket. He said, "Swadesh is fine. I've come to take you to him. I want you and your children to leave with me tomorrow." I later learned that on 19 May 1971, Swadesh and Hasan Imam had crossed the border to India safely at Tripura after a harrowing journey, walking miles and miles on foot, wading across a river, and hiding in rice fields.

I said to Rahmat, "I can't go with you now. It's not possible, I have only my younger daughter with me, everyone else is in the village."

We decided that I would come to my Mama's house in Rampura by 15 June. At 8 o'clock on the night of 15 June, Rahmat would pick us up from there. The plan was that we would stay at a certain place with him that night, and the next day we would start the journey. Rahmat didn't tell me that day where we were going. After talking to him, I woke my younger daughter Anita and went straight to Mama's office. I told him, "We have to go to Noapara right now." I also told him I would come back the next day with the other children. Then Mama and I went back to his house.

On the one hand, I was glad to be going to join Swadesh. On the other hand, I felt bad to leave the people who had given us shelter in this dangerous time. I had spent two months in their house. My children played all day with the village children, roaming all over and reminding me of my own childhood. My children were very safe and had a great time at Holde Nani's house.

In the morning of 15 June 1971, we left Noapara for Dhaka. I hadn't been able to sleep the night before because I had decided that I would leave Jaseem in Dhaka. Jaseem was sixteen years old. I had learned from Rahmat that the military had their eyes on boys of that age, because many of them were joining the Mukti Bahini. Rahmat had said we would be leaving Dhaka by bus. On the way, the Pakistani Army had several check-posts where they would make the men get off the bus, line them up, search them, and interrogate them. If they were suspicious of someone, they would detain them. Sometimes they would make women get off the bus too and take them away in cars or jeeps. People had no way to protest. Under these circumstances, I didn't have the courage to take my darling Jaseem with me.

When we reached Dhaka from Noapara, I sent word to Jaseem's Phuphu, Bela Nabi. When they came, I told them my plan. She was shocked to hear I wanted to leave Jaseem with her in Dhaka. She asked where I was going off to, leaving my son in this dangerous city? I had no answer to this question then. I handed Jaseem over to his Phuphu along with some clothes and money. I couldn't look Jaseem in the face. I felt like my heart was tearing in two. Bela Nabi lived in Gulshan. Her son was the same age as Jaseem. I thought if Jaseem stayed with Bela, he would be fine. Still, I was worried to leave my son. I told my younger sister Runu to go to Noapara the next day. I was very worried about her too.

At the end of the evening, Rahmat came and set off with the three of us—me, Anita, and Mini—on a rickshaw. When we went out on the street, it looked like it was late at night. We had to take the rickshaw from Rampura to the main road to get a taxi or baby taxi. Rahmat said, "We have to go to Gulshan." At that time, there weren't as many roads in Dhaka as there are now. Gulshan seemed far away. To get to Gulshan from Rampura, you had to go to through Malibag, Mogbazar, Bangla Motor,

Farmgate, and finally Mohakhali. There was almost no one on the roads, only military jeeps and trucks. It would take a long time to get from Rampura to Gulshan by rickshaw, and it would be risky too. So when we got to the main road, we waited there for a taxi or baby taxi. Finally, a baby taxi came. The driver was an Urdu/Hindi speaker or "Bihari";[5] that made me a little nervous, because many "Biharis" were helping the Pakistani military. Once we got in, Rahmat started talking to the driver in Urdu and deliberately praising the Pakistani government. So, talking with Rahmat all along, the driver took us to Gulshan.

Two people were waiting for us that day in the house in Gulshan. I didn't know then who they were. They were Sidhu Bhai and his wife Rose Bu. Sidhu Bhai's full name is Mokhlesur Rahman Sidhu Miya. Rose Bu's name is Shamsun Nahar Rahman Rose. Rose Bu was Rahmatullah's Khala. We took shelter that night at Sidhu Bhai's house in Gulshan and ate dinner there. Then Rose Bu and Sidhu Bhai explained to us the route we would take. They also told me how to get to our destination on my own if anything happened to Rahmat on the way. They said it was possible Rahmat might get caught.

I had some money with me. Rose Bu sewed a moneybag with her own hands and tied it around my waist. I packed a few clothes for the three of us in a small bag. We couldn't take a lot of baggage, because we didn't know where we would have to walk, what we would have to do. Besides, we might need to carry my two children on the way.

When I finished talking things over with Rose Bu and Sidhu Bhai, I went straight to bed, but I couldn't sleep. While I was lying there, I suddenly saw Rose Bu muttering something like a mantra and blowing on our bodies. I lay there quietly, pretending to be asleep. I didn't know someone could have so much compassion for unknown people. My eyes filled with tears.

*Crossing the border*

We got up at the crack of dawn and left. Sidhu Bhai drove us in his car to the bus stand. Rose Bu wrote an *ayat* of the Koran on a slip of paper for each of us. At the time, she didn't know I was a Muslim woman. She asked me, "If you don't mind, please pin these *doa* [prayers] to the inside of your own and your children's shirts. Maybe this *doa* will protect you from harm. I feel you will reach your destination by Allah's will."

Later I learned that Sidhu Bhai and Rose Bu had risked their lives to send many people to safety during that time, including Swadesh. It's impossible to repay our debt to them.

At that time, the Pakistani government was trying hard to make life in East Pakistan look normal, so there was more traffic and more people around than usual. We got on the bus and left Dhaka. Rose Bu had asked me to wear a burqa, but I wasn't willing to wear a burqa in the June heat. I told her I would pull my sari down over my face. When I got on the bus, I sat holding my two daughters to my chest. A little while later, the bus started. Rahmat was sitting in the seat behind us.

After 25 March 1971, I had given Swadesh a Muslim name. My children had learned to call him by that name. Still, I thought if someone threatened them, they might accidentally say their father's real name, Swadesh. So I told them to just keep quiet and not answer anyone who might speak to them.

The bus was leaving the Dhaka city limit. After that, I saw big army trucks on the road, covered with tarpaulins. The trucks were mostly leaving Dhaka; some were going toward Dhaka. There were twenty or twenty-five of us on the bus, which was going toward Cumilla. We were supposed to get down at the bank of the Gomati River. Rose Bu had told us there was a ferry there, and she had also said that after crossing the river we could stop if we needed to, but that we should not get off the bus before that under any circumstances. Rahmat had arranged the route and everything beforehand, including people who would help us along the way. I realized this later.

Along the road, there were several Pakistani Army check-posts. In a few places, the army took the male passengers off the bus and interrogated them. It was painful to watch. Each time, I sat with my heart in my mouth until Rahmat came back; then I would feel a little braver.

Rose Bu had given me an address and said to go there if anything happened to Rahmat. She told me to keep calm even if the army killed Rahmat. I had kept the address she gave me tucked into my blouse. She had told me, "If Rahmatullah doesn't come back, go to this address and if you tell the rickshaw-driver, he'll take you on your way later. Don't stop anywhere else."

Along the road, I also saw that many of the jute and rice fields and houses had been burnt down. After we came near Cumilla, I heard gunshots. It sounded like there was a skirmish taking place somewhere nearby.

Then we got down from the bus at a certain place. I didn't know the name of the place. After the bus left, a rickshaw came forward at a sign from Rahmat. We got on the rickshaw and started moving. It was a dirt road, and the monsoon on top of that. The rickshaw driver took us very carefully through the rice fields, past people's houses, sometimes along the bank of a pond. When we went past a house, sometimes people would come out and ask us the news from Dhaka. They wanted to stop the rickshaw and ask who we were and what was happening in Dhaka.

After going a long way on the rickshaw, the driver dropped us off and stood waiting for a signal from the main road. A little later, someone on the main road lifted a hand and said something. The rickshaw driver told us to wait there and quickly went across with his rickshaw. We stood a little way off the main road, under cover. We saw a military convoy roar by on the main road, shaking everything. Then someone raised their hand and signaled to us from the same direction the rickshaw had gone. Rahmat picked Anita up and told me we had to cross the road quickly. I took Mini's hand and almost ran across the road behind Rahmat. On the other side of the road, that same rickshaw was waiting at a little distance. We got on it and started moving again. Later I heard that Swadesh, Hasan Imam, and many others had left by this same route. Many people had died crossing this road. The path we were on now was a beaten track through the rice fields, very uneven and winding. There were other people using the path too, on foot and on rickshaws.

Finally, we reached the bank of the Gomati. We saw hundreds of people waiting there for the ferry. Seeing so many people, I was scared, thinking how long we might have to wait before we could cross! A little later, I heard that one boat had gone down, and that's why so many people were waiting there. They were trying to pull the boat back out of the water. Some local people had gone to get another boat. Signs of anxiety were clear on the faces of every person there. They all had the same question: when will we get across?

It was a very hot, sunny day too. Everyone's eyes and faces were red with hunger and thirst. My children's faces were wilting, but they didn't say anything. A village boy was selling bananas, so I went to buy some. My daughters waved their hands to tell me they didn't want anything, but I still bought a few. What if they were hungry later? Then I asked a local, "If you can get us a separate boat at a higher rate, it would be a big help."

He said, "There's no fee. As soon as the boat comes, I'll take you across first."

And he did. He didn't take a single coin from me, and he took me and my children across first.

After we crossed the river, we had to walk quite a long way through the mud. Ani sat on Rahmat's shoulders. Mini held my hand and walked. Once we got through the mud, there were rice fields. Even though it was hard to walk through the fields, I felt a little less scared, because we had crossed the Gomati. After we had gone a little way, Rahmatullah said, "A rickshaw is waiting for us up ahead."

I walked faster. Soon we came to a small market. I sat in the shade of a tree there, and Rahmat brought us some young coconuts. We'd left very early that morning, and now it was late afternoon. We hadn't eaten anything. We drank the young coconut water. Ani and Mini didn't want to eat anything; they only had the coconut water.

The rickshaw was waiting for us in the market. Rahmat and the rickshaw driver said the Indian border was very close now. I saw Indian citizens freely moving around here and selling various Indian goods. The Pakistani Army hadn't come there; that's probably why these people were there. The market was in full swing, the vendors sitting on the bank of the pond or in people's fallow fields, selling their goods: rice, dal, oil, salt, saris, wraps, mosquito nets, and soap, all the necessary things for everyday life.

Our rickshaw stopped on the bank of a pond, and we got down. Rahmat said, "Look, there's India right in front of you." I couldn't believe it. How was this possible? The same earth on both sides, the same people, no wall or fence. India was just two steps ahead. An Indian rickshaw was waiting on that side, and a Bangladeshi rickshaw on this side. All we had to do was take two steps ahead. The whole thing seemed unbelievable. Before we crossed the border, I took some earth and smeared it on my head and face. I was thinking, who knows when I will come back to Golden Bengal! My heart started throbbing.

We crossed the border and stepped onto Indian soil. We got on the rickshaw that was waiting there, and the driver took us to a small town close to the border, called Sonamura. The town was overflowing with Bangladeshis then. As soon as we entered India, my younger daughter Anita, who was only two and a half, opened her mouth for the first time on the whole journey. She said, "Are we in India now?"

My older daughter Mini snapped at her, "Don't you see most of the women are wearing *shankha* and *sindur*? Where else could this be but India?"

Anita asked me, "Can we use Baba's name here, Ma?"

Tears sprang to my eyes. I said, "Yes, Sona, now you can use his name."

She hugged me with relief. This two-and-a-half-year-old girl had been through so much!

When we reached Sonamura, Rahmat got us a taxi. There were thousands of people around, but not many taxis. The taxi drivers were taking in as many passengers as possible, ignoring the usual rules. But you had to pay whatever they asked. Rahmat had a hard time getting the taxi. The four of us were squeezed into a corner, because there were twelve or fourteen people in that one taxi! It sounds impossible, but it's true. I was scared, thinking what if we've come all this way only to die in a street accident. But we had no choice. Everyone wanted to get where they were going. The taxi finally started. On the way, I saw the schools, colleges, and hospitals were teeming with people. There were Bangladeshis everywhere you looked.

I still didn't know where we were going. Finally, our journey ended. Rahmat said, "We've reached Agartala."

The taxi stopped in front of a small one-story house. When we got out, we saw a lot of people sitting on the open lawn talking and having tea. I learned that this was the house of Anil Bhattacharya, the local editor of *Jugantar* magazine. Rahmat said, "Swadesh-da is staying here in this house."

This was the first time he mentioned Swadesh to me. Later I heard that many well-known people from Bangladesh took shelter at this house when they first crossed the border; then they moved on to wherever they were going. The doors of Anil-da's house were open to all Bangladeshis. A few people got up and came toward us. I noticed that everyone knew Rahmat. There were several Students' League leaders there. When they heard who I was, several boys went on their bicycles to find Swadesh and send him to me. They said, "Swadesh-da was so worried about you, he'd forgotten to eat and sleep." They also said, "You came just in time. Swadesh-da is going to Mujibnagar[6] tomorrow morning."

We sat down on the lawn with them.

The time seemed to go by so slowly. My girls were anxious to see their father. A little later, Swadesh came and took my hand. Everyone on the lawn shouted, "We were all waiting to see your reunion!"

When Swadesh arrived in India, he found that some people had come together with their wives and children. He felt very depressed, thinking, why hadn't he brought us with him? He had been waiting for an opportunity, and when he found Rahmat, he arranged for him to bring us to India. It wasn't possible for everyone to reach India safely. Many people died along the way. Meanwhile, the Chief Minister of the Bangladesh government, Tajuddin Ahmad, was calling Swadesh repeatedly to come to Mujibnagar. But Swadesh couldn't leave without us.

We reached Agartala on 16 June. On 17 June, Swadesh was supposed to go to Mujibnagar. He didn't know we were going to arrive that day. When we finally met, I asked Swadesh, "What are we going to do now?!" He said we would have to stay in Agartala for a few days while he made arrangements, and then he would come get us. I objected strongly to this. I told him, "Wherever you go, we're going too."

I learned that an Indian Army plane was going to take Swadesh from Agartala to Kolkata. I told him, "However difficult it may be, we're going with you."

Swadesh repeated, "They're taking me to Kolkata in an Indian Army plane, they won't allow women and children."

I didn't say anything more.

That night, we somehow swallowed a few bites, thanked Anil-da and his wife, and went to sleep at the *Jugantar* office in Agartala. Swadesh had been sleeping there along with Debdas Chakrabarti, a renowned artist from Dhaka. There was not an inch of space left in Anil-da's house. There was a small single bed in the office. I tucked Ani and Mini in there, under a small mosquito net, and we sat up all night talking. It was hard to sit still, there were so many mosquitoes.

In the morning, I went to the airport with Swadesh and brought the girls with me too. When we got there, I saw that it was a very different kind of airport. Everyone was startled to see us with Swadesh. Swadesh made a special request to the pilot to take us too. The pilot immediately rejected this proposal and said that women and children were not allowed on the aircraft under any circumstances for safety reasons.

Then I talked to the pilot myself and said, "We've been reunited after so long, and we don't want to be separated again."

The gentleman heard me out. After a pause, he said, "You won't be able to get onto the plane."

I hadn't paid attention to the plane before that. I looked and saw that it was very high off the ground and there was no stairway to get up there. A thick rope was hanging from the door, and everyone was climbing the rope to get in. Even after seeing that, I still pleaded with the pilot to let us on, but he kept saying it wasn't possible. I watched the military personnel swinging up and down that rope, getting in and out of the plane.

I used to climb coconut trees as a child. So I made a bold proposal to the pilot: "If I can get into the plane, will you take us?"

At that, the pilot didn't seem to know what to say. Before he could answer, I took my sandals in my hand, ran over to the plane, climbed the rope, and got into the plane. Everyone stood there, speechless with shock. When I got to the top of the rope, I saw the plane had a small door; you had to bend down to get inside. Once I was in, I said, "I'm not getting down."

After that, the pilot didn't argue. Swadesh got on the plane nervously, with a lot of difficulty. The soldiers carried my daughters up. Inside, everyone looked at me, open-mouthed.

This plane didn't match any of my ideas of what a plane was. There were no seats inside, no food or drinks. The inside of the plane was like a big hollow shell. Everyone was sitting on the floor. We sat down too. There were seatbelts attached to the floor, and when we saw everyone putting them on, we put ours on too. The inside of the plane was very hot. We were soon drenched in sweat. There was no air. Later I learned it was a cargo plane.

There were Indian soldiers sitting in the plane. At first, my children were scared of them. They knew something about the atrocities that the Pakistani Army was committing. They thought these soldiers must be like that too. I explained that wasn't true, and they finally calmed down. Then Mini struck up a conversation with the soldiers. I hadn't brought any food or water with me. I hadn't even thought of it. We hadn't eaten anything in the morning either. So we had to go hungry. We learned that Indian planes weren't flying over Bangladesh at the time, so the plane would have to take a roundabout route to Kolkata. The plane landed in Guwahati, the capital of Assam, to get oil or something. I got down there for a little while, but I didn't find any food to buy except biscuits. I bought biscuits for the children. The soldiers had given the girls a share of their water.

The plane trip lasted all day. We had got on the plane in the morning, and the plane kept circling around who knows where, all day long. I thought the journey would never end. We landed in Kolkata Airport at around ten at night. Then we took a taxi to No. 8, Theatre Road. This was Mujibnagar, the central office of the Bangladesh government during the Liberation War. Swadesh left us in the taxi and went inside to see Chief Minister Tajuddin Ahmad. When he came back, he told me that Tajuddin Ahmad had congratulated him on reaching Kolkata safely with the family.

Tajuddin Ahmad had also given Swadesh the address of a place to stay in Kolkata. It was the India Hotel. We went there in the taxi and found a lot of known and unknown people from Bangladesh there. We went into our room, took baths, ate, and went to bed. I felt like I was in a dream; we had such good luck. But I couldn't sleep thinking of Jaseem. Once we reached the hotel, I kept thinking, my son who lost his father before he was even born, whom I raised with such hardship and care, where have I left him behind! When will I have him in my arms again?

Before we left Agartala, I had written a letter to Jaseem and given it to Rahmat, telling him to give it to Jaseem and to bring me Jaseem's response when he came this way again. Rahmat fulfilled his promise. I can never repay my debt to him. He didn't save only my life; he brought many families to safety during the Liberation War, and he also risked his life to bring important papers and news from the country on Tajuddin Ahmad's orders. If he had been caught, he could have been killed. Sidhu Bhai's house in Dhaka was their secret headquarters. Sidhu Bhai's wife Rose Bu's father was Rahmat's Nana. He was a Muslim League boss. Maybe that's why the military didn't suspect Sidhu Bhai and Rahmat. Even then, there was always a danger.

### *Refugee life in Kolkata*

As refugees in India, Swadesh could now use his real name. But now it was my turn to hide my name and my religion. At the suggestion of a friend, I started using the name "Joya" instead of

Noorjahan. "Noorjahan" is a Persian name meaning light of the universe, and it would immediately reveal that I was from a Muslim family. Muslims are a minority in India, and Hindu–Muslim marriages were (and are) not looked upon favorably.

We were in the India Hotel in Kolkata for about a month. The room for the four of us and meals three times a day cost us 20 rupees a day. *Ruti-torkari* (flatbread with vegetables) and tea for breakfast, and rice, dal, vegetables, and *macher jhol* for lunch and dinner. Occasionally meat. It was a great arrangement. We had left Dhaka in April with 8,000 taka. Now we didn't have much left. As soon as we had been in Kolkata for a few days, I started thinking, if we spent 20 rupees a day, this money wouldn't last us very long. One day, I thought of Atul Babu (Atulchandra Das), my teacher from Patuakhali. He lived in Kolkata now, and I knew his address. I wrote a letter to him and to my college friend Jhuntu. I didn't hear from Jhuntu while we were in Kolkata, or after that. Maybe he's not alive, or maybe he didn't get my letter. Atul Babu came to see us and said, "You can't live like this. I'll take you to another place where the rent is only 10 rupees. If you can budget 5 rupees for food, then you'll save 5 rupees a day. But you'll have to cook yourself."

But before we moved, there was one thing I had to do. I insisted that Swadesh contact his siblings, who I knew lived somewhere in West Bengal. He completely refused to do it. I told Debdas Chakrabarti, "You have to convince Swadesh. I want to go see them."

Swadesh was born in Kashipur village near Barisal. His two brothers and sister left their ancestral house after the riots of 1950 and migrated to India. Swadesh was only nineteen or twenty and was enrolled as a student at BM College and involved in student politics. He was supposed to take his BA exam and then go to India to live with his siblings. But fate was against him. Before he could even take the exam, the government of East Pakistan arrested him on charges of participating in the Language Movement of 10 March 1948. After that, he was in jail for almost eight years. When he got out of jail in terrible health, he jumped back into politics. By this time, he had no relationship with his relatives, and they didn't have the courage to contact him. Swadesh never tried to get in touch with his relatives in India; I don't know why. Right after our wedding, we left for England. Swadesh entered a PhD program at Cambridge University. From this time on, I often asked him to try to contact his siblings. Finally, after Mini was born, he gave into my pressure and wrote letters to his two older brothers, mentioning me. Responses came immediately from his brothers and their children. From then on, they were in contact through letters. When we went back to West Pakistan in 1967, he lost contact with them again. I thought we should try to find them now that we were here in India. I wasn't sure what kind of relationship he could have with people he hadn't seen in twenty-five years. But I thought to myself, it's not so easy to wipe out a blood relationship.

Debdas told Swadesh, "Since Boudi wants to go, why don't you take her?" Swadesh refused. He was afraid his family wouldn't accept me. I said, "So what? Let's go visit them at least. I want to meet them. And I want my daughters to see that your family lives here." One day, I made up my mind and told Swadesh, "You don't have to go. I'll take our daughters Ani and Mini and go to Asansol." When he saw my determination, Swadesh agreed. I put on *shankha* (conch-shell bangles worn by Bengali Hindu married women) and a *sindur* (vermillion dot on forehead and a line of vermillion in part of the hair to signify married Bengali Hindu women) and got on the train to go to my brother-in-law's house. I decided that when we got back, we would move to the place Atul Babu had suggested, with 10 rupees' rent. The place was called the Savoy Hotel.

After a day-long train journey, we got down at Asansol. His two brothers had been working here even before the Partition. After the riots of 1950, they had brought their families here and settled down. When we came out of the station, we got on a rickshaw, and Swadesh told the driver to take us to Talpukur. All this time, Swadesh had told me he didn't know where his siblings lived. The driver dropped us off somewhere in Talpukur. Swadesh stopped at a small tea stall and asked where to find his brother Sukharanjan Basu's[7] house. Someone pointed to a house in a lane and said, "That's Sukharanjan Basu's house."

The man held a light for us and led us there. We went and stood in front of the one-story house he indicated. I saw there was a short curtain on the door, and I could see inside through the gap. An older gentleman was sitting there in an easy chair.

Standing outside, Swadesh asked, "Is this Sukharanjan Basu's house?"

An older gentleman answered, "Who are you?" Swadesh said, "It's me, Swada." I was astonished—this was the first time I learned that his family called him "Swada." The gentleman got up from his chair and started pacing on the veranda. We stood there for a while, then took off our shoes and went inside. Sukhranjan-da kept pacing, and we kept standing there. Finally, I said, "Chorda, why don't you sit down?" He came to himself and sat down. Even after asking us to come inside, Chorda didn't ask us to sit down. I think he was nervous. After all, he was seeing his younger brother after almost twenty-five years! I told him and Swadesh to sit down, and I sat on the floor with the girls.

Then the two brothers started talking about the war. They didn't do any of the usual pleasantries. In my family, if we met someone after twenty-five years, we would be hugging and crying by now! Here I saw they did things differently. The two brothers just kept talking about the war, and it kept getting later. Then I noticed Chorda's daughters Moni, Bulu, Ranu, and Monta were all standing there against the wall, still like dolls. We had gotten letters from them when we lived in Cambridge. I understood that unless I asked them to sit down, they would keep standing there.

Ani and Mini were falling asleep in my lap with hunger and fatigue. I overcame my hesitation and said, "Which one of you is Moni?" The oldest girl was called Moni. She came forward. I told her, "Give me a towel and a sari and show me the bathroom. It's getting late. Put on some rice and potatoes to boil. Everyone's hungry." It worked—the girls started running around. I washed Ani's and Mini's feet, took a bath, and sat down to talk with the two brothers. Late at night, the girls gave the brothers their dinner. I fed Ani and Mini and tucked them into bed.

Then the girls served me dinner on the veranda. When I asked when they were going to eat, they said they would eat in the kitchen. When I went to bed, I found Swadesh agitated. He said, "I knew you wouldn't be able to stay here; we're leaving tomorrow." I said calmly, "What's wrong?" He answered, "Those girls didn't eat with you, how are you going to stay here?" I said calmly, "I didn't expect them to eat with me. They don't know me, after all. You can go if you want. I'm staying here." He fell asleep still muttering with rage.

The next morning, I sent Mini to find Swadesh's oldest brother Kamini Ranjan Bose, whom Swadesh called Ranga-da. Ranga-da came hurrying over. Swadesh was still in bed. I ran and hugged Ranga-da. He lifted my face, looked into my eyes, and said, "You have a face like Ma Durga's." I had forgotten that in Bengali culture women aren't supposed to touch their brothers-in-law. We talked a lot, but Swadesh wasn't convinced that we were welcome. Swadesh ate and left for Kolkata, still angry with his family. I stayed on with my girls in this unfamiliar household. Neither of the brothers' wives were there. The oldest brother Ranga-da had a son and two daughters. He had sent his wife to Ranchi to treat a mental illness, and no one had kept in touch with her after that. The second daughter Chaya seemed fine; she'd done well in school and had a good job. The older daughter Maya hadn't finished her education; she looked after the house. She didn't seem well—she was sickly looking and constantly wrung her hands. She seemed to be suffering from anxiety. The oldest son Nirmal had done his BA and had a job, but he had already been diagnosed with mental illness. He lived alone, but Ranga-da went to sleep at his house at night; still, father and son had a bad relationship.

Ranga-da had lost his mental stability while he was in college. He was an excellent student at BM College and fell madly in love with another top student, Phulrani. When the girl's father refused his proposal of marriage, Ranga-da became unstable and suffered mental illness for the next ten years. My father-in-law took him all over India for treatment and became bankrupt. Later he started using some therapeutic oils and got better. My father-in-law married him into a business family in Jhalkathi, but this marriage never brought any peace or comfort into Ranga-da's household. Later his wife lost her own mental stability and left the household. What a tragedy!

Chorda's household wasn't happy either. After bearing two sons and four daughters in quick succession, his wife died of smallpox in 1954. Chorda began a life of struggle with his six small children. The two brothers raised all these children with incredible effort, but they couldn't think of and plan the children's marriages as was customary. The oldest son Chanchal went to his aunt's house in Kolkata for his education. The oldest daughter Moni took on all the household responsibilities at a young age but still managed to pass her higher secondary exam. Later she finished a teacher training course and started teaching. She still did all the housework and tutored small children in her spare time. The other siblings all got BAs.

Swadesh had gone back to Kolkata and started work with the Mujibnagar government in Kolkata. I slowly acquainted myself with my new surroundings. Ranu and Monta were schoolgirls. Babul had gotten his BA and spent his time hanging out on the street corner and making job applications under pressure from his father and uncle. Moni and Bulu cooked and ate breakfast early in the morning and went to work. I spent most of the time chatting with the two brothers. At night, we all ate together and then hung out talking and having a good time, which was a completely new experience in that family. Even though the two brothers lived on two ends of the same street, they never went to each other's houses, much less ate there. Ranga-da kept inviting me to eat at his house, so I said I'd go along with everyone from Chorda's house. Chorda didn't go, but Babul, Moni, Bul, Ranu, and Monta went with us.

They lived in one room. There was a big bed where I could tell both sisters slept. Ranga-da slept at Nirmal's house. There was a cook. Chaya was the mistress of the house. Maya sat on the bed wringing her hands. She looked very weak and sickly. Nirmal had also come to see me, his Kakima. After a lot of talking, Chaya laid the things out on the floor and served Ranga-da, Nirmal, Babul, Mini, Ani, and me. Up until now, in the other house, they were serving me separately. I suddenly asked Ranga-da, "Ranga-da, am I the wife in this household, or are they?" Ranga-da laughed out loud and said, "What do you mean, you're the wife, how could they be wives?"

I said, "They've been serving me like an outsider for a week now. I can't let this go on. Today you all sit down, and I'll serve you. Are you afraid of losing caste? You lost it a long time ago when you left your Kaku in a Muslim country." Ranga-da agreed. I tucked in my sari-end at the waist and served everyone, then I ate too. We talked long into the night. Ranga-da went home with Nirmal, and we all went back to Chorda's house.

The next Sunday, I invited Ranga-da's whole family to eat at Chorda's house. I took Chorda with me to the market. I bought shrimp, chicken, and all kinds of vegetables and said, "I'm cooking today." Ranga-da came over early. The girls brought me a portable stove on the veranda. They said, "You'll be hot cooking in the kitchen, why don't you cook here?" I let it go.

I fried the shrimp and gave it to the brothers with hot tea. At first, they were startled and said, "We have to eat this now?" I said, "If you don't eat them now, they won't taste good later." As I was cooking, we kept talking of this and that. This was the first time anyone had cooked chicken in that house. I taught the girls how to cut a chicken.

I sat everyone down to eat together. Chorda and Ranga-da unanimously praised the cooking. Then Chorda announced, "From now on Joya [the name I was known by in that house] will cook for us." Ranga-da said, "Chaya, don't cook at home for me anymore. As long as Joya's here, I'll come eat lunch and dinner here and talk with her."

With all these parties and fun, a month flew by. Swadesh didn't come even for Mini's birthday, but we celebrated her seventh birthday on 1 July in grand style. The neighbors came too. Only one thing was bothering me. That I am really Noorjahan—my in-laws kept my name and Muslim identity a secret from everyone. I didn't like that at all. Besides that, they either didn't know or pretended not to know that I had a sixteen-year-old son.

On 2 July 1971, Swadesh showed up. When he saw how well things were going, he was amazed. The house was full of laughter and cheer. When we went into the bedroom, he asked me, "How did this change come about?" I answered, "Magic." Swadesh had come to take me back to Kolkata. I said we had to ask his brothers first. Swadesh said, "I'm taking my own wife and children back with me, why do I need their permission for that?" I insisted, "No, we have to ask them." When I brought it up at dinner, Chorda exclaimed, "No no, they're not going anywhere. They'll stay here. You go back." Now I saw trouble coming. I said, “Dada, eating out all the time is affecting his health. I need to go with him now, but I’ll definitely come back.” That night, it was as if a shadow of grief fell over the house. The next day, everyone from both households came to the train station to see us off. The brothers hugged me and cried, saying, “If it weren’t for you, we’d never have Swada back again, we know it.” I said goodbye with tears in my eyes, promising to come back for Pujo. From then on, I have had a strong relationship with my in-laws. Every year when I go to Bangladesh, I go to see them. As long as the brothers were alive, I went to Asansol. Both Ranga-da’s daughters are now married, and they each have daughters. Sadly, Nirmal and Chanchal died several years ago.

I then went to Swadesh’s older sister Ranga-di’s house in Chakdaha (near Kolkata) for a family reunion. We fixed the date ahead of time, and her children and some other relatives came from wherever they were. But Swadesh’s brothers did not come. We had lunch together and spent the afternoon talking; then in the evening we all went our separate ways.

Two of Chorda’s daughters and his son Babul later got married. The daughters seem happy in their married lives. Two other daughters—Moni and Bulu—had careers in the local schools and took care of their father until he passed away. I still write to his family regularly and visit them.

In 1971, Ranga-di hadn’t seen her other two brothers and their children for more than twenty years. I was the one who took her to Asansol to meet them. The brothers were amazed and said, “How did you do in no time what we couldn’t do in twenty years?” The four siblings met for the first time in more than two decades and soon got to talking about all sorts of memories. I sat at a little distance and watched them, my eyes tearing up with emotion.

Two remarkable things happened while I was staying at my in-laws’ house during the Liberation War. Four or five days after we reached Asansol, we were all sitting and talking on the veranda one morning when suddenly Moni (Chorda's oldest daughter) came and said, "Kakima, come and see what Ani and Mini are doing." I looked and saw they had spread out two *gamchas* and were doing *namaz*. I laughed and said, "They're doing *namaz*. Your Kaku married a Muslim, so why shouldn't his children do *namaz*?" Their faces went pale. I said firmly, "Wait a few days and you'll see them doing *pujo* too." Sure enough, eight or ten days later we found Ani and Mini had collected some flowers and leaves and were doing *pujo* with great seriousness in a corner of the veranda, using a flute instead of a conch-shell. Children's minds are so innocent and beautiful. If only we could be like them!

The second thing was, one day Swadesh, Ranga-di, Ranga-da, Chorda, and I were all busy talking. Suddenly Ani and Mini came running and said, "Ma, the boys from the other street are saying we're Hindu. We're not Hindu, are we?" I looked around and saw everyone staring at them in silence, pale with fear. I said, "Yes, I know you're not Hindu, but what are you then?" Mini said, "We're not Hindu or Muslim, we're Bengalis." Ani said quietly, "Yes, we're Bengalis." The atmosphere lightened immediately, and smiles of surprise and pride broke out on everyone's faces. My two brothers-in-law shouted happily, "Look what a big thing our darlings just said! We had better learn from them." They called their own children and told them, "Learn from your cousins."

There's one other thing I must mention. When we came back to Kolkata from Asansol, we first stayed at the Savoy Hotel, and then Ratna and Amiya Bagchi invited us to stay at their friend Dr Sunanda Sen's small but nice flat in Jadavpur University. The days went by without any improvement in our circumstances. In my in-laws' house, I was known as Joya. I think they hadn't told even their sister Ranga-di, much less the neighbors, about who

I was, a Muslim widow. I told Ranga-di myself, because I don't like dishonesty. After we moved to Jadavpur University, Ratna told me not to use the name Noorjahan; not even her mother knew my real name. When I told Ratna's mother my real name after Bangladesh's Independence, she was stupefied, and I was embarrassed too.

One day in Kolkata, Swadesh was at home during the day because it was a holiday. After lunch, Mini suddenly said, "I'm not going to marry a Hindu or a Muslim. I'm going to marry a *saheb* [foreigner or white person]." She was only seven at the time. When we asked her why she said that, she said, "In Pakistan, we were forbidden to say Baba's name [because the Pakistani Army was killing Hindus], and now we can't say Ma's name." We hadn't realized this had such a big impact on her at such a young age. When Mini grew up, she really did marry a *saheb*.

After Swadesh came to get us from Asansol, we moved into the Savoy Hotel, where Atul Babu had rented a room for us. Atul Babu was very fond of me from my student days in Patuakhali. I bought a small tin pot and wok, two plates, a tin spoon, two glasses, and a small kerosene stove from a pavement shop. It cost me 15 rupees for the lot. That was a lot of money in those days. Our budget for groceries was two to two and a half rupees.

We met a family in the Savoy Hotel who had come there from East Pakistan after 1947. They had been managing to live in one room all this time. This family had thought that they would save up little by little, buy some land somewhere, and build a house of their own—but things didn't go that way. I met several other families like them. Just next door to us lived three siblings, a brother and two sisters. The brother and the older sister were over fifty. The younger sister was thirty-five. The brother and the older sister were schoolteachers. The younger sister did the cooking and cleaning. I used to see the younger sister all the time, and she would always say to me, "When will I be liberated from this imprisonment?"

I said, "You could get a job too, or get married."

She told me, "Why would they let me do that? I'm their domestic help!"

I felt bad for her, but there was nothing I could do. I was myself a refugee.

An older woman lived in the Savoy Hotel with a houseful of cats. You could smell cats whenever you went near her room. A young woman lived upstairs with her two daughters, seven and three years old. They lived alone; I never saw the woman's husband. The woman was very cheerful and came to see me a lot. One day, she said, "Mashima, I think my husband has another wife. He stays with me for a few days, then he goes off on 'business' for two or three months. He gives me money before he leaves, so it's no inconvenience to me. When he's here, he treats me well."

I thought to myself, but what if her husband doesn't come back?

We were getting along fine there. Then suddenly our old friends Amiya Bagchi and his wife Jashodhara, whom we met in Cambridge, found out we were there and called us up. They asked us to move to a flat in the faculty quarters of Jadavpur University. Swadesh objected strongly to this, but I said, "Our money's running out. I can't live like this."

So I accepted the offer.

I had another reason for accepting. The Savoy Hotel was right on the main road. One night, I couldn't sleep. There was a narrow slip of a veranda in front of our room. I went and stood on the veranda. When I looked down, I saw the street had taken on a completely different character. There were rows of people sleeping all up and down the street. Whole families, with husband, wife, and children. Next to them lay their household items, bundles of this and that.

I had read a lot about refugees in stories, novels, and in the newspaper. But seeing this sight in real life, I was shaken. I thought, if our country doesn't become independent soon, we could end up like this too! I thought about this a lot. After that night, I kept worrying what we were going to eat and where we were going to stay when our money ran out. That's why I accepted the Bagchis' offer. Then they came and took us to the flat at Jadavpur University.

The flat belonged to Dr Sunanda Sen. She was an economics professor and unmarried; she moved to her brother's house to make the flat available. Hundreds of Bengali Hindu families in Kolkata and Agartala gave up their own peace and comfort to make room for Bengali refugee families during the Liberation War. Not only room, but many people also gave financial assistance. A few professors from Rajshahi University had also taken refuge in Jadavpur University with their families.

After we moved to the Jadavpur faculty quarter, a former leader of Barisal's Communist Party, whom everyone called Sarba-da, found out we were there and suddenly showed up one day. After 1950, he had come to live in West Bengal. Sarba-da was now a full-time worker for West Bengal's Communist Party. He had never married; he lived in the Party office. One day, Sarba-da brought Manorama Mashima and Nalini-da to our flat in Jadavpur. We were so glad to see them, and to know they were alive!

Before the trip to Asansol, I worked for a while in Kolkata's Salt Lake Camp. Whenever I went there, I searched for people from Barisal, but I didn't find anyone. I heard that people hadn't started coming from Barisal yet; they came to Kolkata much later. When I saw Mashima and Nalini-da, I felt a little better. They gave me news of people I knew in Barisal and told me stories of the indomitable resistance of the people of Barisal, who had come together irrespective of community, religion, caste, and political ideology to take a stand against the Pakistani Army's atrocities of March and April. Sadly, they were overpowered by the Pakistani Army's modern technology.

After that, Mashima and Nalini-da visited me often. One day, the old comrades from Barisal got together, and Nalini-da rented a bus to take everyone to the Barasat Camp. He took me and Swadesh along too. There was a camp in Barasat for Communist Party organizers and Muktijoddhas, soldiers fighting for Bangladesh's independence. My older daughter was sick with jaundice at the time. I left her in Jashodhara Bagchi's care.

In Barasat, I met many Muktijoddhas from Barisal. They were all very young men, wearing *lungis* and undershirts, who were fighting against the Pakistani Army. A group of them were sleeping, exhausted from the fight, and another group were getting ready to go. I couldn't believe these young boys were going to fight a war. Many of them probably never returned. Who knows how many mothers lost their sons? I saw that many of them were Jaseem's age, and I felt like crying. We ate lunch with them—coarse red rice and *kochur ghonto* (taro root). They were satisfied with that.

After lunch, Nalini-da called a meeting. There were about forty or fifty people there. Nalini-da introduced us to everyone. At one point, he got carried away and said it was a mistake to kick us out of the Party when we were married and that he had invited us here to make amends.

After seeing the Barasat Camp, I decided to put my mind to improving the quality of food the Muktijoddhas were receiving. I started raising funds. Many people helped me; one of them was Sabita-di, to whom I had grown close. Sabita-di introduced me to many of her friends and went with me to many storefronts to collect money, clothes, medicines, and so on. I met with an unexpectedly warm response. Mashima came regularly to collect all these aid items. Nalini-da sometimes came too.

One day, Nalini-da asked me, "Noorjahan, how are you getting all these things in this unfamiliar place?"

I said, "With the mantra Mashima taught me, it doesn't matter if the place is familiar or unfamiliar. Besides, I'm not doing this for myself, so I don't feel shy or ashamed to ask anyone for help. I think the people I ask know this too, and so they don't turn me away empty-handed."

A few days after the trip to Barasat, I had to go to the police station. The Indian government had decided to register the refugees and issue them ID cards, so every refugee had to go to the local police station. Swadesh and I went to the Jadavpur police station. A police officer asked me all kinds of questions. One of the questions put me in an uncomfortable situation. The police officer kept asking me if I was Swadesh's wife or not! It would have been natural for Swadesh to answer this question, and I had thought he would be answering the questions. But I'm sorry to say that Swadesh was silent. In these kinds of situations, Swadesh keeps quiet, and I have to do the talking. That day too I had to talk to the police officer. This made me very upset.

A few days later, a question started to bother me. I thought, how long will we have to live here, away from our country? We had come to take refuge in India along with a vast number of people who had lost their homes, their identities. If we didn't win this war, we would have to live the rest of our lives in exile, where no one knew us, our names, our family histories.

Ever since we came to Kolkata, I had kept myself busy, but having two small children imposed some limits—I couldn't go very far, certainly not to the battlefield, so I chose Salt Lake to do my service. There were a huge number of refugees there. I went to serve them and keep up their spirits. This was important at the time because due to Pakistani government propaganda and the hardships of refugee life, a few of the refugees had gone back home, and others were ready to follow their example. If this went on, it would hinder the war effort.

I think the Bangladesh government was looking into this also. That's why political leaders were going around to all the camps to give rousing speeches to the refugees. I joined in this task, sometimes by myself and sometimes with a group—what they call "motivational speaking." We had to explain to the refugees that this was a struggle of life and death, it was a war for our existence, our language, our culture, and our heritage. We had to win this war. In Salt Lake, we often sang in unison the Bangla version of Joan Baez's inspiring song, "We Shall Overcome." Young and old, everyone joined in, and the little children were very happy. My daughters Mini and Ani, who were seven and three, often came with me and joined in too. Almost every day, we sang this song before leaving for home.

The days went by like this, and amid pain and sadness, uncertainty and death, Eid came around. I hadn't even thought of it. On the day of Eid, I had gone to the camp with Mini, and they told me it was Eid. I looked around the refugee camp and saw that the little children had taken baths and worn whatever clothes they had and were flitting around with *kajal* around their eyes.

There were over 100,000 refugees in Salt Lake Camp. Many of them were Muslim. There were a lot of health problems there, especially fever, measles, and irritation of the eyes. Measles was rampant in the camp. The sick refugees lay on the damp floor on palm-leaf mats, moaning. Their mothers' eyes were dark with anxious tears.

The day of Eid, I was looking around the camp. A Muslim family brought me a plate with a little dry *semai*, made without milk, and a few dal fritters. I asked them, "Where did you get all this?"

They said the local authorities had distributed a small ration of sugar and *semai* to the Muslim families for Eid. Besides that, they had been saving up dal and oil little by little to have a bit of festivity in the gloom.

Many foreigners came to see the Salt Lake Camp. A lawyer from Kushtia, Amirul Islam, sometimes brought foreign dignitaries there. I had gone to Salt Lake for the first time with Amirul Islam, and after that I started to go regularly. I remember Edward Kennedy's visit to the camp,[8] which was pivotal in bringing attention to the humanitarian crisis caused by Pakistan's refusal to accept the election results. During the Liberation War, Swadesh worked all over the border region to ascertain the number of refugees and their condition.

### *Barisal's Prashanta Dasgupta*

I saw Prashanta-da at a seminar in the Bangiya Sahitya Parishad during our refugee period in Kolkata in 1971. When I was in Barisal, I'd gone to Prashanta-da's house many times. One of his sisters went to school with me. Prashanta-da was a friend of Chacha's too. He was a small-built, sweet-natured person. I've written about Prashanta-da earlier too; he was a student leader at one time and spent long years in Pakistani jails. When he got out, he went to Kolkata. I saw him toward the end of the Muktijuddho. It was a meeting to remember.

Amiya Bagchi, Swadesh, and I had gone by bus to the seminar at the Bangiya Sahitya Parishad. Swadesh went and sat at the front of the seminar room. Amiya and I sat a little farther back. A little later, a middle-aged gentleman in a *dhuti-panjabi* came in, looked around, and sat down in the front. As soon as he sat down, he turned around and looked at me for a few moments. After that, he kept looking back at me. Swadesh started giving his speech, but the gentleman kept turning back. At some point, Amiya said, "Noorjahan, why does this gentleman keep looking at you?"

It was obvious he was looking at me. At the end of the program, he came up to me and said, "Aren't you Noorjahan? I'm Prashanta. I'm seeing you for the first time in twenty years, Noorjahan! You look like a proper housewife now."

Then we both went to meet Swadesh. The way they hugged each other made a lot of people stare. They were friends from childhood, meeting after a long time. He had come there from Sodpur when he saw Swadesh's name in the paper.

Prashanta-da invited us to his house the next Sunday. When we went there by train, we found Manorama Mashima there. It felt good to see Prashanta-da's wife Bela-di and their sons. Bela-di is a very good cook. We spent the whole day there in a very festive atmosphere. Swadesh and Prashanta-da were engrossed in talking about their friends in Barisal and the state of the war. We went home after dinner. I felt like we had found our own people after so long!

Before we went back to Bangladesh, we had to visit Prashanta-da's house several more times. Even though he was busy with local politics, he'd left his heart in Barisal. Together with some other old Communist worker-friends from Barisal, he had established an organization called "Samanbay" (Synthesis). Prashanta-da taught at a college. He had found a good flat in Sodpur. His sons were good students, and they also believed in his ideals and dedicated themselves to Party work.

Once, there was a terrible flood in Barisal. Prashanta-da worked tirelessly to raise money for the people of Barisal. But how was he going to send it? He heard that Rani Chakrabarti, the wife of the Party leader Hiren-da in Barisal, had come to Kolkata to treat an eye problem. Prashanta-da wanted to give the money to her, so he put it in his pocket and got on the bus one morning to go see her. On the way, he had to get off one bus and on another one. He was run over by the first bus and died. The passersby took him to the hospital. The bundle of money in his pocket was untouched. Even though the people of Barisal did receive that money later, they lost one or their accomplished sons forever.

## *Nabaneeta Deb Sen*

During that period in Kolkata, I also met Nabaneeta Deb Sen.[9] Nabaneeta invited us over for lunch one day in her ancestral house, called "Love." Nabaneeta's mother Radharani Debi lived there, and Nabaneeta lived there too with her two daughters. Our two daughters were the same age, so they made friends right away and were soon busy playing.

That was the first time I saw Nabaneeta. I had heard about her from many people. She was beautiful and talented. Nabaneeta introduced me to her mother Radharani Debi. She was a writer; in fact, both Nabaneeta's parents were writers, Radharani Debi and Narendranath Deb. I had read both their writing and heard the story of their marriage. Radharani Debi was a child widow. She and Narendra Deb fell in love and got married. Their biggest supporter was Rabi Tagore himself. He also chose Nabaneeta's name.

I liked Radharani Debi on the first day I met her, and she made me her own on that first day too. From that day on, Radharani Debi and I were friends for life. She told me, "Noorjahan, I took a liking to you right away. Somehow, I don't like ordinary homebodies."

I was widowed at eighteen with a child, and later I married Swadesh. I think that was one reason she liked me.

We ate lunch together: *ilish shorshe* (hilsa or shad with mustard paste), *puishak* (a kind of greens) with *ilish* bones, meat, thick moong dal, and various side dishes like chutney, curd, and sweets. After lunch, we lay down on Radharani Debi's huge bed and talked all afternoon. She opened her basket of stories on the very first day, all kinds of stories of her life: her love story, the role of Rabindranath Tagore and Sharatchandra in her marriage; she even showed me letters from them. I was impressed. While I was talking to her, I noticed Nabaneeta was bustling around, tidying up the house. In between, she was talking to foreign friends on the phone. I was impressed by her too that day. She was so beautiful and talented, and she had Amartya Sen for a husband! She was so lucky!

On my way home, as I was going down the stairs, Nabaneeta was coming down with me. Suddenly I said to her, "Nabaneeta, you're so beautiful and talented. Amartya is very lucky to have a wife like you."

She turned to look at me and said sadly, "I see you don't know anything. Amartya doesn't like me at all. He cleared out our home in Delhi, left me here, and went to England with his lover."

I was astonished. Then Nabaneeta told me Amartya was coming to Kolkata that evening. She would go to pick him up from the airport, but he would be staying somewhere else. Later I became close to Nabaneeta. We saw each other often, ate together, talked together. I liked her writing a lot. It made me sad to know that she still had a weakness for Amartya. Maybe it's hard to forget someone like him. I kept in touch with Nabaneeta's mother Radharani Debi until the end of her life. After Independence, every time I went to Kolkata, I went to see her even if Nabaneeta wasn't there. She always hugged me close and fed me herself.

The last time I saw Radharani Debi, she was very weak because of her age, but she kept a keen eye on everything. She put sweets on my plate herself and kept aside sweets for everyone in my family. When I left, she took both my hands and said, "You live in America, if you see Bablu [Amartya Sen], tell him I love him just like before. And tell him that there's no other man in Nabaneeta's life. Nabaneeta loves only him, and she always will."

Maybe Mashima had an idea that since Amartya and I both live in America, we must see each other all the time. I never had a chance to give Mashima's message to Amartya Sen.

*Victory: an independent Bangladesh*

Before we knew it, December came around. The war started in earnest on 3 December. After that, we kept track of events with bated breath. We kept the radio on every day. No one could sleep. The Indian Army was bombing Dhaka. I was more scared than glad to hear this, because so many of my friends and relatives were in Dhaka, and with them the light of my eyes, my beloved Jaseem. At the same time, it was clear that independence was almost here. The Pakistani Army and their supporters had no choice but to withdraw to Dhaka and other cities, but that didn't stop them from spreading destruction along the way.

On 14 December, Swadesh came and told me that Amirul Islam was leading a large group to Kushtia, now a free zone, the next day. They had asked Swadesh to come, but he couldn't go because of other work. If I wanted, I could go along. I agreed right away, but then I thought, where am I going to leave my children?! Our young friends from Dhaka Pratima and Kanutosh Pal had come to see me that day; they used to visit me often, and Ani and Mini had taken a liking to them. When I asked Pratima to stay with the girls, she agreed immediately.

On the morning of 15 December, I left with the group for Kushtia. I didn't have any decent sari to wear, so I remember borrowing a nylon sari from my friend Pratima. We left for Kushtia in seven or eight cars. In my car were artist Debdas Chakrabarti's wife Saleha, the economics professor Anisur Rahman, and another gentleman whose name I can't remember. An Indian woman was with us too; she was a social worker.

As soon as the cars entered Bangladesh, we could see the signs of destruction inflicted by the Pakistani Army. Here and there, the Bangladeshi flag was flying. People of all ages came flocking over to us. In one place, they crowded around the car, and we got out. They were so excited! Shouts of "Joy Bangla" (Victory to

Bengal) shook the air. It was a bittersweet moment. I've never seen anything like it.

We heard many sad stories everywhere we went. I'll never forget what I heard that day. Sons killed in front of their mothers, mothers in front of their sons, sisters raped in front of their brothers. All the women of the household raped in front of the elderly father. We went forward, listening to all these hair-raising stories. I've read the history of various wars, but I've never seen such destruction and atrocity with my own eyes. This was my first taste of such a terrifying experience. Even after all that, the people were so happy and excited! They hugged us and cried, but they also puffed up their chests with pride to be citizens of an independent country. The area was lit up with the light of a great hope. Amirul Islam was wiping his eyes repeatedly and hugging everyone.

We reached Kushtia at night, by way of Magura and Jhinaidaha. The news had gone ahead of us; the local leaders were cooking in tents. After a long day, Saleha, another woman, and I went to sleep on Red Cross blankets on the ground. Late at night, they woke us up and gave us *khichuri*. I don't remember anymore what time it was. The local leaders were busy with discussions and meetings, and we three women were sleeping in a half-ruined post office.

One incident in Kushtia still burns in my heart. When I woke up and looked around me, I saw some thirteen- or fourteen-year-old boys there. They were all wearing *lungis*, with *gamchas* around their waists and guns in their hands. They were our Mukti Bahini, standing there to guard us. When I first woke up, the boys said to me, "Khalamma, you can sleep peacefully. When we're here, you don't need to worry, you won't come to any harm."

I wasn't afraid, but I just thought, these boys have given their lives for the country's independence. So many sisters have lost their brothers, wives have lost their husbands, mothers have lost their sons. So many women have lost their greatest asset, their honor. Can we ever repay their debt, personally or collectively, or truly assess the value of this self-sacrifice?

Morning came. We all ate breakfast at a little roadside restaurant and got ready. We went around and talked to people in the city and surrounding villages. Our aim was to reassure them and help bring some normalcy back to their lives. We listened to their experiences during these long nine months. The local people could hardly believe that this unnatural life was about to end. Fear still reigned on their faces. There were signs of cruelty all over the city of Kushtia; it made us shudder to see this in the light of day. In one part of the city, there was a huge hole made by a bomb. We went door to door talking to people all morning.

The other members of our group were also busy. Amirul Islam held several meetings. When we had done whatever was possible to do in one day and were ready to return to Kolkata, we suddenly noticed something funny. We saw that Professor Anisur Rahman was covered from head to foot in cotton fluff from the Red Cross blanket. We all laughed out loud. When we had woken up in the morning, all of us had looked like him, but we had each cleaned the fluff from our hair and clothes before anyone saw it. He hadn't done that.

This was 16 December. We were all anxious to hear the latest news of the war. On the way back, the cars stopped at Magura. The local government officials met with the political leaders. They came running to tell us the news that the Pakistani military was getting ready to surrender in Dhaka. The Indian Army, General Arora, and all the high officials of the Mujibnagar government were on their way to Dhaka.

Hearing this news, we quickly got on our way to Kolkata. On the way, we saw people happily distributing sweets. Our cars could hardly move forward. When we reached Kolkata, it was nighttime. We saw the whole city awash with light. All this time, they had kept it dark for fear of an attack from the Pakistani military. Firecrackers were going off and sweets being given out everywhere. Even inside the city, our cars could hardly move. The convoy split up, and each car went off in a different direction to drop people off at their destinations. Our destination was the faculty quarters of Jadavpur University.

I was in the same car as Professor Anisur Rahman. He got down ahead of me. He was staying in Sunanda Sen's brother's house, and I was staying in Sunanda Sen's own flat. As soon as the car stopped in front of Sunanda Sen's brother's house, everyone came running to welcome Anisur Rahman. He got out of the car still covered in fluff. Everyone was astonished. He had told us in the morning that he would wear this sign of Bangladesh's independence as long as he could. And when we reached Kolkata, he said, "This sacrifice for the independence of Bangladesh will make history." Then I understood why he hadn't shaken off the fluff all day—he wanted to show it to his friends! He struck me as a very emotional person.

The next day was 17 December. That day, Swadesh left for work as usual and came back in the evening. I think it was the next day, 18 December, that Professor Anisur Rahman came to see me and said he was leaving for Dhaka. He told me that the Planning Commission had been established under the leadership of Professor Nurul Islam, Rehman Sobhan, Mosharraf Hossain, and himself, Anisur Rahman. They were all going to Dhaka, and so he had come to say goodbye. Swadesh wasn't home then. When he came back, I told him what Professor Anisur Rahman had said. He was disheartened, but he didn't say anything. It's sad but true that the members of the Mujibnagar Planning Cell and Swadesh's friends who had gone abroad went back to Dhaka without him. There was no place for Swadesh in the Planning Commission of independent Bangladesh. No one even came to see him before leaving. I believe he was left out because of religious discrimination against Hindus, and perhaps also because of our interfaith marriage. Swadesh was the only Hindu among the prominent Bengali economists at the time, and he was constantly being overlooked despite his hard work and brilliance.

When the Liberation War started, most of Bangladesh's economists had taken refuge in India at first, and later they had gone abroad. As far as I know, only Dr Mosharraf Hossain and Swadesh stayed in Kolkata and carried on important work as members of the Mujibnagar Planning Cell. Among those who went abroad was the PIDE director Professor Nurul Islam. He wrote a letter to Swadesh from abroad telling him not to waste his time in Kolkata and to go abroad right away. He thought that Indira Gandhi was not going to help with the Liberation War. Professor Anisur Rahman had left Dhaka and come to Kolkata on the very first day of the Liberation War; then he too had gone abroad. He came back to Kolkata right when the country was about to gain independence. Professor Rehman Sobhan also went abroad during the war and came back after independence and joined the Planning Commission. The funny thing is, those who left first during the war were the first to come running back to join the Bangladesh Planning Commission. No one thought of Swadesh then.

After 17 December, I was in tears, wondering if my son was alive. But I had no way to get news from him. A few days later, Swadesh also went to Dhaka, leaving me in Kolkata. When he left, he told me, "I'll go straight to Jaseem and put him on the phone with you."

After Swadesh left, I waited anxiously for the phone call. As soon as he reached Dhaka, he went to see Jaseem, called me, and said, "Here, talk to Jaseem."

When I heard my son's voice, I cried. He cried too.

After that, the days went by quickly. After talking to Jaseem, I was almost crazy with eagerness to go back home, but it wasn't possible then. Swadesh borrowed money to rent a house and came to get us almost a month later. We had to stay in Kolkata until then. I had left home on 16 June, and on 16 January I came back with my two daughters to independent Bangladesh.

When we reached Dhaka, I was reunited with Jaseem. I was so happy! Swadesh had rented the downstairs of House No. 362 in the old Road No. 27 in Dhanmondi. When we first arrived from Kolkata, we went to Karim Chacha's house and ate there, then went to our new house in the afternoon. I had left the country with Ani and Mini during very dark days, when I was afraid even to breathe loudly. The day we returned, the skies of Dhaka were tinged with gold, and it was exhilarating to take a breath standing on free, independent soil. I felt as if we were flying around like a bright flock of pigeons. At Karim Chacha's house, I met that same Dulu Mama who extorted money from me by threatening to turn us over to the military. Here he was being hailed as a Muktijoddha or freedom fighter! He was describing his heroic deeds to everyone in detail. Later he occupied a Bihari family's house and lived in comfort. It wasn't only Dulu Mama, there were thousands of "Dulu Mias" who acquired Muktijoddha certificates after Independence and grabbed a piece of the country's wealth.

In Dhaka, we heard more horrible and heartbreaking stories about life under the rule of the Pakbahini. Many well-known professors at Dhaka University lost their lives cruelly at the hands of the Pakistani Army. Hearing all this dampened the elation of homecoming. Two of the professors who died were very dear to me, Dr Jyotirmoy Guhathakurta and Professor Munir Choudhuri. I went to give my deep condolences to their families in Dhaka. I had a picture of Jaseem and Munir Sir's son Bhashon listening to songs on the radio. I gave the picture to Munir Sir's wife.

PART 6

# POST-INDEPENDENCE IN DHAKA AND ABROAD

## *Breaking and building*

After Independence, when everyone was busy dividing up the big posts in various institutions, Swadesh went on silently working for his old institution. After Independence, PIDE was renamed BIDS (Bangladesh Institute of Development Studies). He was the most senior and accomplished economist at BIDS and ran the organization but was never officially made its director; he was only given "Acting Director" status. Again, he faced discrimination because of his religion and perhaps because he had been part of the interim government in Mujibnagar/Kolkata. At that time, naturally, the country was caught up in the game of breaking old institutions and building new ones. The governmental administration had fallen apart. The Awami League and other political groups had experience leading movements, but they had no prior experience with shaping or governing a country, so it became difficult to reestablish the broken administration. Besides this, when hundreds of thousands of homeless refugees came home, housing them, treating the injured Mukti Bahini and civilians, and rehabilitating victims of rape and their unwanted children became big problems. There were shouts of dismay all around: we need this, we need that. Already, the country split in two: those who had suffered all kinds of pain and stayed in Bangladesh, and those who had been forced to flee until they reached Mujibnagar or India. These two groups began to suspect and mistrust each other. Those who left began to suspect those who stayed of being sympathizers with the Pakistanis, "Pajis" or "scoundrels." And those who stayed began to mock those who went to Mujibnagar, calling them "Haji" or those who go on the Hajj to Mecca. Widespread problems arose between the "Hajis" and the "Pajis." Meanwhile, everyone grew anxious to know when the Indian Army would leave our country and go back to their own. Even though we had attained independence swiftly with their direct support, people didn't look positively on their presence in Bangladesh after Independence.

We were under a lot of financial strain then. Some housewives I knew started small businesses and asked me to join them, but I had no interest in that, so I took a teaching job at Udayan School. My two daughters Mini and Ani were enrolled there, which was very convenient for me. After I took the job at Udayan School, I got to know Salma Sobhan, and we became very good friends.[1] Salma's middle son Babar went to the school along with my daughters. Salma taught at Dhaka University, and she couldn't pick Babar up on time, so I would take him home after school. Ani, Mini, and Babar would eat and play together. When Salma arrived, we would talk together, and so we became friends.

I often talked to Salma about the problems village women faced, especially legal problems. I told Salma, "If we don't make legal knowledge available in every house in language they can understand, our village women's troubles will never be over." I told Salma a few stories about my own family. My Chacha's daughter Kohinur had been married to my Phuphu's son Alam, who lived in the next village. After Kohinur had a girl child, her marriage broke up. My father and uncles married Kohinur off again to a teacher in our village. Alam also married again. That's all I knew about it.

A few years after that, I went home to Katakhali for a visit. Some men and women came from our village and the next village to see me. After talking to them, I felt tired and lay down. The place was teeming with people, and my family couldn't get them out of there. Even so, I was lying down with my eyes closed. Suddenly I realized our Kohinur was sitting next to me breast-feeding her baby and sobbing. Kohinur was extremely beautiful and intelligent.

I asked my mother, "Why is she crying?"

Ma said, "No wonder she's crying. The whole village has come to see you, and your Phuphu and Phupha even brought their domestic help, but they didn't bring Kohinur's daughter."

Kohinur's daughter lived with her Dada and Dadi, that is, my Phuphu and Phupha. So that's why Kohinur was crying—Kohinur's daughter Piyara was eight or nine then. I asked Ma, "Why didn't they bring her?"

Ma said, "Your Phuphu and Phupha are afraid she might want to stay with her mother or give her some comfort. They don't want that."

At that, I sat up and called my Phuphu and Phupha. Ma told me, "Let it go for now, the house is full of people, what will they think?"

I said, "What will they think? It's not time to think of that now, Ma."

My voice is already harsh and deep. Hearing me shout that day, everyone in the house got scared. I told Phuphu and Phupha, "Send Piyara here right now. Piyara will live with her mother from now on until she is sixteen years old. Then Piyara can decide whom she wants to live with." I informed everyone of this article of the law and explained it in simple terms, so they understood.

After Independence, we couldn't stay in the country for long. Swadesh was planning to take his study leave or sabbatical from BIDS and spend a year doing research at Queen Elizabeth House in Oxford. It was exciting for all of us except Jaseem. He had just passed his Senior Cambridge (O Level) exam and enrolled at Dhaka College. Jaseem had also applied to Notre Dame College in Dhaka and was among the top ten in the entrance exam, but after he got into an argument with the Fathers of St Joseph School about our independence, they didn't want to enroll him there. We also decided he shouldn't go there. Yet again I had to leave Jaseem with Bela and go to Oxford, although this time we brought Jaseem over to Oxford a few months later.

In September 1973, we left Dhaka for Oxford. Our friend Ian Martin met us at the London Airport to drive us to Oxford, where Swadesh had rented a furnished house from a professor who was away in Australia for a year. The house was in the southern part of Oxford, right off Abingdon Road. The River Thames divides Oxford into two parts, North and South. The South is supposed to be a poorer area. We loved our new home in Oxford. It was two stories and had a beautiful garden with flowers and fruit trees (pear, apple, blackberries, and rhubarb). The children's school was just ten minutes' walk, and the girls could walk alone.

We had met Ian Martin in Dhaka after the independence of Bangladesh. At the time, he was working at the Ford Foundation. Later Ian spent many years at Amnesty International. We have stayed good friends for all these years. When we were in Oxford, Ian wanted us to meet his parents in Gloucester. He drove us in his car since we did not have one. We spent a whole day with Ian and his parents. They lived in a beautiful house called Laurel Cottage, surrounded by gardens. We were served a delicious lunch of roasted leg of lamb, roast potatoes and carrots, salad, and fresh mint sauce, followed by homemade apple pie with whipped cream. We spent the whole day with this gracious and generous couple. They were genuinely interested in our lives and our culture. We invited them to come to our home for a meal one day, and they promised to come. The drive to Gloucester and back was also an opportunity to see the gorgeous English countryside. Ian's parents came to see us in Oxford before we left for Washington. I made them a Bangladeshi meal of beef curry, *mach bhaja* (fried fish with turmeric), dal with vegetables, chutney, and *payesh* (Bengali rice pudding) for dessert.

*About my father*

After we went to Oxford, my father died suddenly. My siblings did not send me the news of my father's death.[2] I found out several days later when I called Jaseem. Baba, along with many other wealthy and middle-income farmers, had been impoverished financially and in mind and body by repeated cyclones and floods. Defeated by these disasters, they began to suffer from depression and low self-esteem. They lost not only loved ones, but everything they had in the floods and storms: their houses, jewelry, cows and buffaloes, goats and sheep, ducks and chickens. Above all, the soil that had once yielded gold became infertile due to increased salinity. They never received any government or non-governmental assistance.

I have lost almost sixty of my loved ones in various storms and floods. Among them are my loving Dadi, my youngest brother, my Nana and Nani, numerous uncles and aunts, and cousins. I can't make anyone comprehend this loss by quoting numbers. When I think of those I lost, my heart still bleeds.

Baba was a dynamic, playful, music-loving person. His life was full of fun, adventure, and excitement. The sons of *jotedar* families in our area usually lived lives of leisure, but Baba was something of an exception. He was always trying to do something to liven up his boring life. He busied himself not only with his own happiness, but with bringing cheer to everyone in the village.

There was one thing we loved in our household: music. Baba was central to organizing music and other performances. A harmonium, a record player, *dhol*, cymbals, we had everything. There would be *jatra*[3] and plays, and many kinds of festivities centered on these performances. Costumes for the *jatra* troupe were always ready. But these were only for the men to use. Baba was the main organizer of the troupe. In the winter, we enjoyed music and *jatra* all night long.

There wasn't much to do in our village in the monsoon season. Every year when I was small, Baba would plan out all kinds of programs for the winter even before the winter months of Agrahayan and Poush arrived. For example, he would pitch huge tents in front of the gate of our house for a month-long fair. Hundreds of people came by boat from far-off villages to the fair, many of them bringing various goods and opening shops or stalls. Some made *jilipi* and many other kinds of sweets all day and night. Some were little restaurants making a wide variety of dishes. Some sold fancy saris and bangles. Music, singing, plays, *jari gaan* (laments on the theme of the siege of Karbala, usually sung for the festival of Moharram), and *kobi gaan* (a competitive, improvisational form in which the singers carry on a debate through song) went on twenty-four hours of the day. Gambling went on too. Baba walked around the fair and enjoyed everything except the gambling. There was one interesting thing about this festival: for three to four days, it would only be open to women. Then my relatives would come pouring in—my Khalas, Phuphus, and Mamis would bring all their women relatives and friends, and our house would be full of festivity, like a wedding.

Once Baba brought in a huge Kamala Circus troupe from Barisal. One morning, we woke up to the roars of lions and tigers. We ran to the riverbank and stared wide-eyed at the boat full of real lions, tigers, bears, zebras, giraffes, elephants, camels, and monkeys. There were eight or ten women in the troupe too, who performed various acts. This event had the whole region in great excitement. In one day, they put up a huge tent. Everyone in the village crowded around the cages of the tigers and lions. Some members of the circus took elephants, zebras, and camels door to door for tips. I ran proudly ahead of them with my gang of other children. It was thrilling! By evening, Katakhali was full of bustling shops. The fair happened every winter, but that year was beyond everyone's expectations. I think there were tickets, but the price was nominal.

Another funny thing happened during the circus. Wherever I went with my friends, people would pull out chairs for us with great respect and feed us. No one asked us for money. I gave all my friends bangles, and I didn't have to pay for them. There was a tea stall in the fair. When we all went and sat there, they gave us tea in little glasses. I'd never had tea before, nor had any of my friends. They were all looking at me. I thought, I can't accept defeat now. As soon as I took a sip, I burnt my tongue. It was bitter too. I thought, "Ish, why do people drink this stuff?" But if I wanted to be a leader and uphold my reputation as the Boro Mia's eldest daughter, I had to drink the tea, no matter how bad it tasted. Finally, I managed to drink it, and the others followed suit. After that, I decided never to go near that tea stall.

Most people on our island never went beyond their familiar village, forget about going to the city! They felt extremely lucky to see so many live animals and watch the city women and clowns perform their acts. The fair went on for a month. The last week was for women only. My mother never went out, but this time she gave in to our request, got dressed up one evening, and went to see the circus, holding my hand. I was overjoyed. I think Baba was happiest of all. At least one day of her life, Ma left the house, breaking the rules of her world.

I've written all this to try to show my Baba as a human being. Baba sometimes left home without warning. After a few weeks, my Dadi would start wailing. I think Baba found village life boring. He would come back suddenly after two or three months. He never told us where he had been and what he had been doing. Maybe he told Ma, but her mouth was sealed. She never said anything about it. The village people made up their own fantastic stories about Baba, but he just laughed.

One time when Baba had vanished for months, my Dadi was doing her usual wailing and Ma was silent. Suddenly one of Baba's followers in the village came with news. Baba had several of these followers, who were always hanging around him. Ma couldn't stand them, but there was nothing she could do. That day, this follower came running and said that a sanyasi was meditating under the big old banyan tree by the riverbank. Everyone but Ma went running to the banyan tree and saw there really was a sanyasi, dreadlocks and all, sitting deep in meditation. Baba's followers were all falling at his feet and crying. Dada and Dadi came and broke down too, asking him to help them find their eldest son (Baba). Meanwhile, Ma sent someone to tell me secretly that the sanyasi was likely to be none other than my Baba. I shoved my way through the crowd, went and sat in the sanyasi's lap, and said, "Baba, why are you acting like this? Talk to me!"

Then the sanyasi hugged me to his chest and started bawling. A wave of jubilation went through the crowd—everyone's favorite Boro Mia had come home! Without Boro Mia, there was no cheer in the village.

Dada and Dadi quickly went home, rubbed down their biggest cow, and released her, telling the villagers, "Anyone who wants can take her."

Dadi didn't stop there; she bathed Baba with the water of seven ghats and the milk of seven cows, made his face wet with hundreds of kisses, dried it with her sari-end, and took him into the house. Dadi said she would hold a feast for the whole village.

But Ma was stiff with rage. She thought Baba had done this mischief because he was afraid if he came home normally after so long, he would get a scolding.

But who was going to scold him now? It was no small thing that he'd come home safely! No one dared to ask Baba any questions. Some said maybe Baba had gone to Agra to see the Taj Mahal; that's great, not many people get a chance to see the Taj Mahal. Some said maybe Baba had gone to Kamrup Kamakhya Temple[4] and the sorceresses there had turned him into a goat or sheep; that's what they do there, people say. Through good fortune and intelligence, Baba had broken the web of enchantment and escaped. There was a storm of storytelling around this incident for several days.

Baba was well known and respected for other things as well. Whenever anyone fell sick in the village, Baba would run to treat them; he even performed minor surgeries when needed, so he kept scissors, knives, clean bandages, and Dettol antiseptic handy. Sometimes there were cholera outbreaks in the village. Baba and my Chachas took turns attending to the sick and imposed strict rules such as drinking boiled water, keeping food safe from flies, and not washing the sick person's clothes in the pond. In our house, we always drank boiled water. After cooking, the food was always kept on a *chouki* covered with a mosquito net, and we ate it as hot as possible. For these reasons, no one in my family ever got cholera.

Baba had other talents also. New wives in the village were often possessed by ghosts or *jinns*. Our area was known to be under the watch of *jinns* and ghosts. People called on Baba to free their wives and daughters from these spirits. When I was old enough to know what was going on, I went along with Baba. I saw that Baba began by talking alone with the possessed woman, then with the mother-in-law and husband. The whole village would come to watch the spectacle. If it was a minor case, all he had to do was burn a dry chili and hold it under the nose of the possessed woman; she would sneeze and cough herself into a faint, and then when he sprinkled her with water, she would sit up perfectly normal and have no further problems. Sometimes if Baba gave the woman or her husband a few slaps in the face, the *jinn* would go away. If the case was complicated, Baba would say he was going to talk to the *jinn* in the night. Then he would go home, telling everyone to wait. After talking to the *jinn* at night, he would come back the next day and advise the husband and in-laws of the possessed woman to arrange for a divorce immediately or for the husband and wife to live separately. People followed his advice. Baba's orders came directly from the *jinn*, so the question of disobeying didn't arise! I now understand how intelligent Baba was.

When several cyclones and floods in a row destroyed all we had, I saw that my Baba who was so full of laughter, stories, and mirth began to change. A terrible depression swallowed him. This happened not only to my father, but to many others. Our area had a large Burmese population. We were familiar with or close to many well-off Burmese families. As a community, they had many good qualities: their houses were very nicely arranged, each with a flower garden in front; in the afternoon, the women would bathe and dress in beautiful attire, always with colorful flowers or combs in their hair; every morning after finishing the cooking, the oldest daughter in the house would take the food in a tiffin carrier to the pagoda or temple. The priest would distribute the food among the poor and eat a share himself. The children went to the pagoda every morning and learned to read and write in their language. On the other hand, many of the men were addicted to opium. The women ran the households while the men lay around all day, high as kites.

At some point, my Baba and many others like him tried to fend off their depression by taking opium. My proud mother was deeply shamed by this, thinking of it as her failure. This destructive addiction ruined many families in our area. All night long, Baba and his followers would sit in the Burmese neighborhood smoking cheroots or cigarettes filled with a mix of *paan* and opium. In the morning, they would come home and sleep all day. When I went home and saw Baba in this state, I broke down. He paid no attention to his health. Before, eating was one of the great pleasures of Baba's life; it made him very happy to eat well and feed people. Many times, he woke us up at night to feed us *roshogollas* he made with his own hands! When the mood struck him, he would slaughter a duck, a chicken, or a goat, cut it up and start cooking it himself. It didn't matter if it was morning, noon, or night. After he became addicted to opium, Baba's health deteriorated, and he had little interest in food. He used to have a glowing face and a handsome figure, but from long years of neglect his body became bony and his skin grew dull. I could hardly recognize him. He was oblivious to his surroundings, and just stayed high all day.

My family was on the brink of destitution, but thanks to my mother's firm grip on the household, it didn't sink completely. I don't know how, but Baba later realized his mistake. After ten or twelve years of addiction, Baba slowly came back to us. It's difficult to free yourself of addiction unless you have immense strength of will. I think Baba reduced his dosage little by little and finally cut it out almost completely; he just had a tiny ball of it morning and evening. Finally, he got his appetite back and started taking care of himself. But by that time, the damage had already been done. They'd had to sell or pawn the land to pay for his addiction, and my younger siblings' education had suffered.

Baba's health was ruined. At only fifty-five years of age, after being ill for only two days, Baba died in the Dhaka Medical

College Hospital. Before I went to Oxford, Baba had come to see me. At the airport, he hugged me and said, “Ma Noorjahan, we might not see each other again.”

I could feel that Baba’s chest was nothing but bones. I cried for him throughout the plane ride. Somehow that day I felt I would never see Baba again. And it was true. After Baba’s death, I thought Ma might not live long. After coming to that house as a seven-year-old bride, Ma had never lived alone. Baba was always with her. She never even went alone to visit her father’s house. And yet she lived for many years after Baba’s death.

One year in Barisal, we all got chicken pox—first I got it, then Jaseem, Taslim, Lina, Runu, Lutfa, and finally Ma. When Ma was at her worst, Baba came from the village. We spent the day talking, laughing, and telling stories together. At night, I made up a separate bed for Baba. We were all sleeping in our own beds, but Baba was still sitting up, chewing *paan* and smoking. It was getting late, but Baba showed no sign of going to sleep. Suddenly Baba said, “You say whatever you like, but I can’t sleep without your mother.”

With that, he lifted the mosquito net and got in bed with Ma, and we all burst out laughing.

### *My mother’s widowhood and freedom*

In 1974, after the sudden death of my father, my mother was alone. She was only fifty then. Her children were all grown up: some had married, and the two youngest were studying in the city. My mother was married at the age of seven and came to live with her husband and in-laws at age thirteen. Since then, she had always been with my father. We thought my mother would probably not survive for long in that remote region. There were no relatives to look after her in that storm-, flood-, and cyclone-prone desolate area. It would be difficult to live only with the household help.

When I got back to Bangladesh later in 1974, my mother came to meet me in Dhaka. My brother and sisters also came to meet me. We had long discussions about what we could do with Ma and where and with whom she could live. We felt she should live with one of us. We siblings finally decided that she would stay with our youngest sister, Runu, who was working with the government's Rural Development Unit. Runu was divorced and would be living alone in a small town with her young daughter. If my mother stayed with her, it would be good for everyone. So we siblings announced our decision to the whole family. Surprisingly my mother did not agree to this plan. At one point, I even rebuked her for being selfish. She kept quiet while we talked and was busy sewing. Drops of tears fell from her eyes. All of us thought that her behavior was selfish and impractical. We tried to persuade her to live with one of us, but it was no use. She spent the rest of her life living alone in Katakhali. But she was surrounded by her community.

After I left Bangladesh, my mother went back to her home in Katakhali. I decided to send her money every month. After two years, I went to Bangladesh for a visit and went to our village home in Katakhali also. I was worried about my mother and concerned that I might find her in terrible shape.

When I reached Katakhali, I found that my mother was thriving. She had planted quite a few trees and had changed the look of the house. We already had mango trees, jamun, jackfruit, tamarind, berries, custard-apples, and coconut trees in our garden. But she had now also made small plots for guavas, pomegranate, papaya, and a good variety of banana trees. The trees were full of fruit. The pond was teeming with fish. My mother's house was brimming with four or five cows, and lots of goats, ducks, and chickens. Ma couldn't eat all these things by herself, so all the villagers got a share. Ma was very content. She would share out the milk of her four or five cows before drinking any herself.

One day, she smiled and said, "I know you all wanted me to leave all this and go and look after one of your families. It was my duty to raise all of you, which I did. It is not my duty to raise your children. Why should I leave my huge family here and go and stay with you all? I am a part of the lives of these people—the good and the bad. I will never leave them and go elsewhere."

From morning until late in the evening, people came by not only from our village but nearby villages also. They came to visit my mother, help her with small tasks, and take her advice and counsel on a range of issues and problems.

At dawn, the youngest children of the village came to our house to have breakfast. My mother gave them fresh cow's milk or fresh syrup from the date palm. I could see that she was happy. I had never seen such happiness in her face before. We children had thought that at the loss of my father she would perish early. But she seemed to have filled her life and that of her fellow villagers with her energy and generosity. I stayed at home in Katakhali for a full month.

After that, I visited Katakhali every year or two. Every time, I was astounded by the extent of my mother's work in the community.

Without my father, she became very independent. She got some of our land out of hock. Then she built a house of her own liking, complete with a bathroom. Ma never forgot her fairytale life in her father's house. What Baba couldn't do during his lifetime, Ma did afterward. Ma redecorated the house according to her own wishes. Ma's touch could be seen in every speck of dust in that house.

After my father's death, my mother lived for almost twenty more years as a true social worker. Her education came from her hard life—losing her own mother, her child marriage at age seven, giving birth to and raising seven children, and running a huge, complex household. She went from door to door and made people understand that two children were enough, regardless of gender, and that more children were not needed. Ma persuaded villagers not to marry off their daughters at an early age but instead give them an education. She was very concerned about the whimsical divorces (*talaks*) and domestic violence carried out by the local men.

Everybody came to my mother for advice and resolution of their disputes. They used to accept my mother's decision unquestioningly. Due to my mother's involvement, the condition of women and girls improved, and the people of Katakhali village have shifted in their attitudes. Ma used to discuss the importance of women's education and prevention of child marriage even with her own family members and uncles. I can see tangible change in the village from my mother's efforts.

Whenever we went home to Katakhali, the whole village danced with rapture. People came from all over to visit Ma and meet me. Ma was still known as "Noorjahaner Ma" or Noorjahan's mother, and people would come to meet her Noorjahan. During one of my visits, I was lying down after lunch. There were people everywhere. Ma came and said, "The house is filling up with people. Why don't you go sit on the veranda?"

When I came out, I saw our veranda and courtyard full of people too; people were even spilling out into the garden. I brought a chair out into the courtyard and sat there. Ma spread out the mats she wove with her own hands for everyone to sit and started handing out *paan-supari*. The village women came into the kitchen and started cooking themselves. The whole village was celebrating as if there were a wedding, and people had come from nearby villages too. Ma's face was glowing with satisfaction.

She had a fear that after her death my brother Taslim would sell the land and the house, so she told me many times, "I don't want this house to be sold. I want to do something with this house where the village women can come and talk about their joys and, sorrows and if possible, get education and medical treatment. The women of this area have no one to support them, don't forget that." How could I forget? I was later able to fulfill this wish of hers.

We were always worried about Ma living alone. Once when all the siblings went to visit her together, Ma said, "You don't have to worry about me. The village people will take care of my last rites. I've made all the arrangements. None of you will have to go to any trouble." That is exactly what happened.

Ma had kept a shroud, perfume, *surma*, and quite a lot of money in a suitcase for her last rites. We really didn't have to do anything. After my mother's death, all my siblings went home. I was in Washington at the time and couldn't come until later. Amid continuous rain in the month of Shraban, a swarm of thousands of people of seven villages were present at my mother's funeral. It seems even more people came than when Baba or my uncles died.

Ma is no more, at least not physically, but she is there in my heart. That's why I can't forget Katakhali village. I can't forget the earth and the people of this village. My mother lives on in them, and always will.

### *A year in Oxford*

We were in Oxford for about one year. While we were there, I got to know the son of the *jomidar* of Barisal's Kirtipasha village, Professor Tapan Raychaudhuri, and his wife Hashi. They left East Bengal/East Pakistan after Partition in 1948 and moved abroad. Tapan-da was a professor of history at Oxford University. They have a daughter named Sukanya (nickname Khuku). It didn't take long to get to know them well. They were both very friendly. One was an expert talker, the other an expert cook. They were also fond of good food.

The year went by so fast I hardly noticed. Once, I went with Hashi-di to meet Nirad Chaudhuri, who also lived in Oxford. Long ago, I had read his book *Autobiography of an Unknown Indian*. I thought it would be silly not to take this opportunity to meet him. Swadesh absolutely refused to go meet him. Most Bengalis didn't like Nirad Chaudhuri, but I went with an open mind.

Hashi-di introduced me as Mrs Bose. The restless, small-built man asked me a few questions, where I live, how many children I have, what my husband does, and so on. I told him, "You can use 'tumi' [the familiar form of address] with me."

The gentleman started showing off his house, belongings, clothes, even expensive perfumes. He kept bustling up and down the stairs like a twenty-five- or thirty-year-old. He had a big album full of clippings of articles about himself printed in various papers. I had to look at all of them. He took me downstairs and showed me various bottles of alcohol in the cellar and told me their prices. I had to go out and look at the rose garden. Then we went inside again and ate jam tarts and coffee made by his wife.

Nirad Chaudhuri told me many anecdotes, mostly full of criticism of Bengalis. He told me about the death of his older brother's wife and how his brother took a break from crying to choose his second wife right there at the burning ghat. He also told me that if he ate Bengali food, he couldn't write a word of English for a week. Then suddenly he went upstairs again and came down with a copy of a letter. He said, "This letter was written by Queen Victoria to Max Müller after her husband's death." I didn't quite understand. I thought, why is he showing me this? Suddenly he asked me my level of education. What was the connection between this question and the line of black ink around the letter? I didn't get it. He said immediately, "Uneducated graduate! The queen grieved for her husband the rest of her life. The black lines around the letter are the shadow of her grief."

According to him, Queen Victoria's love for her husband was deeper than that of any Hindu Brahmin widow. I just thought, "Yes, that's why Queen Victoria did nothing but love her whole life!"

He also asked me why we were living in Abingdon Road and why our children were studying in a working-class school. He said this wasn't appropriate at all for a respectable family. I told him, "It's only for a short time, and then we're going to America. I'll enroll them in a good school there."

He seemed a little distracted after that. Then I told him briefly about Swadesh's PhD from Cambridge and his job at the World Bank. I immediately seemed to move up in his esteem. He asked me if I could arrange for him to visit America. I said I would try.

At one point during this long discussion with Nirad Chaudhuri, I also went and met his wife. She sadly told me of her life of disappointments. I learned that she spent years wearing a torn sari and under-eating to support her husband's "sahebipana" or lavish Western lifestyle.

A week after I met Nirad Chaudhuri, a local paper published an interview with him. A Pakistani woman journalist had done the interview. I saw that the events of her interview were exactly like my visit. It seems that was his specialty. An unusual and lively man.

I had enrolled my two girls Anita and Mini at a school close to our house. Mini made friends quickly, since she already spoke and understood some English. The problem was with Ani. She couldn't understand, couldn't talk, couldn't even eat the food. The teachers often sent me notes about her not eating. I went and saw myself through the window that Ani just cried through lunch and didn't eat anything. When Swadesh heard that, he said, "The school is right nearby, just bring her home to eat at lunchtime."

I thought about it and decided that wouldn't solve the problem. If I did that, she wouldn't have any motivation to learn to eat the food or speak the language. Later when she got a grasp of the language, she started chattering away and eating just fine. This same girl told me once in Washington, "Do I really have to eat rice 365 days of the year!"

Nirad Chaudhuri's statement was correct: the school and the neighborhood were predominantly working class. There were also Indian, Bangladeshi, and Pakistani working-class families there. They worked in various industries around Oxford.

I went to the school often to talk to the teachers about their learning and behavior. The teachers were amazed to see me. They never saw the other Indian, Pakistani, or Bangladeshi parents or got any answers to their letters. I explained to them that the main reason was probably the language barrier. I later saw the same thing in Washington. After getting my MA in social work, when I was working for various institutions, I was often called on by the courts and the social services department to contact South Asian families and find solutions to their problems or help them cooperate with the schools. Most of the time, the children didn't even give the school's letters to their parents because they knew they couldn't read English. And the parents thought their responsibility was over once they sent the children to school.

While we were in Oxford, Swadesh got a job offer at the World Bank for a one-year position. At first, he didn't want to take the job. It had been a big disappointment back in the Pakistan era when the US authorities had canceled his visa and he couldn't go to Harvard, so he had lost his enthusiasm for the United States. His friend Mark Leiserson kept calling him and sending him letters, but he couldn't persuade him to take the job. Then Mark and his wife Jean showed up in Oxford. They explained to me that Swadesh should not waste such a big opportunity for emotional reasons. It was only for a year after all. Besides, it wasn't right to get angry at the American government and deprive himself of the opportunity to see such a huge country with its diverse geography, people, and ways of life. We would be lucky to get a chance to see these things, especially the children. Finally, we both agreed. Swadesh and Mark would be working together at the World Bank. They talked it over and Swadesh decided to go to Washington, DC, at the beginning of September and find a house and a school for the children.

Meanwhile, I hadn't been able to go home even after learning of my father's death. I wanted to go home first and see everyone, then return to Oxford before going to Washington. So I went home in October 1974 after being away for one year and found my mother, brothers, and sisters grieving on the one hand, and famine throughout the country on the other. It was the month of Ramadan. We were staying in Karim Chacha's house in Naya Paltan. I saw people crying out for food all around. I was almost crazy from hearing them beg, "Give me a little rice-starch, Ma." I felt bewildered seeing the skeletal, half-dead people in the streets. I saw that in some houses the women were making *rutis* to distribute to the hungry, but that was like a drop in the ocean. Right alongside the family, well-off people were eating their fill as usual; there was no shortage of anything in the markets. I kept thinking, why don't these hungry people get together and steal the food so neatly arranged on the shelves of the shops? Why are we putting up with this in silence? But I didn't do anything myself.

A few days later, I got on the plane for London again with a heavy heart. As soon as the plane left Dhaka and got up in the sky, trays full of food came for me and my daughters: roast salmon, salad, cake, tea, coffee, milk, fruit juice. The food they gave for one person was enough for three. Even though the food looked appetizing, I didn't feel like eating. I had just seen skeletal children in the streets, moaning for a little rice. How could I lift this food to my mouth?

## PART 7

# BETWEEN TWO CULTURES

*Building a life in the United States*

On 4 November 1974, I moved to Washington with the girls and joined Swadesh. Jaseem stayed in the UK to finish his studies. We lived for the first year in the Bannockburn neighborhood in Bethesda, Maryland, not far from Washington, DC. Soon after moving to Washington, I met my wonderful neighbor, Rose Wiener. The girls were at school, not returning until 3:30 pm. Swadesh took the bus and didn't get home until 7 or 8 pm. I had nothing to do all day. Our books hadn't arrived yet. I had practically memorized the *Washington Post* from the first page to the last. Every day, I saw an older woman raking the leaves in front of the house behind ours. The leaves had started turning color and falling. I gathered my courage, went out the back door and straight up to the woman, and said, "My name is Noorjahan, and I've rented this house. I just came to meet you."

Rose immediately invited me over for coffee. Rose's house didn't match any of the stories I'd read about America. She had a worn-out sofa and a very small, simple home. Rose asked me if I was going to the newcomers' welcome party that evening. I said

I didn't know anything about it. Rose was upset. She called someone on the phone and gave them a good scolding, then came back and said, "Go home and cook something from your country, then come to the community center with your husband at eight o'clock. You'll meet everybody there, old and new. We do a potluck dinner for newcomers every year." I said I had two daughters, ten and six years old, so we couldn't go. Rose insisted, "You must go. I'll stay with your daughters." I was amazed. Within an hour of meeting me, she was taking responsibility for my children!

I went with Rose to various Democratic Party events and lectures at the Woman's Democratic Club and met political scientists and many activist women. Later I also became a member of the Democratic Party. Rose participated in big rallies until she was ninety years old—sometimes against war, sometimes for women's rights. I often went with her. I'll never forget the first time. A hundred thousand women wearing suffragette white covered the huge area from the Lincoln Memorial to Capitol Hill. Rose was very thrifty in her everyday life. She never spent money on herself. But she donated thousands of dollars to her preferred social welfare organizations every year. We remained close until her death. Until she was ninety-nine, she lived alone and shopped and cooked for herself.

In 1975, Sheikh Mujibur Rahman and his family members were murdered in a *coup d'état*, and the military took over Bangladesh. We decided to remain in Washington and in 1976 bought a house in Bethesda on Redwing Court. At that time, World Bank spouses were not allowed to work for pay. Later, we organized and lobbied and had the immigration laws changed, but in the 1970s my options were limited. So I decided to volunteer. I heard about the organization Planned Parenthood from a friend and called them up. They interviewed me and immediately took me on as a volunteer. Young people came there every day to get advice and help with all kinds of problems. My job was to listen compassionately, give them emotional support, and refer them to the appropriate services at Planned Parenthood and elsewhere. I had to listen without judgment and have discussions with young people about their health, nutrition, sexuality, birth control, safe sex, sexually transmitted diseases, pregnancy, rape, and abortion. I learned so much from my experience at Planned Parenthood about gender and sexuality, topics that were never discussed in Bangladesh when I was growing up. Working at Planned Parenthood with my supervisor and peers and helping all these young people gave me a lot of confidence. I began to feel empowered myself. I helped hundreds of people during my year or so at Planned Parenthood.

After coming to America, I had been in a kind of depression from sitting at home all the time. Volunteering at Planned Parenthood helped me come out of this depression. Several people advised me to get a master's degree in social work. But Swadesh said that we couldn't afford it. So I got the idea to start a school to teach Bengali. I had been thinking for a while that I wanted to make sure our children did not forget our mother tongue, for which we had fought so hard during the Pakistan era. Anita, Mini, and Jaseem could speak Bangla or Bengali very well, and I had also been teaching them reading and writing at home. But they needed others to talk to. At that time, there were no opportunities for young people to learn Bangla in the Washington area.

So I started the Bangla School in 1976 in the basement of our house. The school kept going for ten years and was the first Bangla school in Washington. My children are still proficient in Bangla, and even my granddaughters Tuli and Koli have learned Bangla from their mother. I suddenly had an income from the Bangla School tuition. Over the next couple of years, my savings grew. Eventually, I enrolled at Catholic University.

I was starting a new life, but the sectarianism in South Asia followed us to Washington as well. One day, the phone rang at home. The caller identified himself as Abdullah and started talking in Bangla. He said that by marrying a Hindu I had offended Islam and disgraced all the Muslims of the world. I was to take my husband to the Islamic Center immediately and make him convert to Islam or else my husband, my daughters, and I would all be murdered. He said what I was doing was worse than prostitution. He kept calling and threatening me, and one day he said, "I am a soldier, and I can die if needed, but before that you have to die along with your Hindu husband and your children. If necessary, I will destroy your house." Later, letters to the same effect started coming from Dhaka.

After the first phone call, I went to the house of the Bangladesh Ambassador M. R. Siddiqi and informed him of everything. He said there was nothing he could do and told me to report it to the police. Then I went and told all my Bangladeshi friends in Washington, but no one wanted to risk getting involved in this. Finally, I reported it to the police. First the local police and then the FBI came to investigate. They took copies of the letters, and police were stationed on all sides of the house to protect us. The FBI officers came by regularly to talk to me. One day, one of them said to me in surprise, "If someone from this country had a problem like this in your country, our embassy would have stepped in right away, but your embassy isn't cooperating at all."

The letters kept coming. Whenever the phone rang, my children would hug me and start crying. If Swadesh was late coming back from the office, I would get scared and call the police. I was constantly thinking our house was about to be blown up. I couldn't sleep at night. When I woke up, I'd see the police cars in the courtyard and feel a little safer and try to sleep. The neighbors tried to persuade me to convert to Christianity! I laughed and said, if they could die for their religious beliefs, then

I could also die for mine. This unbearable anxiety made everyday life difficult.

I told Swadesh to inform the World Bank; he was reluctant, but in the end he did. After meeting with us and the FBI, the World Bank understood the seriousness of the matter and asked the Bangladeshi Alternate Director to deal with the problem. Soon the threatening phone calls and letters stopped. It was clear to us that the Alternate Director of the World Bank had managed to talk to the Bangladeshis in Washington who were behind the problem.

That was a terrifying time for my family. We were nervous about leaving the house, and I was constantly scared that my children or Swadesh would be kidnapped or harmed. Just hearing the telephone ringing was stressful. I am still filled with anxiety when I remember those awful phone calls and letters.

Once the harassment against my family stopped, I was able to focus on my studies. In my third year, I was sent to do fieldwork at the local office of Catholic Charities of America. This organization operates all over the world, helping underprivileged people irrespective of ethnicity and religion but according to Catholic religious ideals and following instructions from the Vatican to the letter. Catholic Charities has been silently carrying on their work of conversion in poor countries, taking advantage of poverty, racism, and other inequalities. They gave me my own small office with a phone. People came for various kinds of aid. For example, a twelve-year-old girl comes in with her mother; she is pregnant. An old person comes in because the landlord has evicted them and thrown all their belongings in the street. Countless refugees are coming in from Communist countries, and the organization is giving them aid. There was a lounge in front of my office where people waited to get help.

Catholic Charities had a refugee program for children and youth. There were many unaccompanied youth from Vietnam who were known as "boat children." The office of the Archbishop of Washington and Regional Director General of Catholic Charities was right in front of mine. It was a huge suite: first a sitting room with a bar on one side, lined with whisky and other liquor, then the office with expensive, comfortable padded chairs around a massive table and the director's own revolving chair. I disliked this person at first sight. He had a huge girth, what they call a beer belly. I noticed that the man would come and take the children by the hand, one by one, into his office, then let them out an hour or two hours later. Terror showed clearly on the children's faces and in their body language. Many of them sat there crying. When I saw that, I felt rebellion brewing inside me. I had to do something—but I thought, I'm just a student, and that too from Bangladesh! Who's going to listen to me?

Meanwhile, one day this same director came to my office and invited me to go with him to a seminar. I was afraid, but agreed to go, thinking others would be with us. But it turned out to just be me, and the man told me to sit in the front seat of his huge Mercedes. I sat scrunched up in one corner. At one point, he started talking about poverty in Bangladesh and suddenly put a hand on my thigh. I jerked away and tried to move over even farther. A few minutes later, he reached out again and grabbed my thigh. This time, I snapped loudly, "What are you doing? Stop that or I'll scream." He quickly took his hand away and said, "Sorry, sorry, I was unmindful."

I told my supervisor about this incident and my suspicions about what this man was doing behind closed doors with the young Southeast Asian boys. He praised my powers of observation and told me that everyone knew about this, but no one dared challenge the top director because he was the head of Catholic Charities' branches in Baltimore, Virginia, Maryland, and Washington and had immense power. My supervisor told me, "I'll definitely bring this up at the next board meeting and we'll get to the bottom of it." But nothing happened after that meeting either. When I saw that nothing was being done, I threatened to leak the news to the *Washington Post*. That finally worked, and the Director General was removed in 1979. But he was just shifted to a different community.

In 1981, I graduated with an MSW, or master's in social work, from the Catholic University. This degree was the result of years of hard work and dedication. I was forty-three years old. Despite his initial doubts, Swadesh was very happy to see me succeed. My field work supervisor offered me a job as a social worker with Catholic Charities' Refugee Program. I was elated. I had barely gotten my resume together, and before I could even send any application, I had a job. Around twenty Vietnamese refugee boys and youth were living in two group homes. Our goal was to help them get education and professional training and establish them in American society. I was in charge of monitoring the group homes. The homes were in Bethesda, Maryland, so it was easy for me to get there in fifteen minutes by car. By now, I had my driving license.

I worked with Catholic Charities for eight years, gaining experience with different populations and collaborating with many other organizations. Later I was promoted to the Director of the Ombudsman Program of Office of the Aging. My supervisor was a 6-foot tall impressive Black woman with a PhD in social work who fought to make sure I got the job despite others being skeptical that a tiny Bangladeshi in a sari could manage this job. I was in charge of monitoring five nursing homes for signs of abuse or neglect. I supervised twenty-five volunteers and continued to wear my sari to work. However, a few months later, I overheard an elderly woman resident saying to a nurse, "That Indian woman is so nice! You know, the one who wears a curtain." The nurses were all laughing at this comment. I decided then that I would no longer go to all the effort to wrap a sari when visiting nursing homes.

### *Starting Samhati and ASHA*

While working at Catholic Charities, I was constantly thinking about doing something for the women in Bangladesh. I decided to start a non-profit organization with the goal of improving the lives of poor women and children in Bangladesh. My experience at Catholic Charities showed me the valuable societal work done by non-profit organizations. I had also learned a lot about organizing and fundraising. I called my lawyer friend Ranu Basu to discuss my idea, and we came up with the name "Samhati," which means solidarity in Bengali. Bangladeshi women in the Washington area would be engaged to raise funds for projects in Bangladesh. Ranu assured me that she would help with the legal registration and other formalities. I invited my Bangladeshi women friends to lunch at my home on 10 November 1984. Many of these women were quite accomplished but had moved to Washington with their husbands and were unable to work in their fields.

During the lunch, I told them my idea about starting a non-profit association called Samhati and asked them if they were interested. Almost everyone at the lunch enthusiastically agreed to be part of it. We moved rapidly to put my plan into action. In January 1985, we formed our first board. My neighbors and friends Bill and Linda Goldman gave me a generous check for $500 to cover the costs of registering as a non-profit and opening our bank account. By March 1985, Ranu Basu helped us quickly obtain non-profit status for Samhati, allowing donations to be tax-deductible.

Our very first benefit dinner was on 5 April 1986 at the Bannockburn Club House, near our first home in Washington. From the founding day of our organization until she was ninety-eight, Rose came to every Samhati dinner. Samhati raised money in the United States and worked with the Bangladesh Mahila

Parishad for almost two decades to establish and support Rokeya Shadan, the first women's shelter in Dhaka for women and girls fleeing abuse. I spent a lot of time in consultation with Mahila Parishad and its founder Sufia Kamal in planning the women's shelter. The Mahila Parishad was established in 1971, right after the independence of Bangladesh, and is a national feminist organization of Bangladeshi women with grassroots work in almost all districts and a progressive, secular agenda focused on gender equality, women's empowerment, and ending gender-based violence. The shelter began in 1985 in a rented space and is named after Begum Rokeya, a Bengali feminist writer, educator, and activist and pioneer for women's education and equality. Samhati was instrumental in establishing Rokeya Shadan and erecting its new building in 1997. These were tremendous achievements, and the shelter continues to do wonderful work for poor women and girls from around Bangladesh who come to Dhaka fleeing violence and abuse.

Samhati also raised money to fund nutrition programs for women and children as well as emergency assistance after cyclones. Some of this emergency assistance was coordinated through Mahila Parishad, and other assistance was provided directly to communities by Samhati. For example, in April 1991, Bangladesh was hit by a terrible cyclone that killed around 135,000 people and left many without food, clothing, or shelter. As soon as we heard about the cyclone, Samhati mobilized to gather funds in Washington to send assistance to Bangladesh. We made posters and put them up in churches and libraries. We held a rally in front of the World Bank and asked people to help. We quickly raised over $30,000 in cyclone relief. Then we were interviewed in the local news and were on television, and even more money came in. Samhati sent some of the funds to Mahila Parishad, who efficiently used the funds to distribute rice, dal, salt, clothing, and cash relief to people in areas such as Kutubdia and

Chittagong. Mahila Parishad also established a project to make large batches of much-needed oral saline to distribute to those facing dehydration and diarrhea in Barisal, Bhola, and other coastal areas. After Super Cyclone Sidr in 2007, Samhati members went directly to Barobaishdia Island to provide rice, dal, saris, and *lungis* for the community.

In 1989, I heard that the domestic helper of one of our Samhati members was suffering physical and emotional abuse. I called a meeting to discuss the matter. But I didn't realize how sensitive a topic this would be. Because of the class divide, our members wouldn't accept the idea of domestic workers seeking our help. The incident led to a crisis within Samhati because other members did not want to get involved in this issue.

I then decided to start a different organization to address domestic violence, both intimate partner and domestic worker abuse. I discussed the matter with Ranu Basu, and we decided to expand the focus to the whole South Asian diaspora in the Washington area. Many of the South Asian wives and domestic helpers lived in terrible conditions. In 1989, I co-founded ASHA (Asian Women's Self-Help Association). I worked with Ranu and others to hold our first meeting at my house on 25 April 1989.

ASHA means "hope" and was a volunteer-run organization for many years. Dozens of women would call me or Ranu from all over Washington, DC, Maryland, Baltimore, Virginia, and even overseas. They spoke Tamil, Bangla, Hindi, Urdu, and English and were mainly from Bangladesh, India, Pakistan, and Sri Lanka. We would try to find volunteers who could speak their language. Later we raised money and got funding for a part-time staff member and rented an office. We faced a lot of resistance from the South Asian community. Ranu and I would get calls from other South Asians telling us to stop our meddling in family affairs.

One day, a young Bangladeshi woman named Seema suddenly called me. She lived in a small town 50 or 60 miles from

Washington. Seema told me she was married and the mother of two children. Her husband had been living in the United States and had married her in Bangladesh and brought her to the US. Seema had very little education and could barely read and write. Seema's husband wanted to divorce her and leave her penniless. He had gotten a Hindu lawyer in Bangladesh to make him a fake divorce document backdated by two years. He was trying to get this document attested by the Bangladeshi Embassy to submit it in court to deprive Seema of any share of marital property. He was also beating her every day, trying to drive her out of the house. In the United States, when a couple gets divorced, the marital property and assets are divided between the spouses. This is generally not true in Bangladesh. I knew that in Bangladeshi Hindu law, there is no provision for divorce. In India, Hindu family law has changed a lot, but in Bangladesh divorce is still not allowed for Hindus because of resistance from Hindu religious leaders.

ASHA wrote a petition on behalf of Seema and submitted it in court. We asked for help from the Bangladesh Embassy, the Mahila Parishad, and Ain-o-Salish Kendra, a legal organization for women in Bangladesh. We were having trouble getting a letter from the Bangladesh Embassy stating that there is no divorce for Hindus in Bangladesh. Meanwhile, our friend Suranjit Sengupta, who was a member of parliament and minister in Bangladesh, made a sudden trip to Washington and dinner was held in his honor. I brought up Seema's case with both Suranjit and the Bangladesh Ambassador. Suranjit agreed that clearly there was no divorce for Hindus in Bangladesh and instructed the Ambassador to give his full cooperation. Within a week, we got a letter from the Embassy stating that under Bangladesh's law, Hindus cannot divorce. Seema filed this document in court to show that she could not have been divorced in Bangladesh and was later able to file for divorce under US law and obtain equitable property distribution.

The establishment of ASHA has been a huge source of support for South Asian survivors of abuse in the Washington area and beyond. ASHA is now called Ashiyanaa and is still going strong with a new generation of leaders.

Domestic abuse is everywhere, not just in the South Asian community. When I worked at Catholic Charities, I often noticed scratches and bruises on the face and arms of one of my colleagues, Gina. I asked her about it, and she always said she fell or had an accident. Then one day I was taking a Bangladeshi woman to a domestic violence shelter. When we got to the shelter, I saw Gina inside. She ran over and gave me a hug. She finally told me that her husband was abusing her but made me promise not to tell anyone, especially our colleagues at work.

I continued to work as a social worker while managing Samhati and ASHA as a volunteer. In 1991, I started a new position at the DC General Hospital, a public hospital run by the Washington, DC, government. The hospital provided free medical services for Washington's poor. At DC General Hospital, I worked with the patients and families of the Critical Care Unit (CCU) and Intensive Care Unit (ICU). The CCU patients were all older, and most came with heart ailments. There's one funny experience I had at the CCU. An older woman, very plump, often came in to treat her heart problem. Every time she came in, the cardiologist asked me to go over a chart explaining a low cholesterol vegetarian diet with her. I explained to her what she should be eating, but as soon as I finished, she would say, "Sure! I have a fridge full of expensive steak, beef, meatballs, and ice cream. Who's going to eat those?" When the woman recovered, she would go home and then within a week would be back again.

In the ICU, many young men and teens, sometimes as young as twelve or thirteen, would come in with gunshot wounds. Most of them were victims of poverty, lack of education, and neglect. Many of their fathers were not in their lives. My life was enriched by the experience of working with the families of these patients. During that time, I saw the dejection and helplessness of family members, and at the same time the complexities of rehabilitating these young men—those who survived—in society. Many of the patients came in multiple times, sometimes from jail. We had to be careful because they were sometimes attacked even in the hospital. Personally, I never felt afraid of working with them. The faces of those young men and their loved ones are still fresh in my mind.

PART 8

# FULL CIRCLE

*Returning to my roots*

Swadesh retired early from the World Bank in 1993. He was tired of his job and having a hard time focusing. The next year, Mini got married and moved to Tokyo with her Columbia Law School classmate, Michael. Jaseem was working as an economist for the Asian Development Bank in Manila. My younger daughter Anita was a graduate student at Columbia University in New York. Swadesh was always alone at home. Whenever I called home from work, he'd still be in bed. He was never talkative, but now he stopped talking almost entirely. He had no enthusiasm for anything. I thought maybe Swadesh was sinking into a deep depression from loneliness. If I left my job and stayed home with him, maybe he would get better.

In 1996, I left the job I had gotten in this foreign land through hard work and determination. My supervisors and colleagues at DC General couldn't believe it. After quitting my job, I was cooped up in the house again. Swadesh refused to see a doctor. Finally, I forced him to see a neurologist, and he was diagnosed with Parkinson's. Now his early retirement made sense. There is no cure for this disease yet, but we tried various treatments without success. My world went dark; I felt suffocated.

While wondering how to cope, I remembered my mother's face. No storm, no flood, nor any sorrow or despair ever broke my mother. And I was her daughter, the daughter for whom she had the highest hopes and the greatest trust. The life of every person living by the Agunmukha begins with storms, floods, cyclones, and intense despair. The despair of losing loved ones and belongings is their constant companion. And yet every person living on the banks of the Agunmukha wants to begin life again, conquering hardship. My strong desire to go home after long years of living abroad grew even stronger.

In 1997, I bought an apartment in Dhaka on the old Road No. 26 in Dhanmondi, walking distance from the home of Sheikh Mujib Rahman on Road No. 32. It is near Dhanmondi lake and has wonderful balconies. I started spending several months of the year in Bangladesh. I became immersed in the cultural, political, and intellectual life of Dhaka. My Dhaka home is just one block from Chhayanat and two blocks from the Bengal Foundation, two leading cultural institutions in Bangladesh. I started walking to all the openings, concerts, and performances. I also became active with the Liberation War Museum, which was established in 1996. I did fundraising to build its permanent building. It was wonderful to finally have my own home in Bangladesh. I filled the house with books and the balconies with plants. We had more household help there, so it was easier to manage with Swadesh's health problems. By around 2003, Swadesh was in Dhaka full time as he was no longer able to travel.

After first getting my Dhaka apartment, I used to enjoy walking almost every morning to the home of Sufia Kamal, who lived on Road No. 32 in Dhanmondi near Mujib's house, which is now a museum. I called her "Khallama." She was a huge feminist leader in Bangladesh, and I really enjoyed discussing women's issues with her. We often discussed my work with Samhati and ways in which we could support each other's missions. Khallama died in 1999, and I still miss those morning visits.

Despite many inconveniences, when I am in Bangladesh, I feel that this is my country, that I am a part of this land and these people. When I wake up in the morning, I read the Bangla newspaper and hear Bangla being spoken and sung all around me. I was kept from this satisfaction for so long. I continued to spend as much time as possible in Bangladesh, while traveling annually to Washington, DC, to see my children and my doctors.

My work with Samhati expanded to include long-term women's eco-empowerment projects in Katakhali, as well as in Natore and Rangpur districts. Ever since my mother's death in 1993, I had been thinking about what to do with her house and how to continue the work she had done with the community. While she was alive, she had organized a meeting with me and all the women and men of the village. We started a women's organization, but it was discontinued after Ma's death. In the year 2000, I was finally able to restart the project my mother and I had envisioned.

I discussed my idea of a holistic women's empowerment project in Katakhali with the board of Samhati, which now included my daughter Mini, who had just moved back to Washington. We wanted to create a project that focused on the women in the community and included health care, education, and the environment as core components. I worked with Mini, an environmental lawyer, to formulate the plan. The Katakhali Eco-Empowerment Project began in our family homestead in Katakhali and continues to this day. Our work focuses on women, because studies show that if women are given education and the opportunity to generate income, this has a positive impact on the children and the whole family. We provide literacy classes for women, including education and discussions about health, nutrition, family planning, domestic violence, child marriage, and the legal rights of women. In addition, there are trainings in organic gardening, other income-generation skills, and leadership.

In collaboration with the government, we established a satellite family planning center in Katakhali, which is open once a week. Many of these family planning clinic staff took their government salaries but failed to show up for work. I met with the woman who ran the family planning clinic and told her that she absolutely must come every week and that we would be keeping track. I also told her that she should meet with each woman alone and let the woman decide how to manage her fertility. Often the mothers-in-law and husbands prevented women from controlling their own bodies, and it was critical that the women be the decision-makers over their own bodies. Samhati also set up a small health clinic and funded weekly doctor visits to the island. By 2003, we had raised enough funds to hire a full-time doctor to live in Katakhali and work for our health clinic, and a few years later we built a brick-and-mortar clinic for the community, serving 27,000 villagers in all of Barobaishdia Island. Before we started the Katakhali Project, there was no medical care in Katakhali, and villagers would die from conditions that are easily treatable.

Samhati also provides scholarships for low-income middle school and high school children, who would otherwise not be able to afford to study. A modest scholarship provides enough money for books, supplies, food, and clothing so that a child can attend school and not have to work or be married off early.

The Katakhali Project has been highly successful from the very beginning and continues to this day. Learning to read and write gives the women much more confidence and has transformed their lives. The local women are now managing and running the programs themselves. It is so gratifying to me that I was finally able to realize my mother's vision and use her home to continue her wonderful community work. Samhati has also established similar eco-empowerment projects in Natore and Rangpur districts.

*Farewell, my friend*

By 2008, Swadesh was barely able to speak because of Parkinson's, but he was clearly happy to learn about all that I had been able to accomplish with Samhati. We were living in Dhaka, and our life there was so active and full. I was involved in the pro-democracy movement and many women's organizations. Swadesh was also proud of my writing. I would read to him what I had written. He still enjoyed having visitors and going out. Swadesh was elated to vote for Mujib's daughter in the Bangladesh election in 2008. We took him everywhere in his wheelchair. But later in 2009 he gradually became weaker and unable to eat. He had written instructions that he did not want to live life on machines with a feeding tube.

With the poignant tones of Rabindra sangeet[1] and a house full of white gladiolus and *rajanigandha* (tuberose), I said goodbye to my closest friend for half a century. On 3 December 2009, at 11:15 am, Swadesh left me forever. Swadesh means "homeland," and it is fitting that this freedom fighter died at home in Bangladesh.

# EPILOGUE

It has been over a decade since Swadesh's death and the publication of my memoirs in Bangladesh. I continue to live between Bangladesh and the United States. I now have an apartment in Washington as well as the one in Dhaka. I travel annually to visit the Samhati programs in Katakhali, Rangpur, and Natore. I still cook and travel and read and write, though my eyes are failing me. I am now in my eighties but continuing my quest for a just and equal world for all genders that is free of discrimination, harassment, and abuse.

In my memoirs, to avoid upsetting family members, I only briefly mentioned the sexual abuse I experienced and did not disclose the identity of the perpetrators. The full details are even more horrible. I still have anxiety resulting from those experiences, and it is only two years ago, long after my uncle had died, that I was able to tell my family and his family what happened. Speaking about it re-traumatizes me and brings back all the terrible pain and horrible memories. Writing about it has been especially difficult, leading to nightmares and sleepless nights. Indeed, I was advised by my doctors not to write about my sexual abuse, for my own mental health. But I feel I must now tell the truth. The trauma from the abuse that I suffered in my own life propels me to help others, especially the women and girls of Bangladesh.

I am on the phone daily with people of all ages, trying to find solutions to empower women and uplift struggling communities. Just a few months ago, I went to Katakhali with Mini and Koli to check on our work there. I talked with all the children and told them to study and avoid child marriage and reminded them that they have rights over their own bodies. We organized a huge meeting with all the local government officials in Katakhali so that they could see the real stories of resilience of the women of our region. At that meeting, I spoke candidly about the abuse girls suffer in their own homes and communities and told everyone that I am also a survivor of abuse and was raped in this house.

At that gathering, we distributed bicycles to middle school and high school girls to make them more mobile, empowered, and safe. It was an incredible sight to see girls riding bikes in Katakhali. While women and girls in Bangladesh are faring much better now than when I was young, too many are still subjected to rape, child marriage, and sexual abuse by family members. Four years ago, a ten-year-old girl in Katakhali came to Samhati complaining of abuse by her father. She was helped by Ain-o-Salish Kendra in Dhaka, and the case against the father is continuing with support from Samhati. He served some time in jail, but the sluggish and sexist legal system has so far failed to deliver justice.

I have been so excited and thrilled by the #MeToo movement, which has led to women coming forward to speak about abuse they kept hidden for decades. I am delighted to see that today's young people are redefining gender and calling for the right to be who they are and love anyone they wish. When I feel tired and old, I try to remember my teenage self and the day I led a girls' walkout to fight language tyranny. I know the next generation will keep on fighting for our rights.

# NOTES

## PREFACE

1. Possibly the geography and flora of each area inspired these place names. Agunmukha (literally fire-mouth) may have received its name from the ferocity of the river or from the way the sun reflects on the river. According to my brother Taslim, our father told him that there were many thorn bushes or *kata* in Katakhali, and these had to be cleared to make it habitable. Probably there were many tamarind or *tetul* trees in Tetulia, and many banana plants or *kalagach* in Char Kalagachia. Barobaishdia may have gotten its name from the famous boat racing or rowing competitions between the villages. Rowing a boat is called *nouka bais diya*. Our island men probably won the "big" prize in the rowing competition, so the island got the name "Big Rowers" or *baro bais dia*, while the neighboring island got the "small" or chhoto prize and thus the name Chhotobaishdia. Of course, the stories behind these colorful names are part of a fluid oral tradition.

## Part 1: GROWING UP ON AN ISLAND

1. "Mia" is a respectful form of address, here indicating the high social status of the author's maternal grandfather.
2. "Pujo" or "puja" refers to various Hindu religious ceremonies, where gods and goddesses are celebrated either in small shrines in the home or larger ones outdoors or in temples.
3. "Kulin Brahmins" were considered the highest stratum of upper-caste Brahmins in India's caste system.

4. The prevalent South Asian custom is for women to move in with their husband's family after marriage. The term *gharjamai* or "house son-in-law" refers to the exception to this rule, a man who moves in with his wife's family.
5. Chand Mia had five wives and fifteen children over the course of his lifetime.
6. The *jotedars* were a class of rich farmers, or proprietors of agricultural landholdings (*jot*).
7. Two words for *kohl* or traditional eyeliner.
8. Jaggery or local dark sugar made from date palm syrup.
9. Traditional Bengali homesteads (*bari*) belonging to a large, well-off joint family like this one were composed of several detached buildings (*ghar* or *bari*) arranged around a courtyard. These buildings each had several rooms (*ghar* or *karma*) and their own kitchen (*rannaghar*). The various units of the joint family shared the courtyard, ponds, and other spaces of the homestead. Rented accommodations in the city, as opposed to the ancestral home, are referred to as *basha*, a word that can nevertheless convey intimacy and warmth. The words *bari* and *ghar* may also be used casually for rented houses depending on habit and context, especially as the word *bari* often refers to the "household" or family rather than the physical structure.
10. *Paan* is an after-dinner treat that consists of the heart-shaped betel leaf, filled with chopped betel nut and other ingredients such as dried coconut or tobacco and folded into a triangle.
11. "Chand" means moon, "Lal" means red or ruby, "Manik" means jewel, "Mohan" means captivating, and "Moti" means pearl.
12. There were fifteen children born to four of Nana's five children—one of them had no children.
13. "Munshi" means scribe.
14. This building was at the edge of the homestead and used by men and male guests only. In the morning and evening, it was used for children's tutoring.
15. A very thin, almost sheer, multicolored piece of woven cotton fabric that is usually used as a towel or headwrap.
16. Thin local cigarettes, usually rolled in leaves.

17. *Parda*, literally "curtain" or "veil," refers to the idea of secluding women from the public gaze. Practices of observing *parda* vary widely with community, socio-economic status, time period, etc.
18. A popular outdoor sport with two teams. One person says "hadudu" over and over in one breath and has to touch every player on the other team to get them out before running out of breath.
19. "Choto" means small or young, and Choto Chacha refers to the youngest brother of one's father.
20. A village council.
21. The historic Brojomohun College in Barisal, founded in 1889 by Aswini Kumar Dutta.
22. Chacha or uncle (father's younger brother) is a common form of address for family friends, such as this Mohiuddin Chacha.
23. "Moulubi Shaheb" refers to a Muslim cleric.
24. These phrases, meaning "God is great," were used as slogans during communal riots.
25. Puffed rice mixed with date palm syrup and formed into large round balls.
26. Grated coconut mixed with date palm syrup and formed into small round balls.
27. The "SDO" or Sub Divisional Officer was the head of the local government subdivision (each district was divided into multiple subdivisions). The SDO was considered quite powerful.

Part 2: VIOLENCE AND LOVE

1. A coalition of the Awami Muslim League, the Krishak Shramik (Farmers and Workers') Party, the Ganatantri Dal (Democratic Party), and Nizam-e-Islam (Province of Islam), which won the first provincial general election in Pakistan.
2. The legislature of what is now Bangladesh when it was a province of Pakistan, from the independence of India and Pakistan from Britain in 1947 until the independence of Bangladesh from Pakistan in 1971.
3. The Jubo (Youth) League was a political organization for younger members, formed primarily by the East Pakistan Communist Party along with other progressive parties.

4. It was not customary for women to meet men outside the family.
5. Manorama Bose was a Communist leader in Barisal. Mashima means maternal aunt, same as Khala. Mashi or Mashima is used more commonly among Hindus and Christians in Bengal, while Khala is used more commonly among Muslims. The suffix -da, short for Dada or "elder brother," is a common form of address among Bengalis.
6. Mosharraf Hossain Nannu, a member of the Krishak Shramik (Farmers and Workers') Party and a friend of the author's uncle Abdul Karim and Imadullah.
7. To get around the ban on public meetings in Dhaka, progressive leaders would hold meetings on the steamers, a common form of transportation in riverine East Bengal.
8. Jasimuddin, also known as "Polli Kobi" or the "Village Poet," was a poet from Faridpur, now in Bangladesh, known for his intimacy with the rural landscape and ways of life. He also collected a vast number of folksongs, which were popularized through the radio in the voice of his friend Abbasuddin Ahmed.
9. The "DC" was the Deputy Commissioner, the chief administrative and land revenue officer and government representative in the district, an administrative region of Pakistan. DC was higher ranking than the SDO, as he governed the entire district.
10. Asharh is the third month of the Bengali calendar (June–July), the beginning of the rainy season.
11. The fifth month of the Bengali calendar, August–September, the beginning of the early autumn season (*sharatkal*). Bengali Muslims believe that Bhadro is an inauspicious time for weddings or other important occasions.
12. Abdul Aziz Talukdar was a member of the Ganatantri Dal or Democratic Party. Our families were related and very close. His son Salimuddin or Taloi lived on my family compound and was married to Maoi.
13. A delicate fish curry with sliced whole fish, a central dish in Bengali cooking.
14. Huge flavorful prawns, like mini lobsters, found in the Bay of Bengal. *Galda chingri* are highly sought after and eaten on special occasions.
15. *Ilish* or shad is the favorite fish of Bengalis. *Ilish* from each river is believed to possess its own flavor.

16. Another well-known member of the Jubo League.
17. "MLA" is Member of the Legislative Assembly, or representative to the state legislature.
18. Respectful form of address for a teacher.
19. A *rakkhoshi* or *rakshasi* is a female demon in South Asian mythology.
20. The city of Narayanganj southeast of Dhaka is the closest river port.
21. Known as "Bangabandhu" or "Friend of Bengal," Sheikh Mujibur Rahman later led Bangladesh to independence from Pakistan.

Part 3: STRUGGLE AND RENEWAL

1. An area in the south of greater Dhaka.
2. Bengali *dim bhaja* or "fried eggs" are cooked like a firm omelette with green chilis and onions. *Bharta* is a mashed dish that can be made with various vegetables or, in this case, dried fish, along with chilis, mustard oil, chopped shallots, and other spices. *Chachchari* is a stir-fried vegetable dish, sometimes cooked with a fish head. *Luchi* is a classic Bengali flatbread, made of white flour and deep-fried into a golden puff, while everyday *porota* (Bengali-style *paratha*) is usually made of whole wheat flour and pan-fried.
3. Azimpur is an area in old Dhaka; the Azimpur cemetery is one of the city's largest.
4. Maulana Bhashani (1880–1976) was a pivotal Bengali politician known for his advocacy for peasants and the poor. He was the founder and President of the Pakistan Awami Muslim League, which later became the Awami League. In 1956, Bhashani was President of the Awami League, which was later led by Sheikh Mujibur Rahman. In 1957, Bhashani broke away from the Awami League to start a progressive party called NAP, commonly known as Bhashani NAP.
5. At that time, Abdur Rab Serniyabat worked for the Ganatantri Dal or Democratic Party. I was close to him and his family from my childhood. His daughter married Sheikh Mujibur Rahman's son. Abdur Rab Serniyabat and his whole family were murdered in 1975 along with Sheikh Mujibur Rahman and his family.
6. This is the custom of touching the feet of respected elders and then touching one's own forehead. It signifies putting the dust from an elder's feet onto one's own head as a sign of immense respect. *Pronam* is also

called *salaam* by Muslims, but the same ritual is used by both communities.

7. *Tyangra* and *punti* are two types of small fish.
8. Meat in a thin curry or *jhol.*
9. Distinctive Bengali version of samosas.
10. Pinaki Basu was a leftist politician, born in Barisal. He is known as a freedom fighter and martyr. He was a good friend of Nikhil-da, and they were both very active in cultural activities and loved by the community.
11. In 1954, Pakistan's dictators imposed military rule over East Pakistan by installing General Mirza as Governor of East Pakistan under Section 92-A of a law that allowed "Governor's Rule" to be imposed on a province. The central government took this action right after the 1954 election to prevent the East Pakistan legislature from exercising any power.
12. Educator, philanthropist, and nationalist; founder of Brojomohun College.
13. A poet and nationalist, actually born in Dhaka district but raised in Barisal; a student of Aswini Kumar Dutta. He was called "Charan Kobi" or "traveling poet" because he went from village to village singing patriotic songs, raising anti-colonial fervor. He was jailed by the British for his fiery songs.
14. Needs no introduction as one of the most prominent poets in Bangla. Taught at BM College.
15. A dry dish of minced vegetables. Unripe papaya is treated as a vegetable in Bengali cooking.
16. The Pakistani Army was dubbed the Pakbahini or Pak Army during the Liberation War.
17. An Islamic cultural and literary organization that strongly supported and participated in the Language Movement.
18. *Kantha* are quilts women make by recycling three layers of old saris and stitching designs on them.
19. Interfaith civil marriage was (and still is) regulated under the British-era Special Marriage Act of 1872, which requires public notice to be given before the marriage and allows anyone to object to the marriage. The act also requires most parties to officially renounce their faith.

Family law in India, Pakistan, and now Bangladesh is equivalent to religious law. Civil marriages are not generally available.

Part 4: LEAVING BENGAL

1. Amartya Sen later won the Nobel Prize in Economics (1998).
2. I do not know the caste of Dadi's ancestors, who were Hindu and later converted to Islam. In South Asia, casteism (along with colorism or the belief that lighter skin is more beautiful and associated with higher rank) remains pervasive even in Bangladesh and Pakistan among Muslims and Christians who converted from Hinduism. Because my Dadi was short and dark-skinned, some of my relatives may have assumed her ancestors were of lower caste. Even today, Bangladeshis who were formerly Dalit face incredible discrimination.
3. A gifted scholar and humanist who later became a professor of English at Dhaka University.
4. "Camellia," a long poem written in Rabindranath Tagore's later years.
5. The reference is to a novel by Rabindranath Tagore, published serially in 1928 and in book form in 1929. The title has been translated variously as *The Last Poem*, *Farewell Song*, *Poem of an Ending*, etc.
6. I later got this groundbreaking thesis published in Bangladesh and Jaseem edited it. *Collected Works: Swadesh Ranjan Bose*, The University Press Limited, 2011.
7. Most South Asian Muslims use Arabic or Persian names, and those who use Bangla names are even now sometimes assumed to be non-Muslim.
8. Gifts of food for breaking the fast after dark each day of Ramadan.
9. Pakistan Employees Cooperative Housing Society was a housing complex with a number of apartments. The whole area was known as "PECHS."
10. The Awami League won an absolute majority of 160 seats, all of which were in East Pakistan. The PPP won only eighty-one seats, all in West Pakistan.

Part 5: WAR AND LIBERATION

1. Sabur Khan was a minister at the time and supported Pakistan during Bangladesh's Liberation War.

2. The Shaheed Minar or Martyrs' Monument was built in Dhaka to commemorate those students who died after being shot by police in the Bengali Language Movement demonstrations of 1952.
3. Scooter taxis that then ran on kerosene but now run on compressed natural gas and are called "CNGs" instead of "baby taxis."
4. The Mukti Bahini or Liberation Army was the guerrilla army of independent Bangladesh during the Muktijuddho or Liberation War.
5. It was common in Bangladesh to refer to these non-Bengalis as "Biharis," though they may or may not be from the Indian province of Bihar.
6. Mujibnagar was the capital of the Provisional Government of Bangladesh, which formed in April 1971. The town formerly known as Baidyanathtala on the Bangladesh–West Bengal border in Meherpur district, Khulna Division of Bangladesh, was renamed after Sheikh Mujibur Rahman. However, the Mujibnagar government operated from Kolkata.
7. Swadesh's second brother used the spelling "Basu" instead of "Bose." They are two different anglicized spellings of the same Bengali Hindu surname that is pronounced *bo-shu* in Bangla.
8. Senator Ted Kennedy visited Kolkata in his capacity as chairman of a Senate sub-committee on refugee affairs. He saw the terrible conditions and opposed the United States' support for Pakistan through arms and aid. On Mujib being imprisoned in Pakistan, Kennedy said: "I think that the only crime Mujib is guilty of is winning an election."
9. An acclaimed writer and scholar with degrees from Presidency College, Harvard, and Indiana University, she published more than eighty books in Bengali, including poetry, plays, novels, and essays. She was a professor of literature at Jadavpur University.

Part 6: POST-INDEPENDENCE IN DHAKA AND ABROAD

1. Salma Sobhan was a lawyer and married to economist Rehman Sobhan, who had been Swadesh's teacher at Dhaka University. She later co-founded the organization Ain-o-Salish Kendra, which provided legal information and support to ordinary people.
2. In Bengali culture, people often hesitate to give news of someone's death, especially to someone living abroad. But it was very upsetting to me to find out about Baba's death so late.

3. *Jatra* is a popular dramatic form with music and dance, traditionally performed in the open air by traveling professional or local amateur troupes. The *jatra* played a key role in the development of (stage) theater and cinema in Bengal.
4. This temple in Assam was famous in Bengal, but no one we know had actually been there. Numerous myths and stories circulated about it, including that men who go there may never escape or are put under a spell. The temple is said to be off limits to men and occupied by a sorceress and goddess of desire.

Part 8: FULL CIRCLE

1. Songs written by Rabindranath Tagore.